P9-CEO-218

Grayslake Area Public Library District
Grayslake, Illinois

1. A fine will be charged on each book which is not returned when it is due.

2. All injuries to books beyond reasonable wear and all losses shall be made good to the satisfaction of the Librarian.

3. Each borrower is held responsible for all books drawn on his card and for all fines accruing on the same.

Investing without Wall Street

Investing without Wall Street

THE FIVE ESSENTIALS OF FINANCIAL FREEDOM

Sheldon Jacobs

WILEY

John Wiley & Sons, Inc.

Published by John Wiley & Sons, Inc., Hoboken, New Jersey.
Published simultaneously in Canada.

For general information on our other products and services or for technical
support, please contact our Customer Care Department within the United States at
(800) 762–2974, outside the United States at (317) 572–3993 or fax (317) 572–4002.

Wiley also publishes its books in a variety of electronic formats. Some content that
appears in print may not be available in electronic books. For more information
about Wiley products, visit our website at www.wiley.com.

Library of Congress Cataloging-in-Publication Data:

Jacobs, Sheldon.
  Investing without Wall Street: The Five Essentials of Financial Freedom /
  Sheldon Jacobs.
    pages cm
  Includes index.
  ISBN 978-1-118-20464-1 (cloth); ISBN 978-1-118-22839-5 (ebk);
  ISBN 978-1-118-23927-8 (ebk); ISBN 978-1-118-26560-4 (ebk)
    1. Investments.   I. Title.
  HG4521.J2534   2012
  332.6—dc23

                                                              2011045566

Printed in the United States of America
10 9 8 7 6 5 4 3 2 1

*To my wife, Betté, who has enriched my
journey with love.*

Also by Sheldon Jacobs

Put Money in Your Pocket: The Art of Selecting No-Load Mutual Funds for Maximum Gain

The Handbook for No-Load Fund Investors (20 annual editions)

Sheldon Jacobs' Guide to Successful No-Load Fund Investing (2 editions)

How to Pick the Best No-Load Mutual Funds for Solid Growth and Safety

Contents

A wise man should have money in his head, but not in his heart.
—Jonathan Swift

Preface

With some books the Preface is unimportant. That's not the case with this book. This preface provides an overview of what investors really need to know to prosper in today's markets, which are so very different from the ones we loved in the 1980s and 1990s. But first, I need to quickly touch on two money-making basics.

1. **Do-it-yourself is the real key to lifetime profits.**

   First of all, you need to appreciate the huge difference between doing-it-yourself and hiring professional guidance. Although there is value in a book explaining the best ways to work with a broker or professional investment advisor, the real benefit comes from a book that teaches you, simply and clearly, how to do it yourself.

   The wealth difference is overwhelming. *Over a 40-year investing lifetime, an average earner can make $252,000 more doing it him or herself than a person who has to share his or her profits with professionals.* That's a lot of money going to advisors, not you. That's why this book is titled *Investing without Wall Street*! (See Chapter 4 for the computations.)

   Achieving this wealth increment is within everybody's ability and takes very little time. In addition, by doing it yourself, you will know your self-interest has always been put first. That's no small thing in an era where crooks like Bernard Madoff stalk uninformed investors. *Investing without Wall Street* gives you control of your finances.

2. **Savings are crucial.**

   All the advice offered in this book is academic if you have no money to invest. Money is accumulated by saving. Savings are not just a good idea; they are crucial.

   There is no need for this book to discuss the mechanics of saving. You simply spend less than you earn. If you don't already have savings, *start saving*. Start as early as you can, the earlier the better. If you have some savings, *save more*.

A 12-Year-Old's Commentary on Saving

The top reasons why I think it is important to save are:

1. To help me tell the difference between my needs and wants
2. To gain interest on my money
3. To save for larger things such as a bicycle
4. Currently I am working to raise money to go to camp next summer.

Sarah, Shepherdstown, WV. Reported by Michelle Singletary, WashingtonPost.com.

As Bill Donoghue, the money-market maven, once said, "If you can't live on your income now, you can't live on 10 percent less. So save 10 percent."

Here's a summary of the book's investing advice and philosophy.

Today's Times Call for More Conservative Strategies

In the 1980s and 1990s, the buy-and-hold investing strategy superseded all others. You didn't have to be a brilliant stock- or fund-picker; all you had to do was buy-and-hold stocks, and you could have earned 18 to 19 percent a year.

The market is unlikely to achieve gains of this magnitude again in my lifetime, and possibly yours. That's because secular bull markets, the long-lived megatrends that last 5 to 20 years, usually occur only when there are dynamic new, giant growth industries such as computers, information technology, the Internet, and in earlier eras, canals, railroads, electricity and automobiles. They provide the basic foundation. All these advances had myriad applications over a broad range of industries. I don't see anything comparable on the horizon. Technological advances since the computer and the Internet became mainstream have been more evolutionary than revolutionary. The new social media are evolutionary, even though they have produced several billionaires.

For many years to come, I believe stock markets will be in a secular bear market. They will move up and down, not basically up as in the 1990s. I expect average gains over the next decade or more will be in the neighborhood of 6 to 7 percent annually. That's because I don't see any reason for the price/earnings (P/E) ratios of stocks to expand significantly in the coming years, and they may possibly contract. (In the 1980s and 1990s, 43 percent of all gains came from P/E expansion, as investors paid more and more for a dollar of corporate earnings.) I believe stocks, over the next decade or more, will at best gain pretty much in line with their earnings increases (which will depend to a greater extent on the economy than has previously been the case).

The good news is that this means stocks can still deliver returns superior to bonds or cash, albeit with greater risk (which I'll show you how to control). The best news is that since stocks declined 38.5 percent in 2008, they could easily have double-digit gains over the next five to six years, and return to that estimated long-term average.

A study by Capital Guardian funds found that when the S&P 500 Index had an annual return of 2 percent or less over a decade, stocks gained between 10 percent and 17 percent annually in the ensuing decade. The annualized return for the 10 years ending 2008 was –0.93, and the S&P 500 gained 23.5 percent in 2009 and 12.8 percent in 2010.

Regardless of the volatility, equities must continue to have a place in your financial planning, particularly if you are young.

Sheldon Jacobs' Statement of Purpose

Investing books are commonly written to enhance authors' careers. However, that was not my motivation. I've had two successful careers, each a quarter-century long, and I have no desire for a third go-to-the-office job. I didn't write this book to sell newsletters or obtain managed account clients. I sold both my money management business and newsletter a few years ago, but I continue to work as a contributing editor of the *Investor* newsletter. In addition, I am on the Finance Committee of the Westchester Community College Foundation, in New York, where I help to manage a multi-million dollar institutional portfolio. And lastly I manage my personal investment portfolio.

The purpose of this book is to share with others the important lessons I have learned over a lifetime. I have always written about what interests me. And right now, what interests me is making my investing as simple as possible. *Investing without Wall Street* is a guided tour based on personal experiences. Most of the strategies that I offer in this book, I have tried myself. *I know they work.*

I am not a genius. I have always looked for ways to make money without being a Goldman Sachs-level expert, and I promise you that any ordinary person will be able to implement the profit-making recommendations in this book.

There are two reasons for this. First of all, investing literature commonly attempts to tailor advice by investor demographics (age, wealth, time horizon) and risk preferences. *Investing without Wall Street* does this too, but in addition, it offers advice by degree of desired investor involvement. It speaks to investors who are willing to spend time to obtain the best results, but mostly to the more numerous investors who are simply seeking a comfortable nest egg while getting on with their daily lives.

Secondly, the specific advice offered takes into account what I think investors will actually do on their own, since no matter how wise the advice, it's not productive if investors don't follow it.

Finally, you'll quickly see that I don't always agree with the conventional wisdom, and as you discover how much about investing there is to learn, you also may find you have even more to *unlearn.*

In November 2010, the *Bottom Line Personal* publication observed, "Among financial experts who are able to think with a small investor's perspective, no one is more level-headed than Sheldon Jacobs."

My Approach to Financial Profits

Between 1974 and 2004, I wrote 24 books as well as *The No-Load Fund Investor,* a top-ranked monthly, mutual-fund newsletter that I founded to provide specific investing advice, recommendations, and model portfolios. The books and newsletter basically offered advice within the framework of a secular bull market. Because investor interest was concentrated almost exclusively on profit seeking in those bull market years, like virtually every investing publication in those decades, I placed greater emphasis on profits than on risks. Even though my recommendations in those years were conservative compared to most of my colleagues, long-term bearishness would not have served my readers.

But times have changed, and so has my advice.

In *Investing without Wall Street* I have expanded on the tried and true wealth creation programs to take into account the challenges of the new market climate. *Investing without Wall Street* emphasizes both risk control and profits by zeroing in on five "essentials."

The Five Essentials

The book is divided into three parts. Part One (Chapters 1–5) discusses five principles that are the essence of the knowledge you need to be a successful equity investor. Master these five "essentials" and you'll have the wherewithal to be a successful investor without the need of professional assistance. They are your priorities.

1. Determine the right asset allocation.
2. Properly diversify within asset classes.
3. Understand and control risk.
4. Keep your costs low.
5. Choose the right financial media to follow.

I suspect that at this point some of you are thinking, "I've heard most of these principles for ages." And probably you have, but I will bet that a good number of you have never really understood their importance, or how best to apply them.

You will also notice that security selection (choosing specific stocks or funds)—most advisors' favorite recommendations—is not one of the five "essentials." Notwithstanding its ubiquitous coverage by the media, it's a myth that you need a lot of knowledge in this area.

Security selection can be simplified to the point where you can make good selections effortlessly. Equally important, if you follow the five essentials, security selection won't be a make-or-break factor in your investing efforts. The purpose of this book is to make you a better investor, not to load you up with tips about specific investments.

In the 1980s and 1990s, investors achieved success by mostly just being in the market. Over the next decade, I believe *the key to success will be you*—how you approach investing, how clear-headed is your understanding of the market's underlying realities, and whether your skills and attitudes are right for the times.

Part Two (Chapters 6–12) refines and provides specific ways to implement the five "essentials." Included are my "takes" on surviving bear markets, the latest advance in index fund investing, and model portfolios that put into practice the "essentials." In Chapter 10, I make the case for market timing.

Part Three (Chapters 13–19) discusses important and timeless lessons that I have learned over the years as an investor, investment advisor, money manager, editor, entrepreneur, and observer of human nature. These chapters show how you can profitably expand your general money knowledge. They will give you an overview of personal money management situations seldom, if ever, covered in other personal finance books or periodicals.

Here are some of the topics covered:

Acknowledging that investing is a science dealing with uncertainty, Chapter 13, titled "For Clearer Thinking," shows that it's just as important to learn *how* to think, as it is to learn *what* to think. It offers lessons in clear and critical thinking. Similarly, Chapter 14 discusses behavioral finance, now an important frontier in investing knowledge. With a few exceptions, my take on the subject ignores the academic approach, concentrating instead on practical applications.

The purpose of these two chapters is to help you acquire the skepticism and creative thinking that are important to financial success. Again, "The key will be you" is not just an empty phrase. This adage is just as important as the fundamentals.

Chapter 16 aims to help women achieve their investing goals, and in Chapter 17, I briefly discuss owning collectibles for profit. Another chapter tells you how to invest in a Broadway musical with a relatively small outlay. Few readers are likely to make such a high-risk investment, but my experience as a backer of *Hairspray* was fascinating and brought me so much enjoyment I had to share it with you.

Integrity is so important when you are giving your hard-earned dollars to impersonal businesses or total strangers that I have devoted an entire chapter to it.

Because almost everybody makes far more money in the workplace than they make from investing, I offer advice in Chapter 19 to both employers and employees, based on my personal experiences as the owner of a small business, and as an employee of two large corporations.

Although there is a chapter titled "The No-Work Way to a Comfortable Retirement—Maybe," don't be misled. *Investing without Wall Street* is not a "lazy man's" guide, or even a "permanent" portfolio strategy. Quite the contrary, it's for people who want maximum results for the time and effort they spend investing. It's for young investors who want to learn it right the first time.

Investing without Wall Street also shares stories of interest. As Adam Smith said in the Preface to the *Money Game*, the classic tale of Wall Street in the 1960s, "Enjoy the stories, they always teach more than the rules." That's what Wall Street does to sell stocks to investors. That's what I have done in *Investing without Wall Street:* recounted stories that will "sell" you investment strategies that are profitable for you, not for Wall Street's promoters.

Although I favor funds, the insights I offer are relevant whether your preference is mutual funds, exchange traded funds (ETFs), stocks, or anything else. And for those of you who are wealthy enough to have personal money management, *Investing without Wall Street* provides a valuable guide for riding herd on these advisors, something that every managed account client should do.

Finally, this book contains many of the usual investing and Wall Street terms. If you don't know a particular term, there is a glossary at the back of the book that will make you an expert on this jargon.

Introduction

Take a Journey with Me

You might think that there is only one investing world, but there are many, and their differences go far beyond investing strategies or financial products. There are the separate realms for hedge fund operators, stockbrokers, commodity traders, gold bugs, and day traders. There are perma bulls and perma bears. There are also the worlds of investors who rely on advisors, the do-it-yourselfers, the stock-pickers, asset allocators, market-timers, trendsetters and trend-followers, the involved and the uninvolved.

My foray into a different world explains these distinctions. Back in the 1990s, I was invited to make a speech to the subscribers of an Internet stock market trading system. I knew that investors who traded on the Internet were not the audience for my style of moderate risk, diversified investing. But the invitation had come through a friend who had recommended me, and the sponsor offered me a substantial fee, so I accepted.

Before I was called to the podium, the president of the Internet trading company jumped up and said he wanted to poll the audience, about 100 strong, to ascertain their risk preferences.

Using a scale of one to ten, with ten being the most aggressive investing and one being the most conservative, he asked, "How many people are tens?" About five people raised their hands. "How many are nines?" About 25 people raised their hands. "Eights?" At least 50 responded.

I thought to myself, "Good grief, I'm a *four*, and this audience wants advice that will make them a killing in the market *tomorrow*." Well, I delivered my usual speech and only one person walked out.

1

Although I considered it a moral victory, I tried hard never to repeat that experience again. And, thankfully, I never did. Time is precious and I hate to waste investors' time with advice they are unlikely to accept.

This book is for investors with risk tolerances ranging from about three to seven. It's not for eights, nines, or tens. If you're an eight or higher, and are perusing this book in a bookstore or library, put it back on the shelf. This book is not for you and I don't want to waste your time. By my standards, you are not really an investor. You should be in a casino playing the slots.

On the other hand, if you are a one or two, stick with your bank CDs, savings accounts, or e-bonds, unless you want to learn how to increase your wealth with only a moderate increase in risk.

My world is primarily the world of diversified, low-cost, no-load mutual funds that you invest in for the long-term. I first ventured into no-load funds because I figured that any financial product that is always on sale had to be the right world for me.

A four is right for me, and some other number may be right for you. That's okay—people are different.

In this book I would like to take you on a journey through my world of investing. It will be fun, and you'll find it worth your time. But before we get down to the main business of this book—improving your investing skills—I want to briefly tell you about the town I grew up in, since it has a strong bearing on who I am and how I came by the advice I will be dispensing.

How My Journey Began

I grew up in Deadwood, in the Black Hills of South Dakota. If you drove through Deadwood back in those days, you might have thought it was an ordinary small town. But Deadwood was unlike any other small town in the United States, and everyone living there knew it. Deadwood had been the scene of one of the country's most notable gold rushes, and the town never lost its frontier spirit.

In the forties, when I grew up there, the town had a population of 4,000. There are many small towns where people live because they can't make it in the big city. But that wasn't true of Deadwood. Some of the sharpest people I have ever met lived there. They could have made it anywhere, but they preferred Deadwood because of the breathtaking beauty of the Black Hills, its heritage, its sense of small town intimacy, and its proximity to Mount Rushmore. There was great hunting, fishing, skiing, camping, and mountain climbing, all within an easy drive. For climbing, there was Devil's Tower, which later on gained fame in the Steven Spielberg movie, *Close Encounters of the Third Kind,* and Harney Peak, which at 7,242 feet is the highest peak between the Rocky Mountains and the French Pyrenees.

The town had a strong Libertarian bent. Its Main Street, filled with prosperous stores, was the shopping center for 40 miles around. It was home to seven churches and seven bars, and each bar had a room in back for gambling, usually slots, blackjack, and crap tables. There had always been gambling in Deadwood, ever since the gold rush days. Technically, it wasn't legal, but the state never bothered to enforce the law.

In those days (the 1930s and 1940s) Deadwood also had three houses of prostitution. All were on Main Street on second floors, above the bars. And they all had neon signs at street level advertising their presence. The signs read: Ma's Nifty, the Cozy, and the Shasta.

Everybody in town favored these businesses, including the clergy, because they brought in tourists, which were one of the two lifeblood industries of the town. "Everybody" certainly included my dad, who was born and raised in Deadwood, and was totally accustomed to this environment. He approved of anything that brought in business. The "girls," as everybody called them, did a lot of shopping in my dad's ladies ready-to-wear store.

The other lifeblood was gold mining. The fabled Homestake Mine, once owned by George Hearst (William Randolph Hearst's father) at the time the largest gold mine in the Americas, was located in Deadwood and in nearby Lead, South Dakota. The mine was listed on the New York Stock Exchange (NYSE) in 1879 and continued producing gold for more than 120 years. Homestake became the longest-listed stock in the history of the NYSE and brought millions of dollars of revenue into town.

Deadwood's liquor laws were loose, to put it mildly. Of course, South Dakota had laws regulating drinking, and I guess they applied to Deadwood, too. But the reality was that liquor was regulated in Deadwood not so much by age as by height. If you were tall enough to stand at the bar and pound it with your fist, it was likely you would be served. You could even drink 3.2 beer legally at age 15.

Another convenient thing about Deadwood, and actually the entire state of South Dakota, was that you didn't need a driver's license to drive a car in those days. The sole requirement was to be 15 years old. Consequently, when we all got to be about 14 and a half, we badgered our fathers to teach us how to drive so we could drive on our own as soon as we reached 15.

During my lifetime, things changed radically in Deadwood. In 1947 the state of South Dakota finally decided to enforce the gambling laws, and that had a crippling impact on commerce. The brothels were closed in the late 1970s in an action that drew national coverage. Then one day right after the last brothel closed, hundreds of people paraded down Main Street holding up banners reading BRING BACK OUR GIRLS!

In 1989, Deadwood got a new lease on life when the state of South Dakota made the town an exception to its gambling laws, just as New Jersey did for Atlantic City.

Main Street, which used to have regular stores catering to families, is now wall-to-wall gambling casinos its entire length—139 in all if you count the stores with slots. The ladies ready-to-wear store, once owned by my dad, is now a casino called the Midnight Star, owned by the actor Kevin Costner and his brother.

The new gambling money has spruced up the town. The streets have been repaved, and almost all of the storefronts are new. There are several new hotels and restaurants.

And it was just in time. Two years later, the Homestake Mine, its gold finally exhausted, closed for good. If it hadn't been for the gambling dispensation granted by the state, Deadwood would have become a ghost town. Even with the gambling, the town's population has dwindled to 1,270 according to U.S. 2010 Census. Deadwood will be around for a long time, but it's not the same town now that it was for my generation.

In 1964, Deadwood became the only city in the United States to be named a National Historic Landmark. In 2004, it received a new measure of fame when HBO launched a western TV series, *Deadwood*, set there. In 2009, ForbesTraveler.com selected Deadwood as one of the twenty prettiest towns in America.

And now you need a license to drive in the state of South Dakota, including Deadwood.

When gambling closed in Deadwood, many of the town's gamblers moved to Las Vegas. So the first time I went to Las Vegas I looked up two of them, Virgil Rakestraw (Rakie) and Eli Gasson.

I found Rakie, a big hulk of a man, dealing at a roulette wheel at the Stardust casino. When he took a coffee break, we discussed gambling. "Never gamble in Vegas," he admonished. "It's different than Deadwood."

I knew what he meant. In Deadwood, if the casino saw a local man gambling away the rent and food money, they made him stop for the sake of his and his family's well being. That didn't happen in impersonal Las Vegas.

I found Eli working as a pit boss at a small casino. Over coffee, he also warned me not to gamble in Vegas, though he made an exception for poker. I politely accepted his advice, but it was meaningless to me.

I knew Eli was a world-class poker player. According to legend (probably Eli's), he was the champion poker player of the Pacific fleet during World War II. How he came by this title I never understood, although I believe there was some legitimacy to the claim. If he were around today, I'm pretty sure he would be earning big bucks on TV.

Poker is a game of immense skill, not luck, although in the short run, luck can temporarily overcome skill, just as it can in economic life. I am sorely lacking in the skills needed to win at poker. (I know, because I learned how to play the game at Boy Scout camp—and never won.) In addition, poker, too, is a zero-sum game, and finally, in poker if you lose there is no TARP to bail you out.

For many years I went to Vegas once a year to speak at the Money Show (see Chapter 5). I always heeded Rakie's and Eli's advice, although the real reason I don't gamble is that gambling is a zero-sum game less the house edge, meaning for every winner there's a loser. Stocks, on the other hand, are a positive-sum game. By that I mean it's quite possible, and often likely, for all the players to win, since they can participate in earnings growth over time. I don't like to lose, so I prefer the far better odds of long-term investing.

I have often thought that the world of gambling I had grown up with led me to the world of investing. I bought my first stock, Homestake Mining, when I was still in high school. The money came mostly from summer jobs. I held it

When I asked my eight-year-old granddaughter, Sarah Jacobs, if she knew what a casino was, she said, "Sure, it's a place where you play with real money."

for three years and sold it for a small loss. In retrospect, my mistake was confusing familiarity with knowledge. Just because I could see the mine from my house, it didn't mean I had sufficient knowledge of the politics and economics of the mining industry. I didn't even know Homestake's earnings. And even if I had known Homestake's earnings, I would not have known how to interpret them.

I left Deadwood to attend college, and I never did go back to live there. Had I, I would have become the third generation of my family to operate the family stores.

During the Korean War, the Army called me up and, in its infinite wisdom, stationed me in Times Square. New York hooked me. I liked the theater, museums, and most of all its restaurants, which were far better than Deadwood's. Upon discharge, I decided to stay in New York. Much as I liked Deadwood, New York was my kind of town. But even with my parents now gone, I still return to Deadwood for short visits every few years or so.

Chance made me a New Yorker. But I probably always was.

New York, New York

I have had two careers in New York. The first career was in broadcasting. I worked 25 years for ABC-TV and NBC-TV doing media research. I became an expert in TV ratings. I studied and forecast audiences (which ironically was good training for forecasting mutual fund performance).

This is not the book for broadcasting stories, but there was one time when I was able to combine my broadcasting industry knowledge with my interest in investing.

In late 1965, ABC invited hundreds of advertising executives to a breakfast to preview programming that would premiere in a few weeks. On this morning, a five-minute clip of the show that would become *Batman* was screened. It seemed to me, and others, that this show was certain to be a smash hit.

Back in the department, we researchers discussed how to capitalize on this early information. Buy ABC? No, we reasoned. A single program, even a major hit, wouldn't move ABC stock. The production company, Twentieth Century Fox? No, for pretty much the same reason. What about the company that held the merchandising rights to Batman characters? We checked and found these rights were held by National Periodical, the same company that published Batman comic books. We felt the success of the TV show could have a significant impact on National Periodical's earnings.

Less than an hour had elapsed since we had previewed the film. Several of us bought National Periodical stock at what turned out to be a bottom.

Then, we did a very smart thing. Down the hall from the research department was the ABC publicity department, with about a dozen of the best publicity agents you ever saw in your life.

We sauntered down there and casually mentioned the fruits of our thinking. They bought the stock, too. Then, the most amazing thing happened. Within a week, stories about National Periodical began appearing across the country—in newspapers, magazines, on TV, everywhere. It was incredible.

The stock jumped 50 percent in a few weeks and eventually doubled in the midst of the 1966 bear market. It wasn't the most money I ever made, but it was surely the most satisfying. We had received good information, and we analyzed it correctly. Not bad for a bunch of amateurs.

In January 1979 I launched *The No-Load Fund Investor* in what newsletter people call a "kitchen-table" operation. That is to say, I wrote the newsletter during evenings and weekends while still keeping my day job at NBC. My timing was good. Investors were just getting over the severe bear market of the early 1970s. I published the newsletter quarterly for more than three years, and watched it grow into a real business. Then, in August 1982, a new bull market began with a vengeance. I knew my day had come. When the bull was a week old, I quit my day job at NBC.

I was 51 at the time. Most of my colleagues thought I had been fired. They couldn't imagine anybody quitting a good job (I was a director) so close to early retirement age. But for me it was the moment to go full-time on a lucrative second career as a newsletter editor and publisher.

About 15 years later, the Sunday morning TV show, *The Wall Street Journal Report*, profiled three people who had created notable second careers. The three were Ray Kroc, the founder of the modern McDonald's, Colonel Harland Sanders of Kentucky Fried Chicken fame, and me, Sheldon Jacobs, editor of *The No-Load Fund Investor.*

PART

I

THE FIVE ESSENTIALS

1

The First Essential: Determine the Right Asset Allocation

Now let's turn to improving your investing skills.

Chapters 1 and 2 are the most important in this book. To give you an idea how important they are, over 2,500 books and countless magazine and newspaper articles have been written on the subject of how to spread your money among—and within—classes of assets.

Given its fundamental nature you would think that virtually every investor would be well acquainted with the principles of diversification. Yet I find that such is not the case. I continually run across investors who have only the haziest idea of how to correctly implement an asset allocation and diversification strategy. I use a quick test to gauge their competency in this area:

Question: Do you know what percentage of your portfolio is currently invested in equities? Yes, no, without looking it up? If you don't carry that number in your head, you may not be applying whatever you do know correctly.

There is a tendency to ignore diversification, perhaps because it is so basic. And a fair number invest with the belief that they already know it all. But that's not usually the case. So let's start at the beginning.

The Basics

Asset allocation basically means holding various asset classes whose performance is uncorrelated; that is, they fluctuate independently of each other. That's the whole point. If two investments fluctuate in tandem, they won't provide diversification, or reduce risk.

The three most important asset classes for individuals are: stocks, bonds, and cash. At the institutional level there are many more. For convenience's sake, I'm going to call these classes of assets *baskets.*

The following statistical table shows that there is virtually no correlation among the three basic baskets. Zero is no correlation; 1.00 and –1.00 are perfect positive and negative correlations. This is critical. You want zero correlation, or better yet, negative correlation. If two asset classes have a high positive correlation, then they are really variations of the same asset class, and don't increase diversification.

Asset Class	Correlation
World equity vs. U.S. investment-grade bonds	0.15
World equity vs. cash and cash equivalents*	–0.02
U.S. investment-grade bonds vs. cash and cash equivalents	0.03

*Short-term investments, such as short-term bonds.
Source: Capital Guardian, Sept. 17, 2010 presentation to Westchester Community College Finance Committee.

Now you see why spreading your money among stocks, bonds, and cash gives you superior diversification and risk control. You are always at risk no matter what you do, but with this approach you have dramatically reduced the likelihood that all your investments decline at once. How you allocate these baskets in your portfolio can determine up to 90 percent of your returns. This alone tells you where you should be spending your investing time.

If you own your own business, though, diversification may not be an option. You will probably have all your money in it. But that's not the case when you invest in other people's businesses—that's what you do when you buy listed stocks. There you may have the choice of diversification or concentrated investing. Some people follow the concentrated path in investing—and some of these people become very, very wealthy. But in all likelihood, you will never know enough about the workings of publicly traded companies, or how the actions of other investors will impact your holdings to be comfortable putting all your money in one, or even a few, stocks. This also applies to investing in companies you work for, if they are large enough to have publicly traded stock. Let me be very specific: *Diversification is not about maximizing profits; it's about reducing risk.* And there is no better way to reduce risk. It's not just for individuals, either. Many hedge fund and mutual fund pros have dispensed with diversification and come to grief because it is impossible to be expert in every holding. Expert or layman, when bad things happen there is really no protection other than diversification.

> Diversification is not about maximizing profits; it's about reducing risk.

I think one of the reasons the *Investor* newsletter led the nation in risk-adjusted returns for so many years (we were number one among all newsletters for the 20 years ending June 2008) is because we had the best asset allocation. We were one of the few newsletters that routinely allocated part of our model portfolios to bonds. Most newsletter portfolios recommend stocks only, or even higher risk securities such as options.

Learn from the Big Boys

Even though you may never be an institutional player, it's useful to know what the big boys do. Here's a comprehensive allocation developed by David Swensen, who manages Yale's multibillion dollar endowment. He suggests six baskets with no asset class greater than 30 percent, or less than 5 percent:

1. Domestic stocks: 30%
2. Foreign stocks: 15%
3. Emerging-market stocks: 5%
4. Real estate: 20%
5. Treasury bonds: 15%
6. Treasury inflation-protected securities (TIPS):   15%

For individuals with substantial assets this allocation makes a great deal of sense.

Another asset class to consider is commodities, which are much simpler to invest in nowadays with the advent of sector exchange-traded funds (ETFs).

How the Ancients Allocated Their Wealth

Many contemporary investing strategies such as random walk, modern portfolio theory, index funds, and even growth stock investing were developed after World War II and are relatively new. But asset allocation is not new. It's been around as long as people have had wealth.

The oldest recorded asset allocation advice may be from biblical times. The *Talmud*, a record of rabbinic discussions pertaining to Jewish law, ethics, customs, and history (circa 1200 B.C.–A.D. 500) recommends: "Let every man divide his money into three parts, and invest a third in *land*, a third in *business*, and let him keep a third in *reserve*." Today we would call these three baskets real estate, common stocks, and money funds. You can clearly prosper with that advice right now.

Jumping to more recent history, the fabled Rothschild family had an asset allocation formula that worked well for over a century and, amazingly, remains totally relevant today. The Rothschilds placed one-third of their wealth in each of three baskets: *securities, real estate,* and *art.*

It's interesting that both historic examples allocated wealth into three baskets and that's basically what most individuals do today, except that our baskets are slightly different. Today, we categorize the baskets as stocks, bonds, and cash, but the principle of three endures as a sound minimum.

And here's another historic example of diversification. In Shakespeare's *Merchant of Venice*, Antonio declares, "My ventures are not in one bottom trusted."

And, of course, that's what insurance is all about—spreading the risk through diversification. Lloyds of London was founded around 1688 to insure shipping, so a shipper could put all his cargo in "one bottom."

It's not known when American investors began to allocate their assets to both stocks and bonds, but the first balanced fund, Vanguard Wellington, was launched in 1929. Vanguard Wellington utilized a 60/40 distribution (stocks to bonds), which is still basic today.

Of course, we are more sophisticated now and at the institutional level, some large portfolios have as many as eleven baskets. That's too much for most individuals, but you can certainly consider commodities, timber, foreign bonds, inflation protected bonds, gold, real estate, art, collectibles such as fine wines, rare books, classic cars, jewelry, and memorabilia. Still, the "big three" are all you absolutely need.

Your Most Important Task: Determining the Best Asset Allocation for You

First of all, there is no single "right" allocation. It's essential to choose an allocation that works for you, considers your current holdings and, most importantly, takes into account a long-term market forecast and your personal risk profile, which depends on your financial ability to tolerate risk, and your willingness to do so.

Regardless of what you choose, the important thing is to *know* your target asset allocation and either stick reasonably close to it, or have logical reasons for not doing so.

> There is no single "right" allocation.

Here are some of the factors you need to consider to reach your own personal allocation:

- How many *years* before you need the money, either for retirement or for other purposes such as college?
- How long does the *money have to last* in retirement? An estimate is helpful.
- How easily can market losses be *replaced?*
- How much *inflation protection* do you need?
- *Age:* Generally older people should take less risk, but there are some significant exceptions. For most people age is closely linked to the time horizon.

These factors are really all facets of what is called your *time horizon.* For most people that's the bottom line. In addition consider:

- *Wealth* (more important than most realize): It's dangerous to take substantial equity risks if you don't have a cushion.
- *Family:* How solid is your marriage? What child rearing expenses are you likely to incur (including college costs, and possible wedding expenses)?
- Are there any circumstances under which you would wind up being financially responsible for any other members of your family? Have you ever co-signed a loan?
- *Income* (if you are still working; or cash flow if you are not): How great is it? How stable is it? The more you have, the easier it is to accept risk.
- How much to set aside for *emergencies?*

- How much money do you want to set aside for *charities?*
- *Equity market outlook:* Are you long-term bullish or bearish?
- Are your stocks or equity funds more or less *risky* than the market?
- How much are you *willing to lose* without cutting your losses?
- How much *volatility* can you accept?
- What is your *current allocation,* and how happy are you with it?
- How closely are your earnings *linked to the stock market?* If you are an investment professional, or work for an investment professional, putting your personal wealth in the market can leave you dangerously undiversified.

Putting all these factors together for optimum results is no small job. I suggest some specific model portfolios later on; however here's a shortcut for people who want to do it themselves. Go to the Vanguard "Personal Investors" website and, using the "What are you looking for?" search box, type in "investor questionnaire." Answer the questions and submit. The program will suggest an allocation that might work for you:

Vanguard Investor Questionnaire (summary of multiple-choice answers in italics)[1]

1. When making a long-term investment, I plan to hold the investment for: *(# years)*
2. From September 2008 through November 2008, stocks lost over 31 percent. If I owned a stock investment that lost about 31 percent in 3 months, I would: (If you owned stocks during this period, select the answer that corresponds to your actual behavior.) *(sell, hold, buy)*
3. Generally, I prefer investments with little or no fluctuation in value, and I'm willing to accept the lower return associated with these investments. *(agree/disagree)*
4. During market declines, I tend to sell portions of my riskier assets and invest the money in safer assets. *(agree/disagree)*
5. I would invest in a mutual fund based solely on a brief conversation with a friend, co-worker, or relative. *(agree/disagree)*
6. From September 2008 through October 2008, bonds lost nearly 4 percent. If I owned a bond investment that lost almost

---

[1]©1995–2010. The Vanguard Group, Inc. All rights reserved. Reprinted by permission.

4 percent in 2 months, I would: (If you owned bonds during this period, select the answer that corresponds to your actual behavior.) *(sell, hold, buy)*

7. The following chart shows the greatest one-year loss and the highest one-year gain on three different hypothetical investments of $10,000. Given the potential gain or loss in any one year, I would invest my money in: *(low-, medium-, high-volatility investments)*

8. My current and future income sources (for example, salary, Social Security, pension) are: *(unstable/stable)*

9. My previous investment experience and satisfaction with the following six asset classes are: *(See website for list.)*

10. The information you enter in the following grid will determine your time horizon (how long you plan to hold your investments). Your current allocation is: *(percent stocks, bonds, cash)*

I keep my personal asset allocation on a spreadsheet, and recommend you do so, too. It can be updated any time by just punching in a few closing prices, which you can get online. It doesn't take any time at all. I do mine in less than five minutes. If you are not computer-literate, use a calculator. Check your allocations regularly. This discipline is far more important than keeping track of your favorite stock or fund.

Also, by including cash in a spreadsheet, you are able to take personal spending into account. I suggest benchmarking total financial assets to the previous December 31, so you know at all times if you are spending more than you are making and appreciating.

For an in-depth professional look at asset allocation, read the second edition of *The Art of Asset Allocation* by David M. Darst (McGraw-Hill, 2008). Darst is a managing director at Morgan Stanley. Another good book on the subject is *All About Asset Allocation* by Richard A. Ferri, CFA (McGraw-Hill, 2006).

Important Lessons in This Chapter

- There is nothing more important than asset allocation. Do it first, and check it the most often. Change it when necessary. Your asset allocation should be foremost in your mind at all times.
- Above all, when you get your asset allocation right, you'll be around to invest another day. See Chapters 3 and 7 for specific advice.

CHAPTER

2

The Second Essential: Diversify within Asset Classes

After you've established your asset allocation, the next step is to diversify within each asset class, sometimes called sub-asset allocation or second-tier diversification. In the equity allocation, for example, it means diversifying among large- and small-cap stocks, U.S. and international, and so on. These definitions are not hard and fast. Many people, for example, would consider international stocks a separate asset class.

Sub-asset equity allocations have totally different characteristics than asset allocations. In this case, there is a substantial long-run correlation between most sub-asset class correlations. One institutional study found that when correlating five sub-asset equity classes, the lowest correlation of U.S. core stocks to emerging market stocks was a very substantial 0.82. Most correlations ran in the high 0.90s. The following table shows the sub-asset class correlations within the equity asset allocation.

What these facts mean is that determining sub-asset allocations is far less important than determining asset allocations—and probably even less important than selecting individual funds.

This is the part of investing where you can take shortcuts, and do it the easy way.

Equity Correlations, Sub-Asset Allocations

	U.S. Core	Global	All Country World	Non-U.S.	Emerging Markets
U.S. core	1.00	0.97	0.96	0.90	0.82
Global	0.97	1.00	1.00	0.97	0.89
All country world	0.96	1.00	1.00	0.98	0.91
Non-U.S.	0.90	0.97	0.98	1.00	0.90
Emerging markets	0.82	0.89	0.91	0.90	1.00

Source: Capital Guardian, Sept. 17, 2010 presentation to Westchester Community College Finance Committee.

Global includes U.S. and developed countries. All country world adds emerging markets. Non-U.S. is EAFE (no emerging markets).

Diversify Stocks with Broad-Based Index Funds

The best way to begin the sub-asset allocation process is to pick a broad-based index fund for your core holding. Index funds, compared to the alternatives, are no-brainers. Here are some of their advantages:

- Index funds are easy to select.
- Index funds have *lower costs* because their portfolios are traded infrequently and they don't incur management and research costs.
- Index funds, which track a known index, *are not dependent on managerial expertise* the way actively managed funds are. It doesn't matter if an index fund manager leaves his fund; it may matter greatly if the manager of an actively managed fund quits. That means index funds have a *more consistent performance.*
- You don't get fooled into buying because of great performance, and then find out the active manager just had a hot streak.
- Index funds have less of a problem with assets growing to an unwieldy size.

Still, in this business all the good reasons in the world don't mean a thing if the investment doesn't perform. Great risk-adjusted returns are pretty much everything. Forget the concept, forget the academic theory—the proof is in the performance (see the following table). The fact is that over any decent period, indexing outperforms the average mutual fund.

Percentage of U.S. Equity Funds *Outperformed* by Benchmarks

Fund Category	Comparison Index	One Year	Three Year	Five Year
All large-cap funds	S&P 500	65.7	57.7	61.8
All mid-cap funds	S&P Mid-Cap 400	73.8	83.9	78.2
All small-cap funds	S&P Small-Cap 600	53.4	70.1	63.0

Source: Standard & Poor's, periods ending December 2010.

One major disadvantage of index funds has become less significant over time. Index funds are always fully invested so they have no bear market protection. It used to be that a sizeable number of actively managed funds would go to cash in bear markets, so their bear market performance could be considerably better than that of index funds.

This isn't true any more. After the secular bull market of the 1980s and 1990s most actively managed funds found that they had to stay reasonably fully invested at all times to be competitive. At year-end 2008, a very bearish moment, the average stock fund had only 5.2 percent of its assets in cash, and a good part of that was necessary to meet redemptions, not because of an investment strategy.

Let me conclude with a story that brought home the advantages of index fund investing to me. In the late 1980s, I received a call from Jonathan Clements, then a columnist with *The Wall Street Journal.*

"Sheldon," he said, "If you could only recommend one fund, which one would it be?"

I tossed out a name and forgot about it. Five years later Jonathan called me again and said, "Congratulations, Sheldon, you're in second place."

"Second place in what?" I asked.

"The contest," he replied. "Don't you remember I asked you to pick one fund?"

I should have asked, "What contest?" But instead I asked, "What fund did I pick?"

"The Vanguard Total Stock Market Index Fund."

I breathed a sigh of relief.

Sequel: In late December 2009, the results of a different year-long contest in the *Chicago Tribune* (and syndicated elsewhere) were announced. I came in second out of eight contestants. My picks?

Two index funds: PowerShares FTSE RAFI US 1000 ETF (PRF) and Vanguard Total Stock Market Fund (VTSMX). I beat six pros—with index funds! Only one beat me. The most surefire way of participating in any up market is VTSMX (or VTI, the ETF version).

I am frequently asked to recommend a fund for a child. I always suggest a total stock market fund. It's the best single investment you can find for the kid.

In this book, I primarily recommend broad-based index funds. I do not recommend index funds that focus on narrow sectors such as tech, or actively managed portfolios. Those recommendations belong in periodical literature that can be updated frequently. There are a few exceptions, primarily specialty funds that complete recommended themes. In all cases, if any of these recommendations—or mentions—interests you, check them out carefully before buying.

Defining "Broad-Based"

My definition of a broad-based index fund is one that invests in the total stock market by holding 1,000 or more stocks. These broad-based index funds are available from several no-load fund groups with very low continuing management fees.

For all practical purposes, Total Stock Market Funds own all listed stocks, even though they may just sample the smallest ones. Check Vanguard, Fidelity, Charles Schwab, and T. Rowe Price for these funds. (Some of these funds go by names other than "total stock market," so you may need to talk to a phone rep at these groups for details.)

There are other ETFs that also offer wide diversification. Three in this category are the iShares DJ US Total Market Index (IYY), the iShares Russell 3000 (IWV), and PowerShares FTSE RAFI US 1000 ETF (PRF), which is discussed in Chapter 8.

My definition of "broad-based" deliberately excludes S&P 500 funds. That's because the S&P 500 is a large-cap index that omits dynamic small companies that are often market leaders. Moreover, the Index has greater turnover than I would prefer (about 20 stocks a year, on average).

Some professionals argue that the 500 is actively managed by Standard & Poor's. There is truth to this assertion. It's an interesting quirk that the new stocks that S&P has added over the years have done worse than the stocks they replaced.

For whatever it's worth, 55 percent of my own equity portfolio is invested in broad-based index funds. (Plus another 24 percent is invested in low cost narrow-based index funds.)

Sometimes diversification can be employed in odd situations:

The Smartest Diversification Ever

As a 26-year old investor in 1939, at the outset of World War II, the late Sir John Templeton borrowed $10,000 and bought 100 shares of every stock trading at $1 a share or less on the New York and American Stock Exchanges. He wound up with a total of 104 companies, 34 of which were in bankruptcy at the time he bought them. Four years later he sold these stocks for more than $40,000 (that's $500,000 in today's money); only four turned out to be worthless. Templeton went on to found the Templeton Funds, now Franklin-Templeton, and become one of the best and most respected fund managers ever.

Forget Style Diversification

Diversifying by *style* has become a big deal. Many advisors and many investment publications will go into great detail explaining style diversification. They will admonish you to diversify between growth and value stocks, and between large-, mid-, and small-capitalization stocks. They will try to make this all seem very necessary by explaining the system popularized by Morningstar in 1992. Morningstar categorizes stocks or funds into nine different style boxes. Their matrix, which looks like a tic-tac-toe board, has three cap sizes on the vertical axis and growth, blend, and value on the horizontal axis. Blend means the security has both growth and value stocks.

In my opinion, diversification by style has been tremendously overemphasized. I think the biggest benefit of this strategy is that it gives investment advisors the opportunity to justify their fees by forecasting which styles will be the best performers, and making recommendations in each style box. The fund groups benefit by having more products to sell.

This, by the way, is a relatively new development. Years ago, funds had ordinary names like the Dreyfus Fund, Babson Fund, Magellan, or the Manhattan Fund. Only two funds had "Growth" in their names in 1949. Today, there are many, many funds devoted to a specific style, such as Fidelity Small-Cap Growth Fund, or T. Rowe Price Mid-Cap Value Index Fund.

There are a number of reasons why fund sponsors find differentiating their funds this way to be advantageous, none of them having much to do with you:

- With more than 5,000 equity funds extant, they need to distinguish their products for marketing reasons. Style designations in their names are one way to accomplish this.
- If a large group has narrowly focused funds in every style category, it will almost always have some winners that can be promoted. And as for the laggards, poor performance can be excused by noting that the style is out of favor.
- Since advisors will put their clients' money in several of these funds to achieve style diversification, the group has a greater chance of gathering assets.

It's Hard to Forecast Styles

It is extremely difficult, at best, to forecast the future and that certainly includes trying to forecast which styles will be the best performers. Performance leadership in these "style-based" asset classes may run in cycles, but these cycles are far from regular, and difficult to predict.

Furthermore, styles don't really qualify as asset classes. Stocks and bonds are clearly different asset classes. They often fail to move in sync with each other. But the differences between styles are usually a matter of degree. If large-caps are going to gain, chances are so will mid- and small-caps, just to different degrees, and at different times in the economic cycle. The same is true on the downside.

It's a little-known fact that correlations among sub-asset classes are not necessarily the same in bull markets as they are in bear markets. Two examples: According to a significant study by Mark Kritzman, president of Windham Capital Management, published in Peter Bernstein's *Economics and Portfolio Strategy* newsletter, *growth* and *value* both *go down* in bear markets, but they *don't gain to the same degree* in bull markets. Similarly, U.S. and foreign stocks are highly correlated during bear markets, but far less correlated in bull markets.

That's a shame. In both cases, we would vastly prefer the reverse: no correlation in bear markets to minimize our losses, and high correlation in bull markets when we want everything to go up.

Here's a Morningstar study that shows the correlations among their "style boxes" over a 10-year period. With 1.00 as perfect correlation, over half the style boxes correlated to the others at a 0.95 or higher level, and 89 percent had correlations of 0.90 or higher. The lowest correlation was 0.85; that was between large-cap growth and small-cap value. These correlations are all very high and positive. Asset classes that are really good diversifiers can have negative correlations in the range of 0.00 to −0.20.

Correlations can be computed over various time frames. This study (see the following table), used a very long time frame to give maximum opportunity for the various styles to interplay.

Correlations between Style Boxes

Style Name	Cat	LB	LG	LV	MB	MG	MV	SB	SG	SV
Large blend	LB	1.00								
Large growth	LG	0.98	1.00							
Large value	LV	0.98	0.92	1.00						
Mid-cap blend	MB	0.97	0.95	0.96	1.00					
Mid-cap growth	MG	0.95	0.98	0.89	0.97	1.00				
Mid-cap value	MV	0.96	0.91	0.97	0.99	0.92	1.00			
Small blend	SB	0.92	0.90	0.92	0.98	0.94	0.97	1.00		
Small growth	SG	0.92	0.94	0.88	0.96	0.98	0.92	0.97	1.00	
Small value	SV	0.90	0.85	0.92	0.96	0.88	0.97	0.99	0.93	1.00

Source: Morningstar, 10 years ending December 2010.

The Solution

While having lots of styles works for the industry marketers, it's an investing no-brainer for you to have some exposure to all of these styles while maybe making some minor adjustments for the current environment.

The solution to style diversification is simple. *Buy them all.* Buy both growth and value, and all cap sizes. Never hang your hat on one style.

Once again, the easiest way to do this is to simply buy the Total Market fund that we described earlier. But there's one minor hitch.

Most Total Market funds are capitalization weighted—which I explain in Chapter 8. Therefore, these funds wind up being effectively large-cap funds. In the case of the Vanguard Total Market Fund, which is representative of the genre, 64 percent of its assets are in large-cap stocks, 27 percent in mid-cap stocks, and only 9 percent in small-cap stocks.

Over the long run, small-caps are outstanding performers and you must not neglect them. To rectify this small-cap underweighting, add a small-cap index fund or an extended market index fund to the portfolio. (Extended market funds own the smaller stocks outside of the large-cap S&P 500 universe. SMID-cap [small-mid] funds also buy essentially the same universe.) I would bring the small-cap weighting up to 20 percent of your domestic stock portfolio.

See, we've taken care of style diversification with two funds. Now isn't that a lot easier than trying to own something in all the nine style boxes, or guessing which style will lead? Leave the style guessing to the fashion world.

Think Globally

There is one other diversification imperative: It's essential to allocate a portion of your equity investments outside the United States. People have long maintained it's one world, but now that has actually become a reality. In sharp contrast to the world before the demise of the U.S.S.R., today virtually everyone everywhere is a capitalist, or trying to be one. The opportunities overseas have grown geometrically. In 1970, world trade accounted for about 12 percent of world GDP. By 2009 it had grown to 34 percent of world GDP.

In 1970 the market value of all stocks worldwide was $936 billion, 68 percent in the United States and 32 percent outside the country. At the end of 2010, global equities were valued at $54.9 trillion, and the stocks of companies outside the United States accounted for 69 percent of the total. You just can't ignore a large majority of the world's economic activity.

That's only one of the reasons for investing overseas. Long-term growth opportunities abroad are enormous, particularly in the emerging markets. Foreign companies are usually now as well managed as American companies. And their stock valuations may be better. Moreover, international investments denominated in foreign currencies provide a hedge against a weak dollar.

There are no sensible arguments for restricting your investments to the United States. Most of the reasons investors overweight U.S.

stocks have to do with the home-country bias: familiarity and inertia, combined with discomfort and lack of experience with foreign stocks.

That said, what percent of your equity allocation should be invested overseas? I've seen a lot of answers. I read that your international equity allocation should be 15 percent, 25 percent, 40 percent, 50 percent+, (and others) of your total equity allocation. There is clearly no universally agreed upon number.

Since I believe international equities are basically a sub-asset class, my advice is to set your international allocation *opportunistically*. By that I mean, if foreign markets are outpacing the United States, increase the international allocation. If the U.S. stocks are doing better, lower the allocation. The strength of the dollar is a factor. With a weak dollar, overseas markets will do better in dollar terms, and vice versa. For whatever it's worth, my own international stock allocation is 14 percent (of all equities).

Here are some tips to guide you in your allocation:

- Take into account any international exposure you may have as a result of owning domestic U.S. mutual funds. The average domestic stock fund now has 7 percent of its assets invested overseas, and 153 diversified domestic-equity funds have more than 25 percent of their assets in overseas stocks.
- Consider gaining international exposure by buying funds that invest in multinational corporations. It's increasingly difficult to distinguish a U.S. company from a foreign company. Coca-Cola, while headquartered in Atlanta, gets 72 percent of its revenue from non-U.S. operations. And here's a real shocker: More than half the profits of the S&P 500 companies in 2008 came from outside the country. And that fraction is destined to increase.
- Understand the nomenclature. In the jargon of the mutual fund industry, an "international" fund usually does not include any exposure to North American equities. A "global" fund invests all over the world, including exposure to the U.S. and Canadian markets.
- Consider developed market funds and emerging market funds separately.

Diversify by Time

In addition to baskets and boxes, you can diversify in many other ways. All reduce risk.

One other way is by *time*. It's never a good idea to put a huge lump sum into the market on any given day. You can reduce risk by spreading purchases over months, if not years, particularly if you are in an aging bull market.

That said, there are many exceptions to this rule. If the market has been in a bear mode for 18 months or more, I think a case can be made that it's worth the risk for a long-term investor to make some large equity purchases. Even if you're wrong, time will usually bail you out.

This leads into a subject called dollar-cost averaging (DCA), which is a well-known strategy whose goal is to increase your chances of buying when the market is low.

When to Use Dollar-Cost Averaging

Advocates of dollar-cost averaging make it seem like it's the ultimate mechanical system to ensure profits when applied consistently over a long period. It's not that simple, and it's not a panacea.

In its purest form, DCA is a discipline that requires an investment of the same dollar amount at regular periodic intervals, such as each month or quarter. Thus, when stock prices are high, you buy fewer shares and when prices are low, more shares. Over the years, the chances of obtaining a lower overall cost basis increase greatly.

DCA should be used primarily to invest regularly from earned income or through regular retirement plan contributions. Funding a 401(k) or an IRA with periodic purchases of a fixed dollar amount is a classic application that is highly recommended. Secondarily, DCA can be used to spread out lump-sum investments, but there are pitfalls.

In the 1990s, we once landed a new client for the BJ Group, a managed account company I co-owned with another advisor. Since the market seemed fairly high when we received the client's money, we decided to invest half as a lump sum, and DCA the remainder over a period of about four months. We thought this was a sensible compromise.

After two weeks, I got a call from the new client asking in an irate voice: "Why haven't you invested the other half of my money?"

I explained our strategy.

"Listen," he responded, "I'm 82 years old. I don't have time to dollar-cost average. Dump it in."

He had a point, and we were, perhaps, a bit too cautious. In a bull market a lump-sum investment will usually beat DCA because you will have more money working for you longer.

The real value of dollar-cost averaging is psychological. It makes it easier for you to make at least some investments during bear markets when prices are low. But the bottom line is that deciding whether to invest using DCA or lump sum is really a market timing call. Since up years outnumber down years, investing a large sum of money as a lump-sum will more often than not turn out to be the superior strategy for the long-term. One study found that from 1976 through 2007, dollar-cost averaging beat the S&P 500 Index. However, an investor would have been 11 percent better off by investing the whole sum in 1976.

Finally, I would never DCA into individual stocks because you never know whether an individual company will continue to perform well over time.

Diversify the Source of Your Income

You also need to diversify the source of your income, if at all possible. This mandate can affect a number of occupations. Stockbrokers, or almost any financial professional whose job security is largely dependent on a good stock market, should only invest a small portion of their personal wealth in stocks. Similarly, real estate professionals and contractors should not put all their personal investments in real estate.

In the Bernard Madoff scam, there were "feeder" funds that sent their clients' money to Madoff—and sent their own money to him as well. That was an epic mistake. Even worse, some of Madoff's own employees invested with him. They probably lost everything.

Where most laymen go wrong is in funding their 401(k) plans with too much of their own company's stock. You can be dangerously undiversified if this investment grows too large, because not only will your current income be dependent on your company's fortune, but also your savings. My guideline is that you should never put more than 10 percent of your retirement money into your company's stock. And if you don't understand corporate finance and accounting, limit your ownership to 5 percent.

Unfortunately, reality is quite different.

Company Stock as % of 401(k) Assets

Coca-Cola	51%
General Electric	42%
Johnson & Johnson	28%
McDonald's	45%
Target	42%

Source: Pensions and Investments, February, 2010.

Enron employees had 62 percent of their retirement assets in the company's stock shortly before it went under. Familiarity is not the same as knowledge.

And finally for investors who prefer active management, if your account is large enough, it may make sense to diversify among different money managers. The big institutions commonly do this.

In this chapter we focused on diversifying your equity basket because it is so important and failure to diversify carries substantial consequences. Naturally, all the other asset classes require diversification, too.

How Many Funds Do You Need?

It is not necessary to own many funds. You can easily get by with two domestic equity funds, one foreign equity fund, a bond fund and a money market fund. You can do all this on your own and keep it simple.

That said, there is a powerful temptation to own far more. So, as long as each fund is low cost and carries its weight in your portfolio, I don't see anything terribly wrong with acquiring more. You may get some additional diversification. With modern capabilities for monitoring your investments, you can easily own up to 20 to 25 funds.

Here's a thought. When Peter Lynch ran Fidelity Magellan in the 1980s, he had as many as a thousand stocks in the fund's portfolio. And Magellan was *not* an index fund! When asked why he had so many holdings, many of them in token amounts, he answered that was his way of keeping track of investments that might have promise.

I think individual investors could adapt Lynch's strategy to their needs. If you hear about a fund that may be promising, buy the minimum if it's not too high. (With ETFs you can really buy cheaply.) That will make it much easier to follow. Otherwise, if you are like most people, the fund will soon be out of sight and mind.

Do Individual Stocks Have a Place in Your Portfolio? I Say No

Owning individual stocks is becoming passé. According to industry sources, in 2010 households were net *buyers* of $230 billion of registered investment company assets (mutual funds, ETFs, closed-ends, and variable annuities), *bought* $163 billion of directly held bonds, but were net *sellers* of $187 billion of directly held stocks.

For a generation, particularly since the advent of 401(k) retirement plans, the majority of investors primarily own diversified portfolios. But some investors still continue to own individual stocks. Why?

Why, indeed. Some reasons: Perhaps they heard a story about a stock that they liked. They've always bought stocks. They inherited their stocks. Their friends buy stocks. They do it for a lark. A broker sold them the stock. They find stocks romantic. They need action. They think all they have to do is buy them when they are undervalued, and sell them when they are overvalued like all the professionals say they do. They believe they are above-average stock pickers.

Well, okay, some of the better pickers are hoping for that big score that can set you up for life. Or they're hoping to pick stocks that will gain when the indexes are declining.

These are seldom fruitful reasons for buying individual stocks.

The most important reason for not buying individual stocks is that the market is reasonably efficient, meaning that the prices of securities already reflect all known information that impacts their value. This means it is difficult to get an informational edge, the surest path to riches for some. While the efficient market theory is not universally accepted, and books have been written about pricing "anomalies," it's true enough for us to make our investing decisions based on this premise. It's important to note that the hypothesis does not claim that all that is known about a stock or its price is always *right*. Nor does it mean that stocks cannot be over- or undervalued.

See the following box for an upside-down way to think about this insight.

You Think It's Easy to Lose? Think Again

Random walkers think that winning is mostly a matter of chance. If this is true, then it follows that losing could also be a matter of chance. John Rogers, founder and CEO of the Ariel funds and a *Forbes* columnist, tested this premise by asking 71 of his associates to pick 10 stocks that would *underperform* the market in the second quarter of 2009. As reported in *Forbes*, only 19 of them succeeded, meaning 73 percent of them tried to lose on purpose but weren't able to. Indeed the average return on the try-to-lose portfolios was 30 percent, double the market's return. Rogers looked on the experiment as validation of the difficulties of short-term investing. I see it as validation of the efficient market hypothesis.

You need a lot of stocks to diversify. If you buy a mutual fund you know that, with minor exceptions, the fund will own enough different stocks to diversify away the specific stock risk (leaving just the risk of being in equities at all). To construct your own portfolio you will need to own at least 18 stocks—in various industries—before you are acceptably diversified. To really eliminate diversifiable stock risk, however, 40 different stocks are recommended. Such a large number requires a lot of work and that's why you should be in funds. The following chart clearly spells out these parameters.

Diversification Reduces Portfolio Risk: Portfolio Performance More Closely Tracks Market Performance When More Stocks Are Held

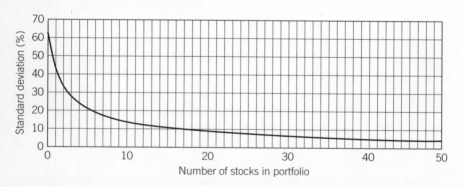

Source: John Campbell, Martin Lettau, Burton Malkiel, and Yexiao Xu, "Have Individual Stocks Become More Volatile?" *Journal of Finance*, February 2001.

Hindsight is easy; foresight is hard, as illustrated here:

Microsoft Executives in 1978: Would You Have Invested?

Why the Fixation on Individual Stocks?

I think the origin of this fixation goes back many years, to a time well before World War II, when "smart" investors bought stocks and "dumb" investors were sold load funds.

It was a different world back then. Commissions were high and fixed by the "Big Board"—the New York Stock Exchange. Innovations like financial planners and investment advisors who are compensated by assets under management were far in the future. Efficient market theory hadn't even surfaced in the universities let alone on Wall Street. And growth stock investing hadn't been invented yet. The understanding of diversification was primitive compared to today.

The so-called sophisticated investors of that day bought their stocks from brokers, who were called "customers men." They worked solely on commission and had every reason to do a lot of recommending.

It's a different world now. We know more, and have different kinds of financial information so we no longer have to rely on brokers' recommendations or stock tips.

A lot of investors see no harm in taking an occasional flyer on a stock. And I do have to agree there is no harm done if the amount invested is unimportant. Nevertheless, investing is serious business, and I believe it's preferable to find other ways to have fun.

I can see only one exception to this rule—and it's rare: Buy only when you have an information edge over other investors. In other words, only buy a stock when you know more about the company than Wall Street does. If you hear about a stock from the media or from a financial advisor, you don't know more than Wall Street and if you buy the stock you are only going along for the ride.

I Buy a Stock

The last time I knew more than Wall Street about a specific stock was in late 1998. The stock was Nielsen Media Research, and it was depressed because the networks, the big users of its famed Nielsen TV ratings, had grown tired of the Nielsen monopoly. They had announced that they would back another company to provide competitive ratings.

This was my area of expertise when I worked at the networks, so I doubted that their initiative would succeed. There had been similar attempts every five years or so, and all had come to naught. Also, I was acquainted with the president of the research company that was being promoted to provide alternative ratings and I didn't believe he had the drive to take on an entrenched giant like Nielsen. I thought the networks were going through the motions to extract concessions from Nielsen, which turned out to be pretty much the case.

No Wall Street securities analyst understood this background. I bought the stock at a price/earnings ratio of about nine and watched the price quadruple over the next year. The gain was mainly due to the market's reevaluating the P/E because earnings remained virtually unchanged. What made the profit even nicer was that Nielsen was a conservative, old-line marketing firm. Most of the other big gainers in 1999 were high-tech and Internet stocks. (Disclosure: Part of the gain was due to a buyout in the final months of the year.)

Smart Amateurs Can Make Big Bucks

Here's a great story on how a person with no financial training whatsoever used his personal knowledge to make big money. Back in the 1950s and 1960s the late Vince Francis was the West Coast time salesman for ABC-TV. In the early days of television there were still industries that had never advertised on TV. Vince noticed that the *first* company in an industry to buy TV time usually saw its profits, and stock price, zoom at the expense of its competitors. Since Vince's job was to bring in new advertisers, he was perfectly positioned to take advantage of this knowledge. No toy manufacturer had ever advertised on TV before Vince sold Mattel a sponsorship. Immediately upon clinching the sale, Vince bought Mattel stock, and made a killing. The point is that smarts and keen observation can reward anybody. The pros don't have a monopoly on brains.

If you study stock market history, you'll see that the great investors of the past, people like Joe Kennedy, Bernard Baruch, and the Rothschilds, all made their fortunes by having superior knowledge.

Today it's illegal to use inside information for stock-trading profit the way these greats sometimes did. So, if an individual investor gains an information edge based on a tip from an insider, and it involves material non-public information, using it to trade may be illegal. That's what led Martha Stewart to spend a winter in a gated community (although her specific crime was lying to the investigating authorities). You need to be careful to get your intelligence legally.

It sometimes can make sense to develop an expertise in the stock of the rare company that you know more about than the markets do. It makes no sense at all to try to put together a 20 to 40 stock portfolio on your own. I wouldn't trust a broker to do it, either. If my equity allocation were over $3 million, I might trust a major investment bank to do it. But, it's so much simpler to buy a fund.

I'd compare stock pickers to astrologers, but I don't want to bad-mouth astrologers.

—Eugene Fama (efficient market economist) in *Fortune*

Important Lessons in This Chapter

- Successfully implementing an overall asset allocation and diversification strategy is the primary way to reduce risk. If you don't diversify you are taking the risk that large holdings of specific securities will go south and cost you more than you can afford.
- One of the most basic rules of risk taking is: Don't take risks you don't have to take. Most people know this intuitively. That's why Russian roulette has never become a popular pursuit.

3

The Third Essential: Understand and Control Risk

The era where taking greater risks almost always got you greater gains is history. It died when the great secular bull market ended. In this new era, the importance of risk management in investing is vastly increased.

So even though the subject of controlling risk overlaps with asset allocation and diversification, managing risk is so important and has such unique aspects that, I believe, it warrants its own discussion.

The goal of this book is not to achieve the greatest gains; it is to achieve the greatest risk-adjusted gains.

Some losses are inevitable when you're investing. So, let's concentrate on avoiding an unaffordable loss, no matter how unlikely the circumstance.

Measuring Risk

Before you can protect yourself against risk you need to be able to measure it. After all, investing is not a gambling game where the odds of winning or losing can be calculated to the penny. Investing deals with multiple unknowns that are virtually impossible to measure. (There was a lot of anguish in 2008 and 2009 when federal regulators couldn't figure out the risk in the mortgage securities held by Freddie Mac and Fannie Mae.)

Basically, risk is simply the possibility of losing money, most importantly at the end of an investment horizon. But that's not precise enough for our, or Wall Street's, purposes. It's important to quantify risk to the best of our ability. So Wall Street has found a solution that provides us with the needed preciseness: volatility. It uses past volatility as a proxy for risk because volatility can be measured easily with simple statistical tools, though actual risk usually cannot.

But be aware that measuring volatility is far from a perfect solution. You can go wrong in a number of ways. After all, it's quite possible for a low volatility investment to be quite risky. As an illustration, bonds have low volatility . . . until they default. Also beta doesn't do a good job of capturing the risk of too little liquidity. Lack of sufficient liquidity contributed to the collapse of Long-Term Capital Management in 1998. Similarly, two other risks not usually captured by volatility are terrorism and unanticipated labor unrest. But it's still a most helpful tool.

Measuring Volatility

Several volatility measures are commonly used, and they can be helpful tools. In the case of stocks, there are betas (the most common measure), standard deviations, Sharpe ratios, semi-variance measures, R squared, and M squared. In the case of bonds, average maturities, duration, and credit quality indicate risk. All these measures have their uses. A word of warning, though: These volatility measures are not inviolate. They can vary under different market conditions.

Also, volatility measures tell you more about short-term risk than long-term risk. How the price of a fund jumps around this quarter or next may tell you little about its long-term prospects. The descriptions of these various measures get technical, so they have been relegated to the Glossary.

Betas Are the Most Common Way to Measure Risk

The most common and easiest way to get a fix on volatility is to check a fund's beta, which is readily available. The following table shows beta's parameters so you will know how to interpret them. A beta of 1.00 is the risk (or volatility) of the market. The usual measure of "the market" is the S&P 500. Funds with betas greater than 1.00 are riskier than the market. Those with betas less than 1.00 are more conservative. The 1.04 beta for the average stock fund is 4 percent more volatile than the market. You can interpret that to mean it's 4 percent riskier.

Fund Averages	Beta
All stock funds	1.04
Aggressive growth	1.09
Growth	1.05
Growth-income	0.95
Hybrid	0.62
Small company	1.18
Technology	1.17
Growth index	1.06
Value index	1.09

Source: *No-Load Fund Investor*, three years ending December 2010.

You can compute betas for individual stocks, and if you are assembling a portfolio on your own, you should do so.

Measuring Fixed-Income Risk

You also need to know the risk in fixed-income investments. The simplest measures are the grades produced by the rating agencies, Standard & Poor's and Moody's. These grades, which run from AAA to C in the case of S&P, are based on fundamentals. Investment grades are rated from AAA to BBB–. Non-investment grade bonds, usually called junk bonds, have lower ratings. (The recent bear market revealed a lot of deficiencies in these ratings, which may result in certain regulatory changes. Or as Warren Buffett put it: "Only when the tide goes out do you discover who has been swimming naked.")

There are a number of common sense measures you can apply to get rough measures of risk. In the case of mutual funds, Aggressive Growth and Growth are the riskiest objective categories. Small company funds tend to have higher betas than mid- and large-company funds. In industry sectors, tech is the riskiest, then natural resources.

Here's another rough way to measure volatility: If your portfolio has an average yield of 2 percent, you can anticipate that it will fluctuate about the same degree as the market. If you are uncomfortable with that amount of volatility, consider funds with higher yields. Or add fixed-income investments to your portfolio.

Managing Risk through Asset Allocation

Asset allocation is the first and most important step in managing risk and failure to allocate properly can be very costly. On several occasions in 2008 and 2009 some retired investors told me they were 75 percent in equities. On one occasion a retired friend told me her advisor had cautioned that 75 percent was too much and suggested selling down to 25 percent. She made the change, and shortly thereafter the market plunged. This story had a happy ending. All too often the ending is painful.

Since the greatest risk is in stocks, you first look at the amount of risk you want to put in that basket. The less you allocate to stocks and the more to bonds, the lower your investing risk should be. Looking at financial assets only, here are my limits on the high side: I would recommend that young people have a maximum of 80 percent in equities, middle-aged people 70 percent, and retirees 50 percent.

The word "stocks" came from an Old English word *stocc* meaning a tree trunk. The word originally connoted a *safe* investment. Times change.

Being totally out of equities is a mistake for most people. Even those who are long-retired should keep 20 to 25 percent in equities because of the need to keep up with inflation given today's longer life spans.

Diversification is the other basic strategy for risk reduction. However, bear in mind that it can't do the job all by itself. It's perfectly possible to have a diversified portfolio of closely correlated, risky equities. A fund invested in a thousand small-cap stocks might be an example.

Additionally, with today's up and down markets, you may not be rewarded for taking more risk, so I think you should now take a more risk-averse stance than you did in the 1990s.

According to a study conducted by T. Rowe Price, for the 15 years ending in 2010, a portfolio 50 percent in stocks and 50 percent in bonds had 100 percent of the return of an all-stock portfolio with only 51 percent of the risk. Similarly, a 75 percent stock/25 percent bond portfolio had 102 percent of an all-stock portfolio return with just 75 percent of the risk. This illustrates my basic principle of investing: Get the best possible return for the amount of risk you are taking. (Because of market conditions in the latest fifteen years, these advantages are somewhat greater than they had been when the study was conducted earlier.)

Another way to look at asset allocation as risk control is to vary your equity allocation depending on your time horizon. When you need the money is a very important consideration. If you need it in, say, three years to fund a college education, then a 10 percent equity weighting should be the outer limits of prudence. If it's for retirement 20 years away, then some of the percentages I will be citing in Chapter 7 would be relevant. This concept can be expanded far beyond retirement needs.

Your wealth is an important factor. If you are old enough so that inflation is not a problem and rich enough to maintain your lifestyle with muni bond interest, why bother with the ups and downs of equities? On the other hand, if you can live on an annuity or pension, you may want to go for further accumulation by keeping more money in stocks.

Five Levels of Risk

Unfortunately, volatility measures are at best a crude way of telling us much about inherent risk. Volatility is more a symptom of risk, rather than risk itself. There are, however, underlying principles that determine risk. The following insights are adapted from an article by the late Peter L. Bernstein and will give you a totally different understanding of risk:

> An asset is risky when we are uncertain about how much we will receive when we liquidate it, and how uncertain we are that interim cash flows (interest or dividends), if any, will be received during the holding period. Thus, the investment's time horizon and the reliability of the ongoing cash flows are the principal determinants of the riskiness of an asset.

All assets can be put in five risk categories:

Safest: Assets in which there is a known and guaranteed maturity and the interim cash flows are fixed. Example: Bank savings accounts, CDs, fixed annuities, and Treasury bonds.

Second safest: Assets in which there is a known and guaranteed maturity but interim cash flows are not fixed. Examples: Money market funds (their portfolio holdings have fixed maturities, but since they are constantly being turned over, the interest paid by the fund varies). Adjustable-rate bonds also fit into this group.

Third safest: Assets where there is a known maturity but no interim cash flows. Example: Zero-coupon bonds. You don't get a penny of income before maturity, which is why you should only buy U.S. Treasury zeros.

Fourth safest: Assets that have no maturity but do have interim cash flows. Example: Dividend-paying common stocks, preferred stocks, and consols (a British bond which pays interest but has no maturity).

Least safe (riskiest): Assets that have neither maturity nor any interim cash flows. Example: Non-dividend paying common stocks, gold, raw land, and collectibles. These assets are worth only what a buyer will pay for them. Gold, by this definition, winds up in the riskiest category, which is where it should be. Gold doesn't pay interest like bonds; it has no earnings or dividends like stocks; and it can't shelter you or provide rental income like real estate. Disregard the pervasive advertising to the contrary. Gold's worth as an investment really depends on people's nervousness. Its value as a hedge is less than absolute.

In conclusion, there are only two sources of potential revenue from investments: interim cash flows and the sale of holdings at a profit. Whereas the owner of a business has some control over cash flows, investors in public companies have none. The bottom line is that the degree of risk in each investment depends on the extent that you can control its two variables.

Five Levels of Risk

Risk	Maturity	Price at Maturity	Interim Cash Flows
Safest	known	known	fixed/guaranteed
2nd safest	known	known	variable
3rd safest	known	known	none
4th safest	none	none	yes
Riskiest	none	none	none

Source: Peter L. Bernstein, *Economics and Portfolio Strategy* newsletter.

Important Lesson in This Chapter

- In order to risk-adjust your investments you need to know your risk.

4

The Fourth Essential: Keep Your Costs Low

It's vital to keep your costs low. Studies done by Morningstar, Vanguard, myself, and many others show that the lower the expenses, the better the long-term performance. In fact, fund expenses predict performance better than any other single factor. That's because overhead expenses directly reduce performance. Low expenses foster good performance; high expenses reduce performance. This is the key reason why index funds do so well.

A corollary to this rule is that while good performance doesn't always continue, poor performance more often does. When poor performing mutual funds have higher expenses, funds find themselves in a vicious cycle. Alert shareholders bail out of these funds. The asset base shrinks but fixed costs stay the same, which drives up per share expenses. The performance worsens; more shareholders redeem. The cycle continues.

It can get pretty bad. Back in the 1990s there was a group of funds called Steadman Funds, later renamed the Ameritor Funds. Ten thousand dollars invested in their American Industry Fund at the beginning of the decade declined to $6,500 10 years later. Mind you now, this was the 1990s, a great decade for huge gains. It was virtually impossible for a fund to lose over a decade in this bubble—but Steadman did it.

With most investors redeeming, assets declined to $900,000. The expense ratio rose to 29.9 percent versus an industry average of about 1.5 percent. The prevailing opinion in the fund industry was that the remaining shareholders were either dead, had moved without notifying the fund, thus becoming "orphans," or were beneficiaries of trust accounts who never knew they were shareholders. If you don't get regular reports from your funds, give them a call and ask why.

Pay attention to fund expenses! You can't control companies, markets, the economic environment, or the fund managers. But you can control expenses. You don't have to buy high-cost investments and you shouldn't. Try to buy funds with expense ratios under 1 percent.

The *Investor* newsletter never recommended Fidelity Magellan in the days Peter Lynch ran it. Magellan was an outlier performer if ever there was one. However, Magellan carried a 3 percent load (sales charge) back then.

Low expenses foster good performance; high expenses reduce performance. This is the key reason why index funds do so well.

Examples of costs you need to be aware of include transaction costs, sales charges, 12b-1 fees, taxes, marketing costs, and advisor and management fees. Every cent that you save on costs goes directly into your pocket. Think of the expense ratio as a hurdle you have to clear before you can earn anything.

These costs have far greater impact on your wealth than the typical investor knows. They reduce investment returns on a dollar for dollar basis. Let's say you sign up with a brokerage house that charges you 3 percent of assets. That covers all management, advisory, and transaction fees. Now if your assets are earning 12 percent annually (and that's higher than the long-term record), then you are giving away one-fourth of your profits. But I don't believe stocks are going to do that well over the next decade. To keep the numbers simple, let's say they average 6 percent annually, which is certainly possible.

DILBERT REPRINTED BY PERMISSION OF UNITED FEATURE SYNDICATE, INC.

That means Wall Street is keeping 50 percent of your return. This is nuts. They're supposed to be working for you, not you for them.

A 40-Year Comparison between Do-It-Yourselfers and Pay-a-Guy (PAG) Types

What about the quarter million dollar advantage for do-it-yourselfers (henceforth DIY) over PAGs that I mentioned in the Preface. Here I use some different assumptions but the conclusion is the same.

This was a lifetime calculation, the real bottom line. I assumed that both the DIYs and the PAGs begin saving at age 25 and save for 40 years, until they are 65. I next assumed both had the same gross return—a conservative 7 percent a year.

Yes, I know your advisor will argue that he can pick securities that will provide a better return than you can. In some cases he will be right, particularly over short periods. In other cases he won't be. Some studies show that the average pro can't beat the market over long periods without ramping up the risk. My comparison assumes the same risk level for both.

Both investors invested the same amounts. From age 25 to 35 they each invested $2,500 annually. (They did this with 12 monthly payments totaling $2,500.) The next 10 years, ages 35 to 45, they increased their savings to $4,000 annually. From 45 to 55, with greater earning power, they invested $5,000 annually, and finally from 55 to 65, $6,000. The total investment for each was $175,000.

So far the two investors have matched each other. But here's the difference. The DIYs had a minimal expense of 20 basis points (0.20 percent), making their net annual return 6.8 percent. The PAGs paid 2.0 percent for advice and administrative and transaction costs. Their net return was 5.0 percent. Given that many investors pay 3 percent or more, 2 percent is conservative.

The results: Over the 40 years, the do-it-yourselfers amassed $723,450; the PAGs, $470,674—more than a quarter million dollar difference!

The Real Bottom Line

	Do-It-Yourselfers	PAGs
Annual investment: 25–35	$2,500	$2,500
Annual investment: 35–45	$4,000	$4,000
Annual investment: 45–55	$5,000	$5,000

(Continued)

	Do-It-Yourselfers	PAGs
Annual investment: 55–65	$6,000	$6,000
Gross return	7.0%	7.0%
Annual expenses	0.2%	2.0%
Net return	6.8%	5.0%
Your retirement nest egg	$723,450	$470,674

The Difference between Load and No-Load Funds

The cost of the average mutual fund is about 1.5 percent of assets annually (150 basis points). Many good, actively managed funds have expense ratios under 100 basis points, and some broad-based index funds have expense ratios as low as 0.06 percent, six basis points. The difference between an index fund and an average managed fund over a number of years is enormous. The simplest way to keep your costs low is to buy low cost index funds, and do as little trading as possible.

Warning: Not all index funds are low cost. Ten index funds have expense ratios of 2.75 percent or more. The worst has a ratio of 4.01 percent. You have to check. Try the Internet, call the fund, or simply look in the front of the fund's prospectus for a table that's usually called "Fees and Expenses."

Avoid Taxes as Much as Possible

Taxes don't show up in the expense ratio, but they are a very real expense. There are, however, ways to mitigate tax outlays:

- Consider tax-managed funds that take taxes into consideration when they trade.
- Don't forget the old standbys, tax sheltered accounts such as IRAs and 401(k)s. Put your tax-inefficient securities (like corporate bonds) in these tax sheltered accounts. Put your tax-efficient investments, like low- or no-dividend stocks, in taxable accounts.
- Hold securities long enough to take advantage of the long-term capital gains rate.

- Some funds have redemption fees of 1 to 2 percent if you sell them shortly after their purchase. It's usually better to wait until the redemption period ends.
- If you have to sell a large holding with a low cost basis, consider giving it to charity instead.

Important Lesson in This Chapter

- Make an extra quarter-million by lowering expenses.

CHAPTER
5

The Fifth Essential: Choose the Right Financial Media to Follow

I don't think it's possible to be a successful investor without relying heavily on the media. Virtually all investors and most investment professionals use the media as their principal source of investing information.

I am a perfect example of a person who learned his investing craft mostly from the media. I never worked on Wall Street, and, unlike reporters, I seldom interviewed portfolio managers. While I took an undergraduate investing and a corporate finance course in the 1950s, outside of explaining such basics as the differences between common stock, preferred stock, and bonds, that sort of thing, neither course taught me anything that is applicable to my work today.

I don't remember whether these courses even discussed mutual funds. Their greatest benefit was to get me interested in the field. My knowledge of practical economics and behavioral finance also comes from the media.

The only way I know how to do without the media is to turn the job over to a high-priced personal counselor. But even then, you are remiss if you don't learn enough to second-guess your advisor.

Where's the Best Place to Get Financial Advice? A Poll

In February 2010 *Money* magazine conducted a poll asking, "Where have you gotten the best financial advice?" The results are shown in the following table.

The media	34%
A professional financial advisor	28%
A family member	22%
A friend	16%

Poll was conducted in New York City. There were 16,494 responses.

The media won hands down. Yet, the financial media are seldom discussed, and when they are it's often disparagingly. This is wrong. Although it's easy to list the media's shortcomings, and I would be remiss if I didn't list a few of them, mainly I want to point out how the media can help make you an informed and successful investor. Knowing how to get the most out of the media is a major step toward investing success.

Of course there are many other worthwhile reasons for consuming media, including general knowledge and pure enjoyment, but these topics are not my concern in this chapter. In the discussion that follows, I have a singular point of view—namely, how to use the media to make you a better investor.

I'm going to cover essentially all the business and investing media because each has its benefits. But before I get into specifics, we need to discuss which media categories are most appropriate for you.

- Broadly speaking, I would say that if you are a real beginner, the best place to start learning is by reading books that teach investing and personal finance basics, and that might possibly include a few college textbooks.
- If you are an intermediate investor who has some knowledge of the fundamentals, personal finance magazines should be appropriate for you. Advanced investors should get most of their information from newspapers.
- Reasonably sophisticated investors can learn from business radio and TV, but I think broadcast has an awful lot of "noise" that may mislead novices. Newsletters also appeal to a wide range of investors, from beginner to expert, but they are most valuable for their specific recommendations. Keep in mind there is considerable overlap between specific mediums. These are not either/or choices.

Cost is a significant factor in obtaining advice. Personal advice from an investment professional is usually the best, but it's expensive.

Much more economical are the general media that can range from free (radio, TV, and Internet) to modest-cost personal finance magazines, and to the relatively more expensive financial newsletters.

So, here's how to use the specific media you are likely to encounter in your quest for sound investing advice.

Newspapers

You need to read extensively to be an accomplished investor. I think the best source is a newspaper. There are three outstanding newspapers that I believe are must-reads for involved investors: *The Wall Street Journal* and *Barron's* both published by News Corp., and the Sunday edition of *The New York Times*. All three are now available by carrier delivery in most major U.S. cities. *The New York Times* usually has special rates for weekend only home delivery. Also *The Times'* columnists and selected business and investing articles are available online for free at: www.thenewyorktimes.com. And once you subscribe for home delivery you have complete online access to the paper. *The Journal* and *Barron's* have introductory offers on the Web.

By reporting breaking news, dailies have a timeliness advantage over periodical competition that publishes weekly, biweekly, or monthly. The dailies are far quicker to report on business and economic events that significantly bear on stock prices, and they often do it more extensively than their competition. As an illustration, in 2009, newspapers (as well as broadcast and the Internet) followed the stimulus bill closely. Periodicals didn't. Whatever little coverage the periodicals provided was after the fact. Similarly, in 2010, newspapers provided page-one coverage of the debt crisis. Newspapers also have more space to devote to subjects such as Federal Reserve policies or changes in the tax code, which can be of critical importance to investors.

Since newspapers are published daily, they may contain more investing advice than the less frequently published magazines or newsletters. *The Wall Street Journal* has a four-page personal finance section "Weekend Investor," published every Saturday that is outstanding; a monthly report on funds, and periodically includes special sections on personal finance. *The Times'* Sunday Business section frequently has worthwhile articles for the investor. The three newspapers all have superb editorial staffs.

The Journal, always good when it was owned by the Bancroft family, is even better now that it is owned by Rupert Murdoch's News

Corporation. It's broadened its news coverage to include political and international news, arts, and sports. Murdoch has transformed *The Journal* from a business-focused second-read into a general-news-driven first-read that is competing head-to-head with *The New York Times* and Gannett's *USA Today*. At a time when virtually all large-city papers are losing circulation, *The Journal* is gaining. It is now the leading global news brand.

There are two other finance-heavy dailies. One is *Investor's Business Daily (IBD)*, which often includes comprehensive investing articles. It's published five days a week with the Monday edition coming out on Saturday. The downside, as far as I am concerned, is that *IBD*'s coverage leans toward stocks. It is also somewhat duplicative of *The Journal*.

The other is the *Financial Times*, which now sells as many copies in the United States as in the United Kingdom and Europe. It's considerate of its readers, featuring terse no-jump stories, many of the most important of them a day ahead of the competition. Its editorials are usually short.

If you don't want to read any of these newspapers, at least read the business section of your local newspaper. Please. If your local paper is any good at all, you'll learn things the other media don't cover.

One other point: Don't expect great profit-making ideas in every issue. If you pick up as little as one idea a month, then the publication is worthwhile. In a monthly magazine, I'd be happy with one decent idea per quarter.

Tip

The media, like the market, is a discounting machine. Sometimes you should read, watch, or listen to them to know what everyone else is focused on. That means watching the news, not for itself, but for the market's reaction to it. For example: when the market holds up under bad news that can be bullish.

If subscribing to a lot of newspapers and personal finance magazines is too much, check your local library. You will be surprised at how many periodicals are available there. You can peruse them quickly and photocopy the articles you are interested in. You can also check online. Sometimes you can find helpful information there with just a free registration.

Personal Finance Magazines

Personal finance magazines are relatively inexpensive, a great read, and have a lot of interesting and useful articles. But they have some important drawbacks.

- Although they offer plentiful advice on when to buy investments, they rarely provide any specific sell guidance. Like brokers, they know that potential buyers vastly outnumber potential sellers, and they want to appeal to as many readers as possible. This imbalance also reflects their generally upbeat attitudes toward markets, which helps to sell the advertising of various financial companies.
- There is seldom any follow-up to their recommendations. Understand that I consider any write-up or profile essentially a recommendation.
- Unlike newsletters, nobody tracks their performance or objectively evaluates the accuracy of their recommendations.
- As with all mass media, they can't offer personalized advice.
- They have relatively little general news, even when it's important. Think of Fannie Mae's and Freddie Mac's travails which were prominently covered by newspapers and broadcast.
- They often lack timeliness.

To their credit, none of the personal finance magazines overly emphasize individual stocks in their investment coverage.

The covers and articles of the personal finance magazines are great examples of what economists call co-incident indicators. Their tone changes with the times. Back in the 1990s, a time of the red-hot bull markets, their emphasis was on how to get rich. Their articles featured the best how-to advice they could find by constantly interviewing experts. In a single issue of *Money* of that era, I was once quoted in five different articles! In that strong bull market, their covers constantly featured teaser headlines offering strong profits. Since the end of the secular bull market in 2000, the three leading personal finance magazines—*Money, Kiplinger's Personal Finance Magazine,* and *Smart Money*—have shifted to a more lifestyle focus. While they still carry many useful "how-to-invest" articles, these features no longer dominate their pages. Articles on insurance, home ownership, smart buying, estate planning, taxes, and cars are more prominent. There are pieces that rank cities ("100 Best Places to live in America," and so on).

These publications also feature special investment issues at least once a year, which are highly recommended. If you don't subscribe regularly, I would make an effort to pick up these editions either on the newsstand or peruse them in libraries.

In the middle of the last decade they even ventured into ultra *soft* articles. To illustrate, in July 2007, *Money* ran an article titled *How to Marry a Billionaire*. The other financial media probably wouldn't do that.

Then, in the 2008 down market, their investing articles became far more conservative. Headlines were on the order of: "Juicy Returns on Your Cash," "Stocks that Pay You 5 percent or More," "How to Cope with Financial Stress," "Protect Your Money," "Time to Buy Gold?"

As the worst of the bear receded, headlines became more factual. December or early January is the time when all the magazines typically feature cover stories forecasting the upcoming year. Here's their cautious take: *Money's* Special Outlook Issue had a conservative headline on its cover: "Make Money in 2011." *Kiplinger's* and *Smart Money* followed with the same cover: "Where to Invest in 2011." There's no market forecast in either title.

One problem, in my opinion, is that these magazines love to illustrate their how-to articles with personal case histories.

Kiplinger's February 2007 cover story was titled "How to make a MILLION." The article consisted of 11 case histories. Nine featured people who made a million by starting successful businesses. Factually, this is how most people do get rich. But it's not actionable news. The article didn't tell how to start a new business successfully. It just chronicled these nine people's experiences. The 10th person got rich by investing in a hot real estate market, not exactly profitable advice in 2007. The 11th invested in stocks based on recommendations from two old-line publications: the *Value Line Investment Survey* and *S&P Outlook*. The article revealed that this person was a big saver, which was probably the real reason he was worth a million. The bottom line was that while it was enjoyable reading, the article really didn't make anyone a better investor.

Words to live by: The plural of anecdote is not data.

You will know that a personal finance magazine has come of age when it publishes this teaser headline on the cover: "Five Index Funds to Buy NOW!" Don't hold your breath waiting for this to happen.

In the 1990s, *Money* would publish a cover story every year entitled "How to Invest $1,000." The idea was to help investors who only had $1,000 to their names. I never understood the point of it, since the average reader of *Money*, if my memory serves me right, had an investment portfolio of $87,000 at that time.

Money would call me every year, requesting my recommendation of a mutual fund with an initial minimum of $1,000 or less. When I inquired why *Money* felt the need to keep repeating the same topic year after year, I was told that it was their best-selling issue on newsstands every year. Effectively, "How to Invest $1,000" was *Money*'s equivalent of *Sports Illustrated*'s annual swimsuit issue.

So each year when *Money* called, I would offer a timely fund recommendation, but I would also add that what I would really do if all I had was $1,000, would be to blow it on a Caribbean island vacation. After ignoring my jest for several years, they finally printed it alongside the serious investing advice. I loved it.

In addition to the three targeted personal finance magazines, there are three other magazines that combine business articles with personal finance information: *Forbes, Fortune,* and *Bloomberg BusinessWeek.*

Forbes' personal finance coverage is probably the most extensive. It has excellent investing articles. It was among the first publications to grade mutual funds using consistent methods. And it doesn't print teaser headlines on its cover.

If it has any weakness, it is its tendency to go overboard on lists. Using a riff on their famous 400 wealthiest individuals ranking, *Forbes* now has a list of the 15 wealthiest *fictional* characters. The 2011 list included Bruce Wayne, Jed Clampett, Scrooge McDuck, Richie Rich, and Gordon Gekko. Even acknowledging that it was a fun article to read, I thought this was a little too much.

Furthermore, on its website, *Forbes* has a ranking of the 25 largest *fictional* companies. *Forbes* says the total revenues of these 25 companies are an awesome $3.6 trillion.

Of course, *Forbes* isn't the only magazine to carry lists. As this is written, a veritable slew of them have picked up list-mania. Note that this book does not offer lists of the 10 greatest portfolio managers of all time, the 10 greatest funds of all time, or the 10 worst lemons of all time. You will have to look elsewhere for these gems.

In sum, if you are an advanced investor give newspapers priority over personal finance magazines. If you're not, enjoy and learn from the magazines.

The plural of anecdote is not data.

I've been an investment professional since 1974, and I still learn from the articles in the six magazines I just mentioned. Don't ignore this convenient source of good investing information.

Newsletters

As a former newsletter editor and publisher, I'm biased. I think newsletters, while priced higher than magazines, are well worth it. Unlike all the other media, *the primary business of newsletters is to make recommendations.* They are not published to provide entertainment; they make do with serviceable prose. They are not advertising vehicles. They are for people who want *actionable advice* that is as bias-free as possible.

- Newsletters are the only generalized source of financial information that provide sell as well as buy advice.
- They are the only medium that publishes model portfolios that you can actually follow. The typical recommended portfolio in a newsletter is updated with each issue, and it's become common to publish Internet alerts in between issues.
- Newsletters typically do not accept advertising. However, a few newsletters do accept advertising inserts, usually for a subsidiary or another newsletter of the publisher. In a few cases it is for products relating to the newsletter's theme.
- In the newsletter business, the first year's revenues from introductory offers are at best a break-even situation because of the high cost of direct mail. This means all the newsletter's profits are made after the first year when the subscribers renew. If the newsletter doesn't fulfill a need and do a job for its subscribers, there aren't going to be any renewals, and soon no newsletter. For that reason, I wouldn't subscribe to a brand new newsletter.
- Unique among the media, the performance of newsletter recommendations is independently monitored and reported on a regular basis by the independent *Hulbert Financial Digest,* the watchdog of the newsletter industry. Newsletters also have this advantage over financial planners, including, of course, those planners who are regularly interviewed by the press.
- Virtually all newsletters are edited by gurus, not reporters. Even though reporters and gurus both spend a lot of time

writing, their skills are very different. The former excel at reporting; the latter at analyzing.

- I think another advantage of newsletters is that they are typically edited by a sole guru with a singular point of view. The mass media—whether newspapers, magazines, or TV—offer multiple (sometimes conflicting) points of view. I think most investors are better off finding a newsletter with an investing philosophy that agrees with their own, and sticking with it.

For these reasons, I believe newsletters are the best source for investment recommendations. If you've never subscribed to a newsletter, call a few. Ask for a free sample issue, and see if they are for you. Even though I sold *The No-Load Fund Investor* newsletter in 2003 to Mark Salzinger, previously editor-in-chief of the Louis Rukeyser newsletters, I still support, recommend, and receive some remuneration from it. Therefore, it would not be right for me to recommend any other newsletters.

However, there is one publication, that's kind of a cross between a magazine and a newsletter that is different. Published by Boardroom Reports, it's called *Bottom Line Personal.*

This monthly publication has just 16 pages per issue, but it is densely packed with very helpful advice that is only partly financial. It contains no advertising. If you've never read it, check into it by calling 800–274–5611 for a free sample. (Disclosure: I am on the magazine's Panel of Experts, but I do not draw any pay.)

Newsletters with Model Portfolios   There are many financial newsletters that publish model portfolios for their subscribers. (There are also many other financial newsletters that make recommendations in copy only or sometimes in lists. They, in my opinion, are generally not as helpful.)

The Appendix to this book lists major newsletters that regularly publish model portfolios, with the accent on those newsletters that offer mutual fund portfolios. I have not made any attempt to screen this list for good performers, something you should do either by analyzing the newsletters' literature or by consulting the *Hulbert Financial Digest,* the source of this list. My list excludes newsletter performance data for much the same reason I excluded it (and recommendations) for actively managed mutual funds. Timeliness is important. Where phone numbers are unavailable, I've substituted web addresses. Also, here's a website that will give you additional information on about 175 financial newsletters: www.marketwatch .com/news/newsletters/newsletters.asp.

In Case You Detest Junk Mail   If you subscribe to a newsletter the odds are very good the newsletter publisher will rent out your name to other direct mailers. You will then receive junk mail. If you don't want this to happen there is a simple remedy. Just ask the newsletter publisher not to do it. He is required by law to abide by your wishes. You can do this at any time, but obviously the best time is when you initiate the subscription.

Mutual Fund-Sponsored Newsletters   A number of mutual funds publish free newsletters for their shareholders. The Vanguard and T. Rowe Price newsletters are well worth reading. Charles Schwab has a fine magazine, *On Investing*, published quarterly that is free to all their retail customers. In addition, the Muhlenkamp Fund has a quarterly newsletter, the *Muhlenkamp Memorandum*, which is accessible online at no charge. It offers informative market insights from time to time. These fund-sponsored newsletters can be very useful for investors who hold their respective funds. They also provide insightful general investing information.

Books

Books are the best way to learn the basics. The first book I wrote, *Put Money in Your Pocket*, which was published during the 1973 to 1974 bear market, at a time when most investors were afraid of equities, showed how stocks could still make sense when purchased in commission-free portfolios for the long-term. I made successful investors out of many people who would have joined the ensuing great bull market much later, had they not read my book.

Among the most gratifying aspects of my work were the many thank-you letters I received over the years. To illustrate, I received the following letter in 1990. It meant a lot to me.

Dear Sheldon,

I feel compelled to write a note to you and send it with my application for a one-year subscription to your No-Load Fund Investor.

One day during 1975, I was drifting through the aisles of my local library. A book entitled *Put Money in Your Pocket* caught my eye. I checked it out, read it, and became fascinated by what you had written. That book planted the seed that was to change my outlook on investing. Through me, it also changed the outlook of quite a few of my friends and relatives.

Five years later, I retired (four years earlier than required) and with a philosophy of investing that began with the seed planted by your book, we have enjoyed seeing our investments grow at a compound rate in excess of 16 percent. So you see, subscribing to your service is really a small "thank-you" for what you started with *Put Money in Your Pocket*, more than 15 years ago. Thank you.

Many thousands of investing books have been published over the years, and most become outdated rather quickly. There are, however, a few timeless and classic books that everybody should read.

My Must-Read Book List   I have several categories classified by subject matter.

Books on Manias   The first book on my must-read list was originally published in 1841, more than a century and a half ago. *Extraordinary Popular Delusions and the Madness of Crowds,* by Charles MacKay, a Scottish poet and journalist who chronicled and explained manias, like the stock and real estate ones we recently went through. Bernard Baruch once said this book helped him make his fortune.

In 1999, it would have been very handy to really understand manias. In the nature of manias, few investors—and professionals too, for that matter—paid attention to the patterns that MacKay had described that were repeating themselves in dot.com stocks.

In November of 1999, I was one of three members of a panel in Tempe, Arizona, sponsored by KFNN, a Phoenix business radio station. The other two were financial planners in their late 30s or early 40s. Both of the planners unequivocally told the audience to buy Internet stocks. They said they were the wave of the future, and that it didn't matter how much you paid for them. You just had to be in them.

When it was my turn to speak, I said those stocks were in a mania, and the top couldn't be too far off. How did I know? By reading the book mentioned previously, a 170-year-old book. For several years after that event, investors would come up and tell me that they had heard me speak in Tempe, and they were very sorry they had not followed my advice. Amazingly the MacKay book is still in print; you can download the Kindle edition (an e-book) from Amazon.com for $0.99.

Maybe these planners just read the wrong books. Three books had come out in 1999 whose titles read in part: "Dow 36,000 . . . Dow 40,000 . . . Dow 100,000." Periodicals aren't the only media that succumb to manias.

There have only been two stock market manias in the last century: 1927 to 1929 and 1995 to 1999. There may not be another mania in U.S. stocks in our lifetime, but other asset classes will experience them.

The stock market mania was followed by a mania in residential real estate. All over the country, there were investors buying up a half-dozen or more homes or condos at a time, on speculation, with vast amounts of borrowed money. They, too, thought the boom would last forever.

One hallmark of manias is that they are often enabled by new techniques or technologies, such as the Internet. In the case of U.S. residential real estate, the new technique was mortgage products that required very little documentation of ability to repay or even make a down payment. Many buyers claimed falsely that they were buying homes for occupancy (to obtain more favorable mortgage terms), when they were actually buying for speculation and had no intention of living in them. Overvalued securities and easy money are usually present, but they are not enough by themselves to cause manias.

If they had read MacKay's book and knew how to recognize manias, recent years would have been different. The facts exposing the real estate mania were just as evident as they had been for the dot-com boom.

Dear God, one more bubble before I die.

—Silicon Valley bumper sticker

Just as secular bull markets are kicked off by new technological frontiers, so are manias, which are often based on legitimate expectations of growth that simply get carried to extremes. The real estate mania began because people couldn't believe the price of real estate could fall. They "knew" the amount of land is fixed; population grows, and nationally, home prices had never generally fallen since the Great Depression. Both the buyers and the lenders bought into this rosy scenario.

Any asset class can have a mania. So when markets heat up, be especially cautious. One clear sign of a mania is when small investors begin to participate in force.

If you want to delve into this subject in depth, there are two fine books available on the same subject. One is a 2005 book *Manias, Panics, and Crashes: A History of Financial Crises* by Charles Kindleberger and Robert Aliber. The other is a 2002 book, *Markets, Mobs & Mayhem, A Modern Look at the Madness of Crowds* by Robert Menschel (listed as a senior director at Goldman Sachs on the cover). The latter is a very easy read.

Remember that markets can stay irrational longer than you can stay solvent.

—Usually attributed to John Maynard Keynes

Books on Random Walk It's an absolute must that every investor today knows something about random walk and efficient market theory. When speaking, I sometimes ask my audience how familiar they are with these terms and I usually find only about half the audience has any knowledge of the subject. That's terrible. Every investor should be totally conversant with efficient market theory. If you are not, then by all means please read one of the following books.

The granddaddy explanation for laymen is *Random Walk down Wall Street* by Burton Malkiel, a Princeton professor. The book, now in its ninth edition, has sold over a million copies. Also check out any book by John Bogle, the founder of Vanguard.

A far more skeptical book on the subject is *The Myth of the Rational Market* by Justin Fox, published in 2009. It offers a complete, easy to read history of efficient market theory and random walk, but also argues that its many "anomalies" have partially invalidated the theory. (I don't think you can ever learn much about a subject without hearing both the pros and cons.)

Another expert to be aware of is the late Peter L. Bernstein, who wrote about capital markets, among many other things. Bernstein was a giant in the investing field. During his long life, he taught economics, personally managed billions of dollars; and was a fine writer who wrote for both professionals and laymen. He was the founding editor of the wonky but influential *Journal of Portfolio Management;* was an in-demand speaker; and wrote a respected newsletter for professionals for 36 years.

A Personal Remembrance

Peter L. Bernstein was one of my heroes. I first became aware of him when I heard him speak at an investment conference. When I learned that he wrote a newsletter, I mailed him a copy of my newsletter, and suggested we swap subscriptions (it's not uncommon for newsletter publishers to do this). Usually these swaps are between similar newsletters. In this case, Peter's newsletter was twice monthly and cost $1,750 a year; mine was monthly and cost $139 a year, so it was hardly an even swap. Nevertheless, Peter saw some utility in the *Investor* and agreed to the swap.

Bernstein's reputation seems to be primarily that of a popularizer and explainer, but people who make that assertion had never read his newsletter, which was heavy on original quantitative analysis of both markets and economics. While I learned much from him, I must confess there were many issues that went well over my head.

In 1999 I wrote an article for *Barron's* about privatizing social security (I'm opposed). Even though I had never met Bernstein in person, I gave him a call and asked if he would vet my article, since I knew he felt the same about the subject as I did. He graciously took the time to do so, which gave me a lot of confidence since I was writing outside my field.

Bernstein wrote 10 books, five of them after the age of 75, and was working on a new book when he died in June 2009 at the age of 90. Two I recommend are *Against the Gods: The Remarkable Story of Risk,* and *The Power of Gold: The History of an Obsession.*

Peter and his wife, Barbara, lived in Manhattan. After 9/11 they decided to always be together. When Peter went to the dentist, Barbara was with him. When she went to the hairdresser, Peter was with her. At work they were a two-fer. My kind of man!

Understanding Wall Street If you want to learn from an insider who knows how Wall Street really operates these days there's one work I recommend highly. In the course of writing this book I read a dozen or so investing books. I read several that were excellent, but there was only one that I thought would perfectly complement this book: *The Wall Street Self-Defense Manual, A Consumer's Guide to*

Intelligent Investing, by Henry Blodget. (The paperback edition was published in 2007.) Its basic prescriptions for the lay investor—diversify and keep your costs low—are the same as mine.

Henry Blodget wrote a surprisingly very good and honest book. It's surprising because back in the Internet bubble days of 1999 and 2000, Blodget's name was synonymous with what amounted to a near larceny of billions of dollars of shareholder assets. Blodget came to fame in October 1998 when he put out a price target of $400 per share on Amazon.com, which at the time traded at a little more than half that amount, and sailed through his price target only weeks later. He was at Oppenheimer at the time, but his audaciousness quickly landed him at Merrill, where he was expected to be a rainmaker for the company's investment banking efforts.

In 2002, Eliot Spitzer, then New York's Attorney General, published Merrill Lynch e-mails in which Blodget allegedly gave assessments about stocks, which conflicted with what was publicly published. In 2003, Blodget was charged with civil securities fraud by the SEC. He settled without admitting or denying the allegations and was subsequently banned from the securities industry for life. So he reinvented himself by going back to his first love—writing. He's a very good writer, and his advice is solid.

Nuts and Bolts Books   The following books answer such questions as: What to do when a fund manager leaves; should you buy a rookie fund; should you buy a fund that's about to close to new shareholders or one that has just reopened; which funds are best in tax-sheltered accounts, in taxable accounts; and how to read a prospectus.

An outstanding book for beginners and advanced investors alike that illuminates these details is *Chuck Jaffe's Lifetime Guide to Mutual Funds.* Even though it came out in 2000, its advice is not dated. (Jaffe currently writes for MarketWatch and elsewhere.) Another book in this genre is *Morningstar Guide to Mutual Funds,* first published in 2005 and available at Amazon.com in paperback as well as some libraries.

Comprehensive Personal Finance Advice   If you're a beginner there are several basic books available. A good place to start is one called *Smart and Simple Financial strategies for Busy People* by Jane Bryant Quinn (2006).

If you want to become an instant investing expert, here's how to go about it. Simply go to your neighborhood library and peruse the bookshelves for all the non-fiction books labeled 332.6. In the universal library numbering system, the Dewey Decimal System, 332.6 means it's an investing book.

Not All Books Are Timely   The downside of books is that they are not timely when it comes to performance information. Publishers put out books with titles like *The 100 Best Funds You Can Buy 2004*, or *The 100 Best Stocks to Own in America*. The latter book is now in its seventh edition and has sold over 300,000 copies since it was first published. Nobody knows whether its readers have made money.

In my opinion, performance information dates too quickly for books. It's even possible that by the time you read a specific fund recommendation in a book, the manager who created that track record will have moved on to another fund. Stock recommendations date even quicker. Whenever you take an investing book out of the library, be sure to check the copyright date.

I have attempted to make this book an "evergreen," one whose lessons and precepts will stay valid and endure.

Why Was This Book Written?   Ask yourself that question every time you pick up an investing book. It's fine to write a book to become better known in your field, to impress your bosses and maybe get a promotion, and, yes, to make some money. However, if a book has been written solely to acquire managed account clients, I would be skeptical about its opinions. Here's what I mean.

One investing book, clearly meant for individuals, spent 74 pages denigrating retail mutual funds, and then turned around and devoted 11 pages to lauding institutional mutual funds, claiming their superiority over retail funds. This puzzled me since I am not aware that institutional funds have any superiority over retail funds beyond their generally lower expense ratios. I further wondered why it would take so much space to laud funds that are unavailable to individuals.

Finally, the author's purpose became apparent. Basically a registered investment advisor whose bread and butter is managing money for individuals, he made heavy use of the DFA institutional fund group for his clients. Laymen cannot buy this outstanding group directly; they must go through professional money managers—like him. Now I have no quarrel with the author's goals, nor would I necessarily advise against hiring him (I've heard him speak; he sounds good). But I doubt if many of the book's readers understood his bias and took it into account. Nor, to the best of my knowledge, did any reviewers take him to task.

How do these books get published? In some cases, the author contracts for a large bulk order to distribute free to his current and prospective clients, assuring the publisher a profit. Or he self-publishes to the same end. In other cases the expert has a "platform," a radio or TV show or column that gives him wide exposure and a pre-sold audience.

I would offer this guidance. Look for a book written by an author who has worked with, talked to, and advised individual investors, or done a lot of investing on his or her own. I qualify on several counts. I used to have managed account clients. I practice what I preach, doing all my own investing. And I learn a lot from the Q and A's after my speeches. That's how a writer comes to learn investors' concerns. Book knowledge or interviewing other experts takes you only so far. So before relying on an investing book, try to determine whether the author has had practical experience. If he hasn't, he is second-class in my book. Also, I'm not implying that there is anything wrong with these books, or that the advice is bad. It may simply be a lack of originality. It may just be a "clip" job.

Vice President Lyndon Johnson, after the first Kennedy cabinet meeting, raved to his mentor, speaker of the House, Sam Rayburn, about all the president's brilliant men. "You may be right, and they may be every bit as intelligent as you say," Rayburn responded, "but I'd feel a whole lot better about them if just one of them had run for sheriff once."

—David Halberstam

Ernest Hemingway's Advice   In the early 1960s an interviewer was trying to get Ernest Hemingway to identify the characteristics required for a person to be a "great writer." As the interviewer offered a list of various possibilities, Hemingway disparaged each in turn. Finally, frustrated, the interviewer asked, "Isn't there any one essential ingredient that you can identify?" Hemingway replied, "Yes, there is. In order to be a great writer a person must have a built-in, shock-proof crap detector."

If you don't have one already, I urge you to start developing one right away. Investors need it just as much or more than writers do, particularly when you're presented with conflicting advice.

Did Einstein Really Say It?   Here's one way you can sometimes verify a writer's commitment to accuracy. Check his use of common quotations that are likely to be or have been proven false. My favorites are the Einstein quotes. The great physicist, Albert Einstein, is frequently quoted in financial books saying that compound interest, or the miracle of compounding, is the most powerful force known to man. Similarly "compound interest is the greatest mathematical discovery of all time." There are many variations on this theme. When you see that quote, you know the author hasn't done his homework.

It's a great quote, so I once wanted to use it. But first I checked all the usual sources and was unable to verify it. So I finally called Jason Zweig (then at *Money*, but now at *The Journal*) for help. This sort of thing is Jason's meat. Jason spent a week trying to check it out without success, and he has a lot more resources than I have. He finally called me back saying that the best he could do was to talk to a physicist at MIT who pooh-poohed the quote. In this professor's opinion, Einstein never thought about anything as pedestrian as compound interest. He was sure Einstein had absolutely no interest in any kind of financial interest. So, I didn't use the quote.

I am also beginning to think that some "quote coiners" may be using Warren Buffett's name for effect. The Internet is rife with his quotes. I have three in this book; however all have been verified.

Finally, and for your information, "There is no such thing as a free lunch," is attributed to the economist Milton Friedman—or to science fiction writer, Robert Heinlein, who popularized TANSTAAFL (there ain't no such thing as a free lunch). In any case, you'll usually see it shortened to "There is no free lunch." No matter who said it first, it's true!

Broadcast

Historically, when it came to investing, broadcast was a minor adjunct to print. Before the 1980s, it would have taken significant news about the market, or major economic updates out of Washington, for any mention to be included in each network's half-hour evening news show. There was little routine coverage. The *Today Show* would only occasionally interview a financial figure, and you could watch a market summary on Louis Rukeyser's *Wall Street Week* just once a week on Fridays. That was most of it. There was no daily business TV until PBS's *Nightly Business Report* premiered in 1979. Most investors relied on newspapers for market news and detailed stock listings. Or they called their brokers.

With the advent of the megatrend bull market in 1982, and better communication technology, broadcast news became more important. But many in broadcasting were slow to see and act on the change.

I Fail to "Improve" the NBC *Nightly News*   Even though I had successfully launched my newsletter, I was still working my day job at NBC-TV at Christmas time, 1981. It was a tradition at NBC that each department threw a Christmas party in its own office, and the parties were open to all. Thus, many of us traipsed from department to department to see colleagues or partake of the libation. (Classic movie fans may remember the Christmas party depicted in the Tracy/Hepburn movie, *Desk Set*. The setting looked suspiciously like NBC.)

When I arrived at the news department's party that year, I spotted the late John Chancellor, then the managing editor and anchor of the *Nightly News*.

I had a beef with the *Nightly News*. Back then it only reported the Dow Jones Average on days when it moved about one percent or more. On days with smaller percentage changes, there was no automatic coverage of market results.

I headed over to Chancellor and explained to him that if you were an investor, no change in the market was just as meaningful news as a large change. I asked Chancellor to run the market averages every night.

"Sir" John's response was short and dismissive. "Go buy an afternoon newspaper, kid," he advised.

I have often wondered what he would have thought of CNBC.

Years ago, most brokerage houses had street-level offices that welcomed their investment clients. The offices located in Manhattan usually had several rows of chairs in the back of these offices facing the "broad tape," a continuously streaming display of stock price quotes and financial news. Invariably, there would be a bevy of older men sitting there, hour after hour, watching the tape. On rare occasions, one would get up and talk to a broker. I could never figure out whether any of them were real customers or just retired people killing time.

A number of firms including Fidelity and TD Waterhouse still have street-level brokerage offices, but the ones I've seen don't have chairs for customers to watch a tape. This tradition has been replaced by business TV and the Internet.

Business TV CNBC is the dominant business channel. This is because they have been around the longest, are available to the most viewers, have a great stable of on-air personalities, and draw knowledgeable expert guests. According to CNBC, 14 million people view the network one or more times a week at home.

One CNBC personality worth catching is Larry Kudlow, an economist with finely honed political and investing instincts. His enormously informative TV show is broadcast weekdays at 7:00 P.M. eastern time. He also has a Saturday radio show.

CNBC now has two competitors, Bloomberg and Fox Business Network (FBN). All three networks are worthwhile. A casual viewer probably won't see a lot of difference between the three.

The new kid on the block is Fox Business Network (FBN), which was launched in October of 2007. Its editorial content is excellent, in part because its president, Roger Ailes, is an experienced TV executive who had previously built CNBC into a hugely successful operation. Secondly, Fox has Neil Cavuto, who directs content and business news coverage as well as being an on-camera host. Finally, Fox's parent company, News Corporation, now owns Dow Jones, publishers of *The Wall Street Journal* and *Barron's*. The *Journal* has a contract to provide financial information and data to CNBC, but that relationship is scheduled to end in 2012, giving Fox Business access to the *Journal's* considerable resources.

To give you a rough idea of the importance of these three networks, CNBC is available for viewing in 98.3 million homes and Fox Business in 58.3 million homes. There are no independently verified data for Bloomberg TV, but I've seen media estimates ranging up to 60 million homes.

Fox Business has taken a number of programming steps to broaden its appeal. They include simulcasting the Don Imus show in the early morning and hiring John Stossel, a long-time co-anchor of ABC's 20/20 prime time show to do hour-long reports, some on business. In late 2010 it hired Lou Dobbs, a 25-year veteran of CNN, to helm a daily program.

The older Fox News cable channel also has a lively, fast-paced two-hour bloc of business and financial news on Saturday morning, then repeated Saturday night on Fox Business channel. The bloc consists of four shows: *Bulls and Bears* (if you like recommendations, this show has them), *Cavuto on Business* (with Ben Stein as a guest), *Forbes on Fox* (with Steve Forbes), and *Cashin' In* (with former actor, Wayne Rogers, a regular panelist). This bloc is an undiscovered gem well worth viewing.

There is also the long-running Public Broadcasting Service alternative, *Nightly Business Report,* which began as a local broadcast in Miami in 1979 and went national in 1981. Seen Monday through Friday, 6:30 P.M. to 7:00 P.M. Eastern Time, it features market reports, company information, CEO interviews, and economic commentary. Long-time host, Paul Kangas, has retired. Replacing him are Susie Charib and Tom Hudson. For many years this show was unique in providing Monday through Friday business coverage, but has since been encroached upon by commercial channels.

The basic problem with cable business news channels is that they have to present business and market news from early in the morning until a few prime time entertainment or opinion shows take over in the evening. This means that they must focus on short-term advice, cover minutia, and follow stocks far more closely than funds.

Business TV has relatively little coverage of mutual funds because there's a limit on how much you can say about them. Years ago, CNBC carried a half-hour show devoted solely to mutual funds for just a paltry 30 minutes once a week on Fridays (with a rerun later that evening). But the show was cancelled because of low ratings. (My former managed account partner, Bob Brinker, was the host.)

It's hard to know what advice to give regarding business television. It is good; in fact its content is extraordinarily good. But how worthwhile is it? How much time should you spend with it and how much action should you take because of it?

Traders will find business TV very useful, and almost everybody can benefit by watching big news events such as coverage of the nation's debt crisis in August 2011. However, if you are a long-term investor, you should just consider it an interesting way to stay on top of current business and economic news, assuming a TV set is convenient. I think buy-and-holders are better off watching the regular cable news shows, particularly CNN, HLN, or Fox News.

For some people, a solution might be to keep the TV on with the sound muted, if that's appropriate in your line of work.

In my case I find it useful to view on days with significant market moves or on days when breaking news affects the markets. I like to hear press conferences with government officials live and in full. Since I have no interest in buying individual stocks, I ignore CEO interviews, company profiles, and stock tout shows like Jim Cramer's *Mad Money*. I never heed short-term advice.

Business Radio

A variety of financial talk show programs are broadcast on talk radio stations and on stations specializing in business and investments. I group their hosts into two categories. The first category consists of hosts who are widely syndicated on as many as 200 stations nationwide. Syndicated radio hosts (in alphabetical order) include Jim Blasingame, Bob Brinker, Phil Grande, Clark Howard, Ron Insana, Larry Kudlow, Chris Markowski, Tom Martino, Tom O'Brien, Dave Ramsey, and John Resnick.

These people offer their listeners straight advice. They are paid by their networks or stations and do not have to sell their listeners any products directly to make a living. (However, if you go to their websites you may find that some do offer additional advice in newsletters or other products, but that's not their bread and butter.)

There is a second group of financial hosts, usually financial planners, who pay the radio stations for airtime. This is quite common in business radio, particularly on the weekends. Business station KFNN, in Phoenix, Arizona, for example, features several shows with local financial planners.

Many of these planners are quite good and their shows can be just as informative as the more widely syndicated programs, and in some cases are carried on more than one radio station. KFNN requires these planners to offer solid advice just as the nationwide hosts do. They don't permit infomercials.

Still, these planners are selling financial services. In that respect, they are no different from any other financial salesmen. They are paying $500 to $1,000 a show for airtime. To recoup that cost, they must sell their listeners financial products or services. Planners host radio shows because these venues have the potential to generate more business than other media, such as print advertising.

While many of these planners are well worth listening to, beware of their high-commission products. The same caveat that applies to all salespeople applies here. You should also be turned off by any hard sell hosts, or anybody offering get-rich-quick schemes.

On the other hand, if the host is basically selling managed advisory services, I would consider him or her on the same basis as any other advisor. Just make sure that the advisor's fees are in line with industry norms. And in all cases make sure there are no hidden expenses.

I also suggest listening to Bloomberg News and CNBC on satellite radio. They have more news and fewer recommendations.

You can learn many important things from radio and TV, but it is not a substitute for reading. Frankly, if you are not willing to do a reasonable amount of reading you should turn your investment decisions over to others, or buy a total market index fund and let it go at that.

I once got a call from a Rhode Island radio station asking about the possibility of my hosting an investing show. They said the price was $600 a show. I told them I would have to be paid more than that if they wanted me to host their show. Dumb me. They meant I was supposed to pay *them* the $600! I'm sure they found somebody else who needed the exposure. I didn't.

Internet

The Internet has transformed America in the way the automobile did a century earlier. It's radically changed shopping and communication patterns, and it's become a nonpareil investment resource. If you are still Internet shy, you will have to change.

The Internet has revolutionized my work as well as my personal investing. I once had to make scores of phone calls to put together a speech or an article. Now, I can find a great deal of valuable and timely information on the Internet, swiftly and easily.

Personally what I find most helpful is being able to put my own investment portfolio online. I once had to wait for the morning paper to get the previous day's mutual fund NAVs, and then update my portfolio by hand, which of course I virtually never did. Today

I get the prices off the Internet, usually just after 6:00 P.M. New York time, with my entire portfolio already automatically updated.

I trade infrequently, but I do believe in constantly monitoring my investments. And when I do trade, I usually do it online since the commissions are lower.

In recent years, many newspapers have either drastically short-ened or completely eliminated their daily stock and fund tables. The Internet is defining a new world.

As the world embraces the digital age, two billion people now use the Internet regularly. Ninety percent of mutual fund investors can now go online to obtain information, and two-thirds do it daily. This has had a great impact on individual funds. At Vanguard, 80 percent of investor contacts now occur online.

When I make a specific recommendation in this book, I include the contact information in some cases. If contact information is not given, check the Internet. Every important financial company or advisor has a website today. (Mine is www.SheldonJacobs.com.)

There are many websites that provide financial information. I'll point you to just a few. First, there are several comprehensive finan-cial websites that are worth checking out, particularly if you are a data junkie. Unless otherwise noted, they are free. These sites offer com-prehensive information, usually including news and opinion, markets, personal finance, portfolio tracking, quotes, funds, ETFs, and stocks.

I'm not going to attempt detailed descriptions of these sites. The best way to select and use them is to visit them yourself and find the ones you like the best. There is something of a learning curve needed to understand each site, so my recommendation is to pick one or two and stick with them.

MSN Money (moneycentral.msn.com). Unbelievably compre-hensive, data divers can have a field day but you may have to dig a little for articles and commentary pieces.

Morningstar.com is comprehensive, with much worthwhile fund advice. The site is not entirely free. Some sections are avail-able just by visiting; others require registration, and still others, payment.

MarketWatch.com has a wealth of data for most any kind of equity financial investigation, but its strength is its outstanding columnists, and up-to-date performance information as well as historical pricing. It's now owned by Dow Jones.

Yahoo! Finance (finance.yahoo.com) pulls together data from eight news sources. Fund data is free, but performance data lags to previous month-end.

SmartMoney.com has the editorial content of the magazine and more. The website is free; all you have to do is register for full access. Those who choose not to register have limited access.

Investinginbonds.com is good for comprehensive fixed-income information.

Information on **indexes** can be obtained from djindexes.com, mscibarra.com, russell.com, standardandpoors.com, and Wilshire.com.

Most general news sites offer some financial information. They include MSNBC (msnbc.msn.com), CNN (money.cnn.com), *The Wall Street Journal* (wsj.com), *The New York Times* (nytimes.com), bloomberg.com, cnbc.com, and foxbusiness.com.

In addition, the major fund groups all have helpful websites with both general and personal information for shareholders. You can usually find them by entering the name of the fund company, for example, vanguard.com, or fidelity.com, or check Google. As of year-end 2009, DALBAR, a financial-services market research firm, pronounced the following five fund groups with the best websites: T. Rowe Price, Wells Fargo, Oppenheimer, Fidelity, and Vanguard.

Do go online to access an expanding wealth of financial information.

Here's my own personal Internet story.

My mother came from a large family. She had seven brothers. You've heard of tight-knit families? Well, mine was a loose-knit family. Upon reaching adulthood, they spread out all over the United States, so that no family member lived within 500 miles of any other. While (with only a couple of exceptions) they didn't dislike each other, they rarely communicated with one another, except of course to borrow money. Don't forget this was way before e-mail and cheap long distance calls. It is in this context that I tell you about my mother's uncle, Harry Lashkowitz, who was a prominent lawyer in Fargo, North Dakota.

It is my habit to occasionally Google myself on the Internet. One time when I did this, I found a link to Harry. How Google realized the family connection is still a total mystery to me.

Following the link, I found a biography of Harry. Some of it was familiar, but what floored me as I read on, was that in 1936, at the Democratic National Convention, Harry had seconded FDR's nomination for President. Now, that was a bit of family lore I had never heard before. It's strange that I found out more about my family from the Internet than from my mother.

Important Lessons in Part One

- That's it. Five principles a kid can master. You can put a whole lot more effort into picking stocks and esoterica without obtaining significantly better results. So don't go crazy with this stuff. Enjoy life.
- Set your investing priorities by developing the right asset allocation, then broadly diversifying within your asset classes at an appropriate risk level, keeping your costs down, and using the media to help focus your thoughts. If you get the big decisions right, the small ones will take care of themselves.
- Your goal is not to invest in individual mutual funds, stocks or bonds; your goal is to invest in a *portfolio* that achieves the best *risk-adjusted* returns.

PART

II

ACTIONS AND STRATEGIES
TO IMPLEMENT THE ESSENTIALS

CHAPTER

Developing Media Expertise

As we have just seen in Part One, investing is inherently simple. Unfortunately, investing is complicated by those with a financial interest in catering to investors. What is presented as analysis may be biased by salesmanship, the advancement of narrow interests, alarmism, or, very frequently, just the desire to be entertaining.

Along the way, you will encounter two kinds of advice: helpful advice that can make you a better investor; and, unhelpful advice that may be interesting reading, but in the end, offers no specific benefit.

Here are some guidelines for recognizing helpful advice, the kind that you can actually implement with positive results.

Guideline #1: Take advice only from people who know more about a particular subject than you. (This is true in life in general, not just investing.) This guideline ought to be obvious, but it's remarkable how often it's ignored.

Recognize that there are many different areas of financial expertise including economic forecasting, market forecasting, asset allocation strategies, and specific stock- or fund-picking skills. Each discipline requires concentrated focus. Many advisors are thought to be generalists, but it's more likely they are far stronger in one discipline than in others.

I once met a woman who was the manager of an Arizona municipal bond fund. I asked her what I thought was a simple question: If you had to choose, which would be better, an Arizona or New York bond fund? (I live in both states.) She had no idea. She probably could have told me almost anything about Arizona bonds, but New York was not within her area of expertise.

Make sure the advice you are seeking is coming from an expert in the field. After all, if you were accused of a felony, you would hire a criminal lawyer, not a corporate lawyer, to defend you. Although there are exceptions, accountants are not qualified to give sound investing advice. If an advisor's expertise is mortgages, 401(k)s, wills, and so on, don't expect him to be a good stock or fund picker.

Listening to Individuals May Be Hazardous to Your Wealth

I am amazed at how many people seek investing advice from close friends or relatives who have no professional expertise. It's hard enough to get good advice from professionals, let alone amateurs.

Guideline #2: Be careful about relying too much on economic forecasts, even when made by top economists.

Very little of the science that economists study relates to forecasting. Economics is essentially the study of how societies allocate scarce goods and services, and that's how the discipline earned its name. Economists seldom correctly forecast recessions, interest rates, or the market, and many successful investors pay no attention to their forecasts. In today's ubiquitous media environment, a constant stream of economic news is reported. Most of it has no long-term effect and should be ignored by the long-term investor. The economist John Kenneth Galbraith once said, "Economists predict not because they know, but because they are asked." (The same could be said of stock market forecasters.)

Trying to learn economics from the popular media (John Stossel excepted) is like trying to learn physics by watching Road Runner cartoons.

—Donald J. Boudreaux, Professor of Economics,
George Mason University

Guideline #3: Academics often offer sound general advice, but their work is less useful in regard to specific recommendations or investment strategies.

The academic world is rife with professors who want to be stock market gurus. Although some make the transition from academia to the "real world," most do not.

I once attended an investment meeting to hear a talk by a college professor who had written a book on closed-end funds. Because I had read the book and was impressed by it, I looked forward to hearing the professor's take on the field.

His speech was excellent, which was not surprising. After all, most teachers are good speakers. Then came the question-and-answer period. First question: "Professor, should I sell my Adams Express Fund?"

Answer: Duh.

Next question: "Should I buy Gabelli Equity Trust?"

Answer: Duh. The distinguished professor was lost when challenged to answer "real world" investment questions.

Guideline #4: There is a subtle distinction between a reporter and a guru, and here's how to spot it: If the investing article quotes a lot of experts, the writer is a reporter, an expert in assembling other people's ideas. I don't mean this as criticism. Reporters perform a valuable service by distilling the wisdom of many people and presenting it to readers in easily digestible forms. Just realize that reporters are sometimes no better than the people they interview, and they, or their editors, may be selective in which parts of an interview they choose to use.

Gurus seldom quote other people, except as data sources. When I wrote *The No-Load Fund Investor,* I rarely quoted other experts, mainly because I wanted subscribers to clearly understand that they were buying and relying on my expertise, not someone else's. Another distinction is that gurus are more likely to buy their own recommendations than are reporters.

Books, however, are an exception to this rule. Reporters quote people because that's what reporting is all about and quotes add credibility to an article. Book authors are different. They assemble and credit a foundation of knowledge built up over many years to enable them to marshal their own thoughts and advance the body of knowledge. As Isaac Newton put it: "If I have seen further, it is only by standing on the shoulders of giants."

The newsletter industry, of which I have been a part for many years, is inhabited almost universally by gurus. There are hundreds of very fine financial reporters, but to the best of my knowledge only three made the transition from reporting to expert. One was Dan Wiener, who wrote for *U.S. News and World Report* and then moved on to write a newsletter on Vanguard. The other two are Bob Runde and the late Bob Klein. Both Runde and Klein went from being writers and editors at *Money* magazine to become financial planners. Successful investment gurus make far more money than reporters.

Then there is the case of Ron Insana, who was for many years the most knowledgeable reporter/analyst/host CNBC had. (When a bald man makes it in front of the TV cameras, you know he has to be good.) In 2006, when times were still good, he left CNBC to become a hedge fund manager running a fund-of-hedge-funds. When the Great Recession hit, his fund went under. In March 2009 he returned to CNBC, and now has a radio show.

I think part of the reason so few reporters make the transition successfully is that writers tend to be better with words than numbers, whereas the opposite is true for gurus.

The Press Lacks Numeracy

Some reporters find it very difficult to deal with numbers, a condition called innumeracy. A few of them remind me of the old joke about a man who orders a pizza pie. When asked whether he wants it cut into six or eight slices, he replies "Eight, I'm hungry."

Statistics doesn't appear to be an important subject in journalism schools. The next time you hear or read a news account of findings on climate change, rising income inequality, the effects of secondhand smoke, or the effectiveness of preschool interventions, pay special attention to any technical material included in the story. Even without being a statistical expert yourself, you will see instances when the article fails to convey the needed information. Sometimes the data are presented in a misleading way. And sometimes the point made is just invalid.

Lack of good statistical skills shows up when articles include inferior charts and tables. Many are so poorly labeled, and sometimes so poorly constructed, that it's hard to understand the point they are endeavoring to make. Print should follow the lead of television news shows where the graphics are far cleaner and can easily be read on the small screen.

Furthermore, many charts are color coded in a way that makes them incomprehensible at first glance. I once saw a chart in a major newspaper coded in five colors. Three of the five colors were various shades of red (which don't reproduce as well in newsprint as in glossies). Since I am one of the 7 to 10 percent of men who are red-green color blind, this chart completely lost me.

Although there are business writers who are exceptions to this rule (thank goodness), most gurus are clearly better at analyzing numbers. Think about this when you are reading.

Here are two examples to illustrate the reporters' condition. The first is a wistful paragraph by Vito J. Racanelli, introducing an article about the market in *Barron's*:

> Back in high school math class one of the problems I hated was this: A bathtub is filling at x gallons per minute, but water is draining at an $(x - 1)$ rate. How long before the 60-gallon tub is filled? The math geniuses—most of whom probably run their own quant shops now—figured it relatively quickly, but I struggled. I'd always think, why not plug the drain?

Another example of innumerate judgment appeared in the *New York Times* business section on April 14, 2001. The article reported that profits increased by 58 percent at Conoco and by 51 percent at Exxon Mobil. The headline that topped the article read: "Profits More Than Double at Conoco and Exxon Mobil." Perhaps the headline writer (probably a different person than the reporter) added the two gains together to get the "double." Or, maybe the headline writer thought +50 percent is a double. Of course, he may have just been sound asleep when he wrote it.

What follows is another example worth pondering.

Why Do Writers Compare "Up" and "Down" Percentages?

You've probably read it a hundred times. A writer will caution you that "up" percentages are greater than "down" percentages. He will illustrate: "If a stock goes from $10 a share to $5 a share, that's a *50 percent loss*. But to go from $5 back to $10 is a *100 percent increase*." I have puzzled over these differing percentages for years, and I confess I have no idea how to interpret them. One possible explanation is that it's harder to gain than to lose, but that's far from an immutable truth.

What's puzzling about this line of reasoning is that I have never heard either an investor or an advisor talk that way. I've never heard any financial advisor say to a client, "Well, Lucile, your portfolio lost 22 percent in this downturn. That means that when stocks come back, you will need to gain 28 percent to break even."

In everyday conversation, people intuitively talk and think in dollars, not percentages. They always say, "I bought the stock at $15 and now it's down to $11. When it gets back to $15, I will be even." Mutual fund investors say, "I bought $5,000 of the fund and now it's worth only $4,000. When my investment gets back to $5,000 I will be even."

> *Counterargument*: Writers who accept the different percentages up and down theory note that since you have less money working for you after a large loss, those fewer dollars have to work harder (that is, gain more) to recoup.
>
> *Counter-counterargument*: It's not the number of dollars that's important; it's the number of shares, which remain the same.

Forget stocks. Let's think of this in terms of crops. A farmer normally plants 100 acres of corn. One year he only plants 90 acres, 10 acres or 10 percent less. Now how many acres of corn does he need to plant the following year to return to his norm? Hint: It is not 10.1 acres.

The comedians Abbott and Costello explained this math far better than I can:

> **Abbott**:　You're 40 years old and you're in love with this little girl that's 10 years old. You're four times as old as that girl and you couldn't marry her, could you?
>
> **Costello**:　Not unless I come from the mountains.
>
> **Abbott**:　All right, you're 40 years old, you're four times as old as this girl, and you can't marry her, so you wait five years. By that time the little girl's 15 and you're 45. You're

only three times as old as that little girl. So you wait 15 years and when the girl is 30, you're at 60. You're only twice as old as that little girl.

Costello: She's catching up.

Abbott: Yes, yes. Now here's the question. How long do you have to wait until you and that little girl are the same age?

Costello: Now what kinda question is that? That's ridiculous!

Abbott: Ridiculous or not, answer the question.

Costello: If I wait for that girl she'll pass me up. She'll wind up older than I am.

Abbott: What are you talking about?

Costello: She'll have to wait for me!

Abbott: Why should she wait for you?

Costello: I was nice enough to wait for her!

—*Bud Abbott and Lou Costello in* Buck Privates,
Universal Pictures, 1941

This is another situation where you shouldn't use percentages. Let's say that you are considering, or own, two money funds. Fund A is yielding 0.2 percent while fund B is yielding 0.1 percent. I don't care how you massage the numbers, fund A is *not* twice as good as fund B. The sole reality is that both yields are lousy.

Watch out for innumeracy. It impedes clear thinking.

Be Aware of Press Biases

Everybody is biased, and that certainly includes me. This world would be a dull place without bias. Nevertheless, you need to be aware of these biases so you can take them into account when making investment decisions. Here are some worth discussing.

You need the media for their expertise, but always take into account that *their time horizons are usually far shorter than yours. Theirs may be their publication dates or broadcast times. Yours can be your lifetime.*

In some cases this can make a huge difference. My time horizon for this book is your lifetime. The time horizon for monthly newsletters may be as short as 30 days, sometimes leading to recommendations within that time frame.

In my case, my mental time frame when making newsletter recommendations was longer than a month. In fact, my average recommendation stayed in my portfolios for over 600 days. Most newsletters had far shorter time horizons. When I was in a contest my time horizon was the length of the contest, often one year. In that case I tried to recommend securities that would do well for a whole year. Television has extremely short time horizons, leading to lots of short-term advice. Most politicians also have short time horizons: two years, four years, six years, or the number of months before their next election.

President Obama has more than once told the press: "I know that everybody here is on a 24-hour news cycle. I'm not." He is smart to point that out at his press conferences.

Consider the time horizons of all advice givers.

An Unbelievable Time Horizon

A number of years ago, Bob White, who published a hard-money newsletter called the *Duck Book* out of Costa Rica, was told by his doctor that he had cancer and only had a half year to live. He immediately sent out renewal letters to all his subscribers offering lifetime subscriptions for only $25. At the bottom of the coupon, in very small print, he wrote "your lifetime or mine." There is a strange ending to this story. The doctor was wrong. White recovered completely, and had to spend a fortune fulfilling subscriptions. This liability went on for about another decade, until it ended abruptly when White was murdered on a street in Belize by a mugger, who believed he was wearing a fat money belt.

I never offered my subscribers lifetime subscriptions, but there are some newsletter publishers who do. They price their lifetime subscriptions at $1,000 to $5,000. At that level, the interest they receive on the premium will be greater than the cost of fulfillment, so they will be assured a profit.

What's Interesting?

Another press bias is anything interesting. New gimmick funds are interesting. Socially responsible and religious funds are interesting. Reporters find them fun to write about. Consequently they get far more press and airtime than they deserve. Social responsibility funds used to get coverage because of they avoided "sin" stocks. Now they get press because their investments are "green."

Social responsibility funds usually avoid liquor, tobacco, and gambling stocks as well as polluters. This I can understand. But many also avoid defense stocks. This is beyond me. What could be more socially responsible than defending oneself and our country? Mind you now, selecting socially responsible stocks is hardly an exact science. Mistakes can be made. A number of socially responsible funds held BP shares in 2010. I guess they found BP's advertising socially responsible.

I have never understood why these criteria have anything to do with investing. I recommended as far back as 1988 that investors should focus more on performance than these "soft" criteria.

Know Both the Pros and Cons

Most articles have a point of view. That's fine, but I wish there were more articles presenting both pros and cons. I seldom see them, and I think they would be very helpful.

I was really pleased when I saw two articles side by side on MarketWatch in February 2009 with the following headlines:

"It's the Best Time to Buy a Home"

"It's the Worst Time to Buy a Home"

Similarly, in October 2011, shortly after Steve Jobs death, *Forbes* had two investing articles: "Buy Apple"; "Don't Buy Apple." I think it would be very helpful if this sort of thing were done far more often.

The Hierarchy of Investing Knowledge

I would divide business and investing information into four categories.

1. General knowledge about the world and current events including economic and political news
2. General business news
3. Information on investing fundamentals
4. Specific security recommendations

For me, the first three categories are more important than the fourth, but for most investors, it's the reverse. When they are exposed to investment advice, they will pay the most attention to the fourth category, specific investment recommendations. That's why almost every investing article concludes with specific recommendations. Check the columnists in *Forbes* or the experts interviewed in *Barron's*, and you will see what I mean. Categories one, two, and three can be likened to deciding which store to do your shopping at. Category four is what you buy when you get to that store.

The hunger for recommendations and new investment ideas explains why the majority of mutual fund investors never make a second purchase into a fund, something that makes no sense at all.

For years, whenever I made a speech I noticed that people generally listened to what I had to say without taking notes—until I offered specific fund recommendations. At that point, they started writing. I always had the feeling that some of these people gauged the success of the conference by the number of recommendations they collected.

I think these people have it all wrong. Making big strategic decisions based on the first three categories of information described above is far more important than implementing specific recommendations. Once you get an investing strategy right, it is no trick at all to find sound specific choices among index funds, diversified managed portfolios, bonds, or even individual stocks.

Now don't get me wrong. I like good recommendations as well as the next person. The point is you have to be very careful to put recommendations into context and accept only the ones that fit into your overall portfolio goals.

Examples of Important General Information

It's not unusual for general information to have more effect on your portfolio than a stock recommendation. There have been years when the price of oil affected the whole market. Similarly, changes in taxation and other government policies also have that kind of influence.

By the same token, weather can sometimes have short-term effects on the market. That's certainly true for commodity investors.

It's the first two media categories above—general knowledge and general business news—that are most useful in making long-term market judgments. You know the old saying that sometimes you can't see the forest for the trees. In this case the trees are individual security recommendations. The forest, which is far more important to see, is the long-term trend, particularly in four key areas: the deficit, the national debt, taxation, and demographics.

The first three require understanding government policies and politics, which basically depend on changes in political leadership. Investors need to follow these trends. They need to assess the importance of new laws and programs. Don't underestimate their importance.

Okay, here's a toughie for advanced media mavens. There are two reasons to read newspapers: for what's in them, and to find out what's *not* in them. It's not unusual for papers to fail to report fairly significant news. In some cases it's because of media bias. In other cases, it's just for lack of space. Some omissions may have news value, and even investing implications.

Going Beyond Media Recommendations

Investment recommendations can make you a winner *if* they are properly used. So here are some considerations when evaluating recommendations.

You first need to ask why this recommendation was made. There is a huge difference between recommendations made for publicity purposes, and recommendations made in the expectation that clients or subscribers will actually buy them. Needless to say, far more care is taken making the latter. That's because virtually nobody tracks the former; but you better believe they'll remember the latter, particularly if they actually buy it.

Second, you need to go beyond the media recommendations that are less than comprehensive. Here are some ways you can check them out.

- Go on the fund's or company's website and see what management says about itself.
- Check other financial websites and see what they say.
- Call up the fund and talk to a rep.
- If you have a financial advisor, ask him or her.

Your questions will, of course, vary depending on your interests, but here are some possibilities: What's the beta? Is the fund leveraged? How often does it pay dividends? Is the fund suitable for you? Are there any unusual tax liabilities?

If you don't want to do this, stick to broad-based index funds, or work with an advisor.

The Perils of Perma Bulls and Bears

If you follow the field long enough, you will be offered advice from *perma* bulls and bears.

Avoid this advice.

A perma bull is a person who is always bullish, no matter what the market or economic outlook may be. A perma bear is the reverse. Now, obviously, markets go in both directions. So, why would it pay to always be one way or the other?

The principal answer is that both types of permas have business reasons behind their biases. Perma bulls often work for retail brokerage firms, which are vocationally bullish. They make money when clients buy or sell stocks, but as a practical matter the big money is in the buying. Brokers can entice anybody to buy a stock, but only investors who already own stock can sell it (except for short sellers, who are a minor factor in the big picture). They are better off staying bullish.

It's a little more complicated for perma bears. Some just have a negative outlook on life or are gold bugs. For them, the glass is always half empty. Even though America has now experienced 60 years of economic expansion and market gains, the perma bears search out negative news and ignore positives. They are fixated on the deficit, the fact that our money is no longer backed by gold, weak currencies, and inflation. Some are perma bears for historical reasons, such as having had families who lived through bad times in Europe. Similarly, gold bugs look for reasons why gold will do well, and ignore any facts that suggest otherwise. They also have a tendency to predict extreme outcomes during bear markets.

Perma bears had a field day in 1999, just before the start of the new century. They were absolutely convinced that Y2K, the notion that the world's computers were not going to be able handle dates in the twenty-first century, was going to ruin the world. Yet, computer specialists ranging from Bill Gates to my computer consultant said otherwise.

You can identify perma bears by their inconsistency. A perma bear might say he was bearish because the housing market is weak. But then, if you check you will find he was bearish when the housing market was strong. He might be bearish because energy prices are high. But then, he was bearish when energy prices were low. A true perma bear is bearish when credit is tighter, and when credit is easy.

Some bearish newsletter publishers are emotional bears just like their readers. I do think that for a few of the older ones, though, the bearish views evolved to meet the needs of their readership. These publishers turned bearish in the 1970s when they correctly foresaw a long downturn. Over a period of time, their bullish subscribers failed to renew, leaving only bearish subscribers. If the publishers had turned bullish when they should have, most of their remaining subscribers, who were now perma bears, would have left and they would then be out of business.

For any investment publication to succeed, it must find its own unique audience.

If you think an advisor is a perma bear, ask when he first turned bearish. Then ask him how much the market has gone up since then.

Advice for perma bears: "Predict catastrophe no sooner than five years hence but no later than 10 years away, soon enough to terrify but distant enough that people will forget if you are wrong."
                                    —Gregg Easterbrook's Law of Doomsaying

---

In January 2006, global warming advocate Al Gore predicted we had only *ten years* left to save the planet!

I Listen to a Perma Bear

I seldom ventured far from my middle-of-the-road world. One time that I did was when I was invited to speak at an investor's conference in Toronto, Canada.

The speaker just before me at this conference was Harry Schultz, perhaps the most fanatical of all the gold bugs. We were just out of the long secular bear market of the 1970s, so Harry and his *Harry Schultz Letter*, which had a sizeable circulation in the United States even though Harry himself lived in Switzerland, were still popular.

One part of Harry's speech really blew me away. He told the audience that the FBI had the ability to monitor all phone calls, so they had to be very careful about what they said on the phone. Never use the word "gold" on the phone, he admonished the audience. Use some code word like "banana."

I started to laugh, but then I saw that the audience was accepting this bit of perceived wisdom with utter seriousness. Several people immediately pulled out their pens and paper and wrote down this gem.

There are, of course, legitimate reasons for liking gold. But for this audience, gold was bigger than an investment. It had become a religion and Harry was preaching to the choir.

Avoiding Unhelpful Advice

The investing world is awash with unusable advice. It's not wrong; it's just too general, too specific, or too vague to be actionable. Here's a sampling.

> "My best idea for 2006 is to buy low and sell high."—Liz Ann Sonders, Chief Investment Strategist at Charles Schwab, in a January 27, 2006 e-mail to Schwab customers.
>
> "Investors need to find some combination of management, execution, and strategy that makes them confident a fund can outperform its peer group on a 'go-forward' basis."—Karen Dolan, Morningstar, in a radio interview.
>
> "Buy well-managed companies."—Henry Paulson, former Secretary of the Treasury and former Goldman Sachs CEO, in a televised conversation with Warren Buffett.

On November 22, 2005, *The Wall Street Journal* interviewed the manager of a fund-of-hedge-funds. This is a man who was in the business of selecting other hedge funds for his own multi-fund portfolio. Here's how he recommended selecting a portfolio manager:

> Know the bull and bear market performance, the people behind the performance, where each had gotten his start, how he had achieved his success, how he views risk and employs leverage, how he treats employees and partners, who he does business with, his clearing brokers and accountants, how his peers view him, how he handles crises, how he handles success, what books he reads, and how he handles his private life.

I don't believe the author of this advice did all that. I know for an absolute certainty that you and I are not going to do that, even if we could. I'm surprised *The Journal* printed it.

Free Come-on Advice

If you are a consumer of financial media and promotional literature you have probably seen headlines such as this: "Three (8, 25, 50, whatever) Funds That Scream Dump Me." Or: "Check Our List of 'Lemon' Funds." These are proven attention grabbers. If such recommendations are made in editorial copy, they can be good advice, particularly if it's November or December and you are looking to harvest some tax losses.

But if you see a similar recommendation in a direct mail brochure for a newsletter, it is seldom actionable advice. More often than not, by the time a fund appears on such lists, it is already down substantially. If you rush to dump it, you may be selling at the bottom. Whether such advice is offered in publications or in advertisements, investigate them carefully. If you've been paying attention to your investments, you should never see a fund you own on these lists. Also, many of these lists are heavy with load funds that were sold to hapless investors who would never have selected them on their own.

Conflicting Advice

After the conclusion of one of my TV interviews, the on-air host said to me, "Sheldon, I just don't understand this business. One day I have a guest who tells me one thing. The next day another guest will say something diametrically opposite. This happens all the time. Whom should I believe?" I told him that if we ever had lunch together, I would try to explain. This is what I would have said.

You will find a lot of conflicting investing advice out there. Unfortunately, there is very little that can be done about it. Since markets need both buyers and sellers, there will always be differences of opinion about investments' merits, and also why many experts think the market is a random walk.

I think the important thing to understand is that investing opinion can be a contrary indicator. If everyone is bullish, then the market may be at a top. Or if everyone is bearish, a bottom may have been reached. The reason for this is simple. If everyone has bought, then there is a scarcity of new money available to come into the market to drive up prices further. Conversely, if all investors have sold, whether because they are bearish or panicky, selling pressure will be alleviated.

If everybody is on one side of the boat, go to the other side.

In between, you simply have to decide which camp is right, although market trends tend to persist until they reach flexion points. The same more or less holds true for opinions on individual stocks.

The media reflect this dichotomy of opinion and are often contrary indicators, bearish at the bottom, bullish at the top. This holds true for newsletter editors, too. One newsletter, *Investor's Intelligence*, tracks the forecasts of all market timing newsletters. It has thoroughly documented that the collective advice of these newsletters is a contrary indicator.

The media are often trend followers to a fault. I once saw an article on the Internet entitled "Ten Stocks to Sell Now." The article appeared online after the market had just declined for the 10th straight day, an unusual occurrence. With that many down days in a row, the odds are very good there will soon be several up days. It was not a time to "sell now."

One other point: Nobody goes to the media unless they have something to sell. Forget about the people who clamor to appear on reality, game, or court TV shows. Professionals only take time off from their busy lives when they have something to sell. Most actors, authors, or singers only go on *Jay Leno* or *Today* when they have a new project coming out. Some, like politicians, go on just for the exposure. They are selling themselves so they can get elected, reelected, gain higher office, or simply accrue more power. I used to seek TV appearances to sell my newsletter. Except for publicizing this book, I don't do it anymore.

Unworkable Advice

Back in 1990 I was a participant at a large investment conference, and after my own talk, I decided to listen to a fellow guru, Jay Goldinger, who was making a big name for himself at the time. I found Jay speaking in the hotel's main ballroom to a rapt audience of close to 400 people. He had drawn far more listeners than any of the other 40 speakers, most of whom drew less than 75 attendees.

I soon found out the reason for the attraction. In one of the most hyper speeches I have every heard, Jay promised that good old standby, the ultimate winner, what every investor wants to hear "wealth without risk." Jay laid out a strategy that seemed to promise the best of everything. My recollection (though somewhat vague) is that he proposed some sort of day trading in which the trade was consummated at the end of the day if you were ahead, but was aborted if the trade shaped up as a loser. You needed the help of a compliant broker, but Jay insisted they could be found, and he assured the audience that the strategy was legal.

However, the implementation of the strategy was complicated; you pretty much had to be on top of the trade all day long. That's pretty tough for those of us who have a life. My reaction was that the strategy might work in theory, but like a lot of ideas tossed out as audience getters, it would be impossible for the average person to execute. Furthermore, I doubted that even a professional like myself could execute it. I suspected that most investors would come to the same conclusion, but snared by the desire to obtain outsized profits without risk, would give Jay their money so he could implement the strategy for them.

I heard no more of Jay Goldinger until February 1996, six years later, when he broke into the news with the announcement that he had gone bankrupt to the tune of $100 million of his clients' money. Losers included large investors such as Pier 1, the retailer, which alone lost $30 million. I would say there are two morals here.

1. Stay away from advisors who want to teach you complicated investing strategies.
2. Don't give them your money to do it for you.

Postscript: In late 2008 I received a financial solicitation via e-mail. The letter was signed Jay Goldinger. I didn't respond.

Read About Scams

The impact of investment scams is far greater than just bad investment decisions. So it is terribly important to have a working knowledge of them. Investors who get taken by scams usually lose 100 percent of their investment with virtually no possibility of ever recouping. Saddest of all are the vulnerable elderly who can least afford to lose money.

The most despicable scams are what are known as affinity frauds and they are, unfortunately, very common. These are cases where the scam artist gains a position of trust in a church, synagogue, or ethnic organization, and uses it to defraud his fellow congregants. In recent years, Armenian Americans, Baptist Church members, Jehovah's Witnesses, African American church groups, Jews, and Korean Americans have all been victims of affinity fraud.

In addition to the many traditional tricks employed by scam artists, the Internet has created a variety of new scams and greatly expanded the audience of potential victims and the speed at which they can be duped. About one-fifth of all scams are stock market–related, and the SEC estimates that 100 million stock-scam messages are sent daily. The FBI and the National White Collar Crime Center reported that Internet crimes hit a new high in 2009, with losses of about $550 million. On any given day you might find several phishing scam emails, usually in the junk mail folder, but not always. Some are easy to spot but some require a careful closer look to recognize the scam. When in doubt, toss it out.

Many publications report on scams, and I make a point of paying special attention to these stories. Aside from the unsophisticated Nigerian e-mails that everyone was getting a few years ago, I've never been approached by a scam artist. . . . But I'm ready.

> The best defense against being scammed is the old cliché: If it sounds too good to be true, it is too good to be true.

How to Game Contests

Back in the glorious bull market years of the 1990s, the media were always having contests. They'd assemble a multitude of stock and/or fund gurus, have them submit portfolios and crown winners.

I participated in several contests over the years, won quite a few, and never did badly. This was due in part to my ability, but also because I made a conscious effort to game these contests. I realized early on that the goal here was quite different from my newsletter goal of providing solid, long-term, risk-adjusted advice to my subscribers.

The goal in a contest is to *win*, period. There is no other goal. If I won, I could use the results in my advertising, and ultimately attract more subscribers. Also quite unlike my regular advisory business, there was no great penalty in losing. No subscriber ever failed to renew because his advisor did poorly in a contest. The vast majority of them probably didn't even realize there was a contest, since the advisor only mentioned it to his flock if he was winning.

So how do you win these contests? Most of the contests ran continuously for a year or more. So, if you weren't winning, the best strategy was to take greater risks than your competitors were taking. If your risky selections came through, you were in good shape. And, if they didn't? Well, it didn't really matter.

The most famous contest I was ever in ran in *The New York Times* from 1993 to 2000. Besides me there were four other contestants: Eric Kobren, then editor of *Fidelity Insight* newsletter; John Rekenthaler from Morningstar; Harold Evensky, a Coral Gables, Florida, investment manager, and Jack Brill, a San Diego investment manager who created a "socially responsible" portfolio. The *Times* published contest results quarterly, and you could make changes in your portfolio quarterly. The initial word was the contest might run as long as 20 years!

I had some hot emerging market funds in my portfolio that enabled me to take an early lead in the contest. None of the other contestants had assumed that kind of risk. I held the lead for 27 consecutive quarters. Then, as we hit the 28th quarter, Eric Kobren pulled ahead of me. He, too, had learned how to play the game. Ironically, just at that point, *The Times* abruptly ended the contest, deciding seven years was enough. I never got a chance to regain my lead.

Harold Evensky's performance confirmed my opinions. Evensky, a well-known investment advisor who is constantly quoted by the press, did poorly in the contest, finishing last over the seven years. Just looking at his portfolios, I got the impression he was hewing to his investing principles instead of trying to win. Still, I don't think coming in last hurt him in the long run, because he is still apparently very successful. *Barron's* says he has $600 million under management. If you want him to manage your money today, his minimum fee is $12,500 per year.

Me, I prefer to win. Being first did wonders for my business. Not only that, my New York friends and neighbors, who never knew my standing among investors, now realized that I actually knew what I was doing. My reputation among them increased enormously, which I found gratifying.

One other contest is worth discussing. In 2001 I was asked to participate in a contest conducted on the Internet. One of the governing rules was that the contestants were not allowed to invest in money funds. This wasn't very sensible given that we were in a bear market. So, what could I do? I certainly didn't want to be all in equities. My solution was to submit a portfolio that included a significant weighting in a short-term bond fund. The sponsor allowed it. The other five contestants all submitted 100 percent equity portfolios. I won this contest by a very wide margin.

The Selling Advice Myth

Investment literature is replete with a point of view phrased something like this:

> It is apparent that anyone who can forecast the trend of stock prices consistently and accurately would become a billionaire

so quickly that he would have no reason to sell his forecasts to the general public.

As a publisher who has sold advice to the public, I don't believe this. I have run the numbers, and although I am not going to document specifics, because this is an area where you can prove anything by how you define your parameters: how much of your own money did you start with, your return rates on one stock or the market, your time horizon, and how successful you are at selling the advice. I find that, using reasonable assumptions, you can make more money selling crystal ball accuracy forecasts to the public, than keeping them secret for personal use. So don't reject advice for this faulty reason.

My grandfather [B.C. Forbes, founder of *Forbes* magazine] liked to say you make more money selling the advice than following it.

—Steve Forbes

Investing Seminars Worth Attending

One good way to obtain helpful advice is to attend conferences, where you can listen to some of the best financial experts in the United States, and usually ask questions. My three favorite speaker organizations are the American Association of Individual Investors (AAII) the Money Show, and FreedomFest. I speak before all three.

The AAII is a national non-profit organization with 46 local chapters. The chapters usually meet once a month and each provides a platform for an investment speaker. On a scale of 1-to-10 risk temperament, most people who join AAII are solid 4s and 5s, my kind of people. Over the years, I've spoken to perhaps 15 of their chapters. Members welcome me graciously, listen intently, and ask intelligent questions.

I once had an unforgettable experience with the Baton Rouge, Louisiana, AAII chapter. I was scheduled to arrive in Baton Rouge at 6:00 P.M. and speak at 7:00 P.M. Due to bad weather in Dallas, my flight was delayed two hours. I called the program director to let him know about the delay. I arrived at the meeting place around 9:00 P.M. expecting to find an empty hall. To my great surprise and pleasure, all of the attendees were still there. I spoke to a full house! Definitely my kind of people.

Money Show

I have spoken at the Money Show for about twenty years. In terms of size and style, the Money Show is worlds apart from AAII, which has only one speaker per meeting.

The Money Show is the big league for advisors and individual investors. It usually has about 100 speakers, including some of the biggest names in investing, and over 200 exhibitors. Held over a three- or four-day period, it's a smorgasbord of talent and philosophies, with something for everybody. In risk temperament, the speakers range from 4s to 10s. There are mutual fund advocates like me, stock pros, hard money advisors, and even people pushing oil-drilling and energy ventures. Take your pick! It's all in one place, and it's basically *free*.

The Money Show hosts three big shows each year. Orlando (near Disney World) in February, Las Vegas in May, and San Francisco in August—and each draws more than 5,000 attendees. See www.moneyshow.com for details. Click on Trade Shows. In addition, the organization sponsors investment seminars in London, Hong Kong, Toronto, Vancouver, and on cruises.

FreedomFest

Different from the above two is FreedomFest, an up-and-coming conference, held in Las Vegas in July. Although its primary focus is on Libertarian issues, the conference organizer, Dr. Mark Skousen, is an economist who writes an investment newsletter. Thus, the seminar features a number of investment gurus and speakers who discuss, in addition to investing, topics as diverse as philosophy, history, geopolitics, science and technology, art and literature, economics, and healthy living. This conference is not free. Its website lists the cost of attending at $495 per person or $795 per couple. The quality of the speakers is very high and diverse; 2011 speakers included Steve Forbes, Senator Rand Paul, Whole Foods Market CEO John Mackey, TV personalities Juan Williams and Dick Morris, and over a dozen investment professionals including this author. Click on www.freedomfest.com.

Important Lessons in This Chapter

- Make sure the advice is relevant to your needs.
- Only accept advice from people who are more knowledgeable than you are.

- Be aware of media biases.
- Put individual security recommendations in their proper perspective.
- Realize that some advice can be valid, yet useless.
- Be a skeptic.

No matter who says what, don't believe it if it don't make sense.

—Don't Squat with Your Spurs On!

(A classic book of Texas wisdom.)

CHAPTER

7

How to Build Mutual Fund Portfolios for Lifetime Profits

In Part One, I discussed the importance of determining your stock allocation and offered some general guidelines on your equity exposure. Working within these guidelines, you first need to decide how much of your equity allocation should go into index funds and how much into actively managed funds.

However, to make my asset allocation suggestions simpler to understand, and to provide an important overview, I have summarized them in an all–index fund portfolio. Later, I'll show you how to introduce some actively managed funds into your mix. All are long-term recommendations. The purpose of these models is to provide both insights and solutions. The insights are more important.

Lifetime All–Index Fund Portfolio

The following table categorizes investors by their willingness to accept risk, but the Low, Medium, and High categories could just as easily be considered stages of life—or the number of years before the money is needed.

I've divided domestic index funds into two categories, capitalization weighted and fundamentally weighted (which I'll explain in the next chapter). For the purposes of this table, I include cash/ equivalents earmarked for long-term investing as part of the fixed-income component. Cash for everyday use and an emergency cash reserve are separate.

	Index Fund allocations		
Portfolio risk:	Low (income bias)	Medium	High (growth bias)
Age:	Older	Middle	Young
Years before money is needed:	0–5	5–20	20–40
Domestic equity			
Cap-weighted total market or large cap	10%	20%	25%
Fundamentally weighted total market or large cap	10%	20%	25%
Small cap	5%	5%	10%
Small cap fundamentally weighted	0%	5%	5%
International equity*	5%	10%	15%
Fixed-income	†70%	40%	20%
Sum equity	30%	60%	80%

*See complete discussion in Chapter 2.

†This can include guaranteed investments such as fixed annuities.

Consider the percentages in the table as midpoints of ranges, not as absolutes. For example, a 20 percent suggestion could range from 15 to 25 percent.

I've not named specific index funds in this first table because the names are unimportant. In reality, you should probably use the index fund offered by whichever mutual fund group you patronize or use low-expense ETFs. Later tables offer specific recommendations for three large organizations.

> As a general rule, the greater a portfolio's risk level, the more attention the portfolio demands.

There's one other distinction between the three categories. As a general rule, the greater a portfolio's risk level, the more attention the portfolio demands. An equity-heavy portfolio needs to be monitored far more closely than a conservative one with mostly bond funds.

Specific Index Fund Recommendations

I prefer Fidelity or Vanguard funds because they have the lowest expense ratios for index funds and offer a wide selection of other funds. T. Rowe Price is also big enough for you to do all your investing, but their index funds have slightly higher costs. If you want to go outside these three groups, I would recommend using either the Fidelity or Schwab fund supermarkets. If a fund is not included in one of these supermarkets, forget it.

Here are specific fund recommendations for three large groups. If the group doesn't have an appropriate index fund in a category, I've substituted ETFs. I've also included an all-ETF portfolio that can be bought from any broker. ETFs are typically index funds. See the earlier table for percentages.

Fidelity Index Funds

	Fund	Ticker
Domestic equity		
Cap-weighted	Spartan Total Market Index, Investor class	FSTMX
Fundamentally weighted	PowerShares FTSI RAFI US 1000*	PRF
Small cap	Small Cap Enhanced Index	FCPEX
International equity	Spartan Int'l Index, Investor class	FSIIX
Fixed-income	U.S. Bond Index	FBIDX

*Through Fidelity Brokerage.

Fidelity has 18 stock index funds. It has a total of 246 no-load funds. Its NTF (no-transaction fee program) offers another 4,586 funds sponsored by other companies. Based on the weightings in the high-risk category, the minimum needed to own this portfolio is $100,000. Individual Fidelity funds have minimum investment requirements of $10,000 and $1,000.

Vanguard Index Funds

	Fund	Ticker
Domestic equity		
Cap-weighted	Total Stock Market Index	VTSMX
Fundamentally weighted	PowerShares FTSI RAFI U.S. 1000*	PRF
Small cap	Small Cap Index	NAESX
International equity	FTSE All-World ex-U.S.	VFWIX
International equity	FTSE All-World ex-U.S. Small-Cap	VFSVX
Fixed-income	Total Bond Market Index	VBMFX

*Through Vanguard Brokerage (separate account).

Vanguard has 25 indexed stock funds and 24 stock ETFs. Based on the weightings in the high-risk category, the minimum needed to own this portfolio is $30,000. Individual Vanguard funds have minimum investment requirements of $3,000.

Charles Schwab Index Funds

	Fund	Ticker
Domestic equity		
Cap-weighted	Total Stock Market Index Investors	SWTIX
Fundamentally weighted	Fundamental U.S. Large Co. Index Investors	SFLVX
Small cap	U.S Small-Mid Co. Investors	SFSVX
International equity	International Index Investors	SWINX
Int'l fundamental weighted	Fundamental Intl. Lg. Co. Idx Inv	SFNVX
Int'l fundamental weighted	Fundamental Intl. Sm-Md. Co. Idx Inv	SFIVX
Fixed-income	Total Bond Market	SWLBX

In addition Schwab's OneSource program has access to over 2,000 funds with no-load or no transaction fee. Based on the weightings in the high-risk category, the minimum needed to own this portfolio is $1,000. Individual Schwab funds have minimum investment requirements of $100.

All-ETF Portfolio

	Fund	Ticker
Domestic equity		
Cap-weighted	Vanguard Total Stock Market	VTI
Fundamentally weighted	PowerShares FTSI RAFI U.S. 1000	PRF
Small cap	Vanguard Small Cap	VB
International equity	iShares MSCI EAFE	EFA
International Small Cap	SPDR S&P Int'l Small Cap	GWX
Fixed-income	iShares Barclays 7–10 yr Treas.	IEF
Fixed-income	Vanguard Intermediate Term Bond	BIV

As you can see, I have tried very hard to broad-stroke my asset allocation advice. That's because if you read widely you will run across many other recommended allocations. Some will differ slightly from mine, whereas others will differ considerably. Since recommendations do vary so greatly, the conclusion I draw is not that mine are necessarily superior, but that the really important thing is to have an overarching plan. That's the bottom line. *Any plan is better than no plan.* Without a plan there's no telling what you will end up with.

In addition, by its very nature, a book cannot take into account the infinite variety of investors' needs. So if the asset allocation advice offered so far doesn't give you the confidence you need to do it yourself, I recommend that you go to a reputable financial advisor and work out a financial asset allocation tailored to your needs.

Finally, there is a commonplace strategy called rebalancing that many advisors consider part of portfolio construction. I believe this is more appropriately discussed in Chapter 10 on market timing.

What About Gold?

I worry about gold. As these pages were being written in early fall 2011, gold may be in a mania with great gains still to come, or it may have already topped out. In any case it has become quite volatile. However, for readers who missed the boat on the big rise in precious metals and believe gold still has a shot at $5,000 (as the ads promise), here's an alternative vehicle to consider.

The goal of the $10 billion Permanent Portfolio Fund (PRPFX) is to preserve and increase the purchasing power value of its shares over the long term by investing in a conservative mix of six target asset allocations, which never change. The minimum investment is $1,000. The expense ratio is .77 percent. From inception in December 1982 through September 2011, the fund has had an average annual gain of 6.8 percent. The fund was founded by the late Harry Browne, a newsletter editor, who was twice the Libertarian candidate for president.

Here are the baskets.

Permanent Portfolio Fund Asset Allocations

Gold	20%
Silver	5%
Swiss Franc assets	10%
U.S. and foreign real estate and natural resource stocks	15%
Aggressive growth stocks	15%
U.S. Treasury bills, bonds, and other dollar assets	35%
Total	*100%*

The benefits of this diversification are obvious.

The fund's long-term record is good. But understand that this is not a short-term hedging vehicle. And again, as this book is written, all but the growth stocks, real estate, and natural resources had soared to all-time highs.

Let's Simplify the Selection of Actively Managed Funds

Actively managed funds are usually higher-cost. Their performance is also less predictable. Still, there are four reasons for investing in them.

1. The fund has a particular investing niche that can't be easily duplicated by an index fund.
2. The actively managed fund is doing well because it is over-weighted in certain styles or industries.
3. The actively managed fund has been outperforming its bench-mark index, possibly because of exceptional management, or because its portfolio is very dissimilar to its benchmark. You believe that its momentum will continue.
4. The fund utilizes performance enhancing investing tactics such as leverage.

Index funds should be the core of your portfolio. I would consider putting 50 to 65 percent of the stocks in your portfolio into broad-based index funds. The remaining 35 to 50 percent could be invested in actively managed funds. Your split may be based on the simple observation as to which type is performing better.

While there is wide latitude in selecting actively managed funds, here's a caveat: You must know why you selected each fund. The simple fact you heard about a mutual fund is not a valid reason to own it. Nor is "my late husband bought it" an acceptable expla-nation. If you don't have good justification to buy actively managed funds, put a higher percentage of your assets into index funds. There is nothing wrong with being 100 percent indexed. By the way, some equity funds from TIAA-CREF will implement this philosophy for you.

You can make choosing an actively managed fund complicated, but you don't have to. Look first to the media for candidates. Newsletters, personal finance magazines, and broadcast business shows all give usable advice. Select a recommendation that seems right for you, which becomes the starting point of the decision making process. Next check them out.

It's not hard. You can find all the information you need from the funds themselves, either by calling them or perusing their websites. If that's not enough, go to personal finance magazines and some newsletters, which provide detailed information several times a year. Much of the data can be unnecessarily comprehensive. So, don't let yourself get swamped.

Here is all you really need to know to get the best possible results. If you don't want to spend your time checking out actively managed funds, then just stick with index funds.

What to Consider, What to Ignore

Your first criterion is always performance. So concentrate on that. I prefer to look at performance over several short to intermediate-term time periods—for up to three years. In a few instances, you can also consider the five-year record. Get this performance data from comprehensive data sources. Do not go by the selected data frequently found in fund company advertisements. And certainly don't be swayed by the impressive performance data in the ads. If it wasn't good, the fund company would never have taken the ad in the first place.

Just as important, don't look at extended periods. It's pointless to look at 10 years of performance. There is just too much irrelevant ancient history. It's something like trying to forecast the winner in an Olympic swimming event. Normally, younger swimmers have the edge, but in a case where the competition includes an older swimmer who happens to have the better *recent* performance, what should the wise money do? My call would be to choose the recent performance—pick the older swimmer. Yes, I'm thinking of the then 41-year-old, 2008 gold medal Olympian, Dara Torres.

What about the disclaimer found in every prospectus, "past performance is no guarantee of future returns"? Of course it's true. But I don't know a better method than past performance for selecting funds. At least it's objective. Most of the other criteria, such as management ability, are highly subjective.

One other approach is to stick with the largest fund groups, though that's no guarantee. Sorry, even the best have their laggards.

Admittedly, many factors influence performance. You can review them if the data are readily available. But most of these factors are already encapsulated in the performance, so don't go crazy with your analysis. I never spent much time on these factors when I was making recommendations.

In the following discussion, I'll review some things that influence performance in two categories: Those that are already in the performance numbers, and those that either aren't or aren't always!

Those in the first category bode well for past performance continuing. Those in the second category, not so much.

The following are already in the performance figures.

Management Ability   Fund mavens always stress it, and it is clearly important. But the only reliable way I know to identify management ability is to look at the performance. How else do we know that a manager is great? Certainly, not by his ability to do a great interview. Think about all the fund managers who have been anointed by the press. What do they all have in common? That's right: superlative past performance.

A sampling of the factors governing performance:

- The manager's style.
- How he picks stocks top-down or bottom-up.
- How often does he turn over his portfolio, frequently or slowly?
- To what extent does he diversify?
- Is he a quant, or does he interview corporate management?
- How much of his own money does he have in his fund?
- Does the fund have one or multiple managers?

There is no need to consider all these factors one by one. As long as they don't change, they are already factored into the performance. It's also totally unnecessary—and perhaps counterproductive—to examine a fund's individual stock holdings. For openers, the data available to you is not current. And, the point of owning funds is so you don't have to do this.

> The only way I know to identify management ability is to look at the performance.

Some factors that may not be in the performance numbers:

Size of fund. Generally speaking a smaller fund with fewer assets is better. Since good past performance may have been achieved when the fund was small, which may no longer be the case, you can't necessarily trust past performance. However, as a practical matter, asset size is the most relevant with small-cap funds.

Style of fund-growth or value. May not be in the performance, because style leadership changes. In other words, don't assume a style-specific or industry-specific fund will have

good performance based on past performance. Use fundamental analysis or short-term trends to see if the style or industry is still in favor.

Hedging. It makes a difference whether international funds
hedge or don't hedge currencies. Depending on currency
fluctuations it may or may not be in the performance.

Age. The age of a fund is not usually as relevant as manager
tenure—how many years the manager has been running
the fund. If the manager is new, the performance record is
probably not relevant because it's someone else's.

Many people consider Peter Lynch the greatest fund manager
ever for his stewardship of Fidelity Magellan from 1977 to 1990.
Under Lynch, the fund's assets hit $110 billion, a huge amount. After
Lynch stepped down, none of his successors approached his record.
Five managers later, Magellan's assets were down to about $15 billion
(much of it in tax-sheltered accounts). Redemptions totaled about
$63 billion. It was not the same fund that it had been under Lynch.
Not a single one of the subsequent managers performed well enough
to stem the losses—and Fidelity can certainly afford to hire the best.
(The current manager took over in September 2011. It'll be a while
before he has a meaningful record.) So, ignore a fund's performance
under prior managers. An exception might be funds co-managed by
several managers. I wouldn't be concerned if one or two members of
a four or five member team left.

If a fund is brand new, you can't rely on its minuscule history.
In this case, I would consider the reputation of the parent group,
the manager's record at a prior fund, or how well the market is
favoring the fund's style or industry. In most cases there is no need
to buy a brand new fund.

Costs   *Costs* may be a consideration. The way I look at it, if a fund has
been around for several years, then the costs are already factored into
the performance. That said, be realistic. If the potential for gains is
big enough, nobody will care about the costs. If a fund is going to
gain 30 percent in a year, we can all live with a 2 or 3 percent, or
whatever, expense ratio. The hedge funds, which usually charge
2 percent annual fees plus 20 percent of profits, are proof of this.
In the short run, costs aren't important. If you buy a fund for a quick
trade, costs are irrelevant.

But costs gain in importance as the holding period lengthens. That's why index funds are best for long-term holds. In the case of active management, we can ignore high expenses when the fund is hot, but the reality is that over a long period of time performance usually cools, regressing to the mean. Then costs become meaningful. ("Regression to the mean" is one of those jargon expressions the investment world loves! In easy words, it just means that over time a series of numbers tend to work their way back to the middle of their range.)

Summary of Active-Management Fund Selection

You'll do okay if you just check the following:

- The short- to intermediate-term performance record.
- Whether performance was achieved by the current manager.
- The size of a small-cap fund.
- The fund's style. (If the fund is specialized, is that specialty currently in favor?)
- Costs.

Think of the media's investment picks as only the beginning of your selection process. And as always, if you don't want to do the work, fine. Stick with index funds.

Selecting Actively Managed Funds: A Brief History

Back in 1973, when I was writing *Put Money in Your Pocket*, subtitled *The Art of Selecting No-Load Funds for Maximum Gain* (a very provocative title at the time), knowledge of how to pick the best funds, was, to say the least, rudimentary. Almost all the people who were then picking funds were selling load funds. No matter what they told their customers, the biggest factor in their fund selection was the size of their commission. In those days the Dreyfus Fund was one of the most popular. It had an excellent performance record and provided salespeople with a 9 percent commission in certain situations, a half-percent higher than most of its competitors. Today, can we even imagine paying—or earning—a 9 percent commission on *anything*?

I spent months searching every fund newsletter published at the time to find out if anyone in the industry really knew how to pick funds. I also read all the magazines and other financial literature

I could get my hands on. (Don't forget, I was still in broadcasting then.) As a trained researcher, I concluded that not one of these financial people really understood how to forecast fund performance with greater accuracy than the proverbial monkey throwing darts.

Then by a stroke of luck I ran across Manhattan financial planner Melvin Roebuck, who had more brains than the rest of the industry combined. He had come up with four guidelines for picking funds. Reading them, I instantly realized this guy was on to something. His four principles were:

1. Top-flight management, as evidenced by superior medium- and short-term performance.
2. Size of fund.
3. New money inflow.
4. An appropriate cash position.

Points 1 and 2, which are still valid, we just discussed.

Point 3: New Money Inflow   One of the truisms of fund management is that having cash coming into an actively managed fund at steady intervals makes it easier for the fund to perform. If, for example, an exciting IPO comes up, a fully invested manager doesn't have to sell an existing stock to buy the IPO. Conversely, the last thing a fund manger wants is money flowing out. He can't buy anything new without selling something first, which can be frustrating. Moreover, he also has the agonizing task of selling existing stock to meet redemptions. At first it's manageable; he can sell losers. But if redemptions surge, he has to sell his winners (or borrow money, which leverages performance).

Back in the halcyon 1980s and 1990s, when cash inflows were substantial, this topic warranted considerable discussion. Today new money inflows are smaller, nor are they a meaningful consideration with index funds, ETF's, and many hedge funds. For these reasons, and because it is difficult for laymen to obtain that data, I have ignored cash inflows and outflows.

Point 4: Cash Position   The percent of the fund in *cash* has a tremendous influence on the fund's performance. Obviously, you want the fund to be fully invested during bull markets and have a high cash position during bear markets. That doesn't always happen.

As with new money inflow, we don't hear too much about appropriate cash positions any more for reasons discussed in Chapter 10, under the heading "Mutual Funds Don't Market Time." Also, most mutual funds no longer provide the media with this information on a current basis. The information is in quarterly reports, but that's too late to be really helpful.

Bond Fund Selection

Bonds outperform equities in some years and have become an important addition to conservative portfolios. There are basically four parameters to examine when selecting bonds—yield, credit quality, maturity, and tax status.

Credit risk is the risk that a bond's issuer will default. In terms of credit risk, bonds range from ultra-safe U.S. Treasuries to investment grade corporate bonds to high-yield bonds and more. Trained fixed-income specialists make detailed examinations of the ability of the bond issuer to make periodic interest payments in full and on time, and pay off the principal at maturity. You and I are not equipped to do this. So do what most people do: Go by the quality ratings issued by Standard & Poor's and Moody's. Even though there are occasional hazards in doing so, you have little choice if you're buying individual bonds. A better plan is to buy a bond fund whose manager will do credit analysis for you.

Unless you are extraordinarily rich, never buy individual junk bonds. Only buy junk in diversified mutual funds where the manager can do expert credit analysis. Bill Gross, the co-CEO of PIMCO, says that investors need at least $500,000 in fixed-income securities in order to buy individual bonds effectively. And even then, you run a high risk of getting eaten alive by the hidden costs that bond brokers build into their wares.

Tax status essentially divides bonds into tax-free municipals vs. taxable corporates, although there are finer distinctions. Your tax bracket tells you which to choose. If it's high, you buy municipal bonds (munis); and if it's low, you buy taxable bonds. Or, to think of it in a different way, buy munis in your taxable accounts and taxable bonds in your tax-sheltered accounts (such as IRAs).

Maturities require a longer discussion. The quick advice is to basically buy intermediate-term bonds or bond funds, either taxable or tax-free. Compared to long-term bonds, intermediate-term bonds provide 95 percent of the return with 37 percent of the risk.

Intermediate term bonds are generally considered to be in the 5- to 10-year maturity range.

If you think there is a possibility of rampant inflation in the coming years due to federal deficits, among many other factors, put 25 to 50 percent of your bond holdings in short-term bonds with maturities of five years or less.

Asset allocation tip: If your home is financed with a fixed-rate mortgage, that mortgage is effectively a short (negative) bond position. Take that into account.

From Here to Maturities

Bond maturities are a critical factor seldom examined beyond the short-, intermediate-, and long-term summary. However, it's very good to know the numbers behind these generalizations because how much the price of a bond rises or falls with a change in interest rates depends largely on the bond's maturity—the date when you can redeem your bond for full value. The longer the maturity, the greater the risk, potential profit, and volatility. Here's what happens when interest rates change just 1 percent.

$10,000 Investment

	Change in Value When Interest Rates Move:	
U.S. Government Security	Up 1%	Down 1%
3-mo. Treasury bill	$–25	$25
1-yr Treasury bill	–98	100
2-yr Treasury bill	–196	202
5-yr Treasury note	–461	487
10-yr Treasury note	–798	878
30-yr Treasury bond	–1,503	1,897
30-yr zero coupon bond	–2,554	3,424

Note: I've tried to keep the tables in this book to a minimum, but sometimes tables explain things in a way that text just can't.
Source: American Century, September 2009.

Duration

While average maturity is useful, a better measure is duration, which you should use when available. It differs from average maturity in that it takes into account a bond's periodic cash flows from current interest payments as well as the principal received when the bond matures. Average maturity doesn't take interest flows into account. It only measures to the due date of the principal.

The previous table illustrates the huge difference between these two methods. The last two bonds in the table, the 30-year Treasury and the 30-year Zero, have the same maturity—30 years. In both cases you get your principal back in 30 years.

But there is a sizeable difference in duration. The duration for the Zero is 30—the same as the maturity—because there is only one distribution, at the end. On the other hand, the regular T-bond pays interest semiannually. That drops its duration to 17. In other words, you will get half your interest and principal back in 17 years.

This makes a huge difference in the volatility. If interest rates drop one percent, your $10,000 investment in the T-bond appreciates $1,897, but the same investment in the Zero-coupon bond appreciates $3,424.

Duration is a far more useful measure of volatility due to interest rate changes. You can multiply a fund's duration by a change in interest rates and get its price movement. A fund with a duration of five will lose 5 percent of its value with a 1 percent increase in interest rates. A fund with a duration of 10 would lose 10 percent of its value. Conversely, a 1 percent decline in interest rates would result in 5 percent and 10 percent gains in total value, respectively. If interest rates change by 2 percent, then double the figures. You can't use average maturity to make these determinations. That's why, if there is any chance of that you may sell the bond before it matures, pay close attention to duration.

Important Lessons in This Chapter

- Think in terms of portfolios, not individual securities.
- Use index funds for your core holdings then fine-tune your portfolio by selecting actively managed funds based on their short- to intermediate-term performance.
- Have a plan.

CHAPTER

8

Index Fund Investing: Beyond the S&P 500

According to the Morningstar database, there are now more than 2,200 index funds (including multiple series) tracking over 500 different indexes. About 250 of them are ETFs. Some indexes are broad-based, covering a wide selection of listed stocks. Other indexes are more narrowly focused. They are indexes of industries or asset classes.

Whereas narrowly focused index funds have a place in the investing universe, they are basically sector funds far more appropriate for professionals or stock investors. Invest in them if you understand the sector or industry. But this sort of specialized investing is beyond the scope of this book.

It's far more important that you understand the ways broad-based indexes are weighted. The different methodologies result in significant differences in performance.

This chapter discusses three of the four most popular ways of weighting indexes: capitalization-weighting, equal-weighting, and fundamental-weighting. We won't worry about price weighting, an archaic system that is still used to compute the venerable Dow Jones Industrial Average. (But the Glossary has a summary of price-weighting for the math inclined.)

Indexing—Yes; Market Cap-Weighted Indexes—Not Necessarily

The most common way to weight an index is by capitalization. The index fund weights each stock in its portfolio based on that company's market capitalization. That includes, but is hardly limited to, index funds based on the S&P 500, DJ Wilshire 5000, and Russell 3000. It is estimated that over $2 trillion in assets were linked to cap-weighted indexes in the United States alone prior to the 2008 bear market. There could also be another $2 trillion overseas. And cap-weighted assets were growing at the rate of a half-trillion a year until 2008.

I have misgivings about capitalization weighting. To understand this type of weighting, you need to understand how a capitalization-weighted index is constructed. The market capitalization of a stock is simply the price of the stock times the number of shares outstanding. Thus, the DJ Wilshire 5000, which essentially includes all listed stocks above the micro-cap level, is a perfect representation of the market as a whole. A stock accounting for say 2 percent of the market value of all listed stocks accounts for 2 percent of the value of the DJ Wilshire index. It's a simple way to do things.

Thus, in a cap-weighted index, large-cap stocks have a far larger market value (weighting) than do small-cap stocks. Of course, weighting doesn't necessarily indicate more profitable companies or even necessarily larger companies by other measures. A company could have a big market cap simply because investors, enamored with the company, have driven up its price. Remember, price is the dynamic part of the formula. The other part of the formula, the number of shares outstanding, changes very little. The bigger a company's market cap, the more it counts in the index.

Cap-weighting worked far better in the 1990s than in the 2000s, because it suffers from an inherent flaw. With price the major variable factor in the index's construction, *cap-weighting tends to overweight overvalued stocks and underweight undervalued stocks,* particularly in bull markets.

The reason cap-weighting worked so well in the 1990s was that overvalued stocks, especially Internet stocks, tended to get even more overvalued. The crazier their prices and P/E ratios became, the more investors wanted them. Until they didn't. Needless to say those days are long gone.

In the five years ending December 1999, a bull market period, the Vanguard 500 Index Fund ranked in the top 20 percent of all the *Investor's* growth-income funds. The fund's technology weighting in 1999 was an astounding 39.6 percent. In sharp contrast, for the 10 years ending December 2009, which included two severe bear markets, the same fund ranked in the bottom 40 percent among growth-income funds. As the prices of its tech holdings collapsed during the bear market years, the tech weighting dropped to under 24 percent.

Advocates of this approach tout one advantage: Cap-weighting an index enables it to perfectly replicate the overall market. In addition, cap-weighting eliminates the need for rebalancing. The index automatically corrects its stock weightings for changes in market prices each trading day.

Cap-weighting accurately replicates the market so it is the perfect index methodology to use to benchmark active management. But that very specialized function has nothing to do with developing an optimum investment vehicle.

> With price the major variable factor in the index's construction, cap-weighting tends to overweight overvalued stocks and underweight undervalued stocks, particularly in bull markets.

It is true that institutions and the very largest fund groups, which have billions of dollars to invest, find cap-weighting is best suited to meet their needs. Their size constrains their stock selections. *Investability* becomes a problem. Thus they find it easier to obtain an adequate number of shares with cap-weighting because large-company stocks predominate, and there are plenty of shares around. Most retail funds don't have that problem. They can weight their portfolios any way they choose.

The reason indexing works so well is because passive investing substantially lowers costs, not because it replicates a universe or because the market is "efficient." Sometimes the market is efficient; sometimes it isn't. Sometimes one universe is better than another.

Not only does cap-weighting not have any inherent advantage for the individual investor, it has some clear disadvantages.

The S&P 500 Index presents a problem for the index funds that track it. It's too popular. Too much money follows it. Whenever Standard & Poor's makes a change in the Index, which it does several times each year, all the index funds must sell, virtually simultaneously, the stock that is being dropped, and add the new stock. It is difficult to do this at advantageous prices because the stock prices are marked up or down as soon as it's known which stocks will be added or deleted. This hurts the performance of the 500 Index funds.

For the 10 years ending June 2011, Investor shares of the Vanguard Total Stock Market Index Fund averaged 3.69 percent annually. In contrast, Investor shares of the Vanguard 500 averaged 2.62 percent annually.

Why do the stocks in the Index change? The explanation is that even though the weighting may be "correct" in terms of replicating a universe, the 500 stocks are actually just lists of bellwether stocks in leading industries selected by a committee at Standard & Poor's. The committee uses several criteria.

For a company to be included in the Index, S&P says it must be an American operating company with a market cap in excess of $4 billion, have four consecutive quarters of positive earnings, adequate liquidity, and sector balance. Stocks are chosen from a list meeting these criteria. If a company no longer meets these criteria, or is merged, it is dropped from the Index. Selection boils down to a judgment call. The 500 is a large-cap index covering 75 percent of U.S. equities.

The Equal-Weight Alternative

One alternative is to construct a fund that gives every stock equal weight. In the case of the S&P 500, every stock then gets a weighting of 0.2 percent (or 1/500th) of the portfolio. This has been an excellent system in recent years, particularly since it gives more weight to small-cap stocks, which are often superior performers, especially early in an economic cycle.

One such index fund, Rydex S&P 500 Equal Weight Fund (RSP), outperformed the cap-weighted S&P 500 in 2004, 2005, 2009, and 2010. In 2010, it gained 21.4 percent versus 15.0 percent for the cap-weighted 500. That's an incredible difference when you consider the two funds held exactly the same stocks, just in different proportions. On the other hand, the equal weight fund trailed from 2006 through 2008 when large caps did well.

What's more, these funds need to periodically rebalance each stock (back to the 0.2 percent weight in the case of RSP), which increases expenses. RSP rebalances quarterly, and its turnover is 20 percent annually, compared to 5.4 percent turnover for the cap-weighted SPDR S&P 500 (SPY). Consequently, RSP's expense ratio is .40 percent, which is low in absolute terms but not in the same league as the cap-weighted 500, which is .09 percent.

Rydex is on a roll. In January 2011 they added six more equal weight ETFs to their lineup, covering the following indexes: Russell 1000, 2000, and Midcap, as well as three international indexes.

The Fundamental Indexation Alternative

Now, there's another way to index stocks. The fundamental index approach can outperform in some types of markets, and perhaps in the long run. Fundamental indexation, originally developed by professionals for institutional portfolios, is now available for retail investors, too.

The idea is to weight an index using the true fundamental measures of a company's size. By not using price in the weighting formula, fundamental weighting takes the influence of manias, bubbles, and overreactions to good or bad news out of the equation. It aims to measure the inherent importance of a company.

The pioneer in developing this fundamental-weight concept is Rob Arnott, the chairman of Research Affiliates, a Pasadena, California, institutional-money manager with a million dollar minimum. (However, Arnott also advises PIMCO All Asset and PIMCO All Asset All Authority, two funds with relatively low minimum investment requirements.) Arnott is also a former editor of the prestigious *Financial Analysts Journal*. His firm employs some specific metrics in constructing a fundamental index:

- Book value
- Cash flow
- Sales
- Dividends

Weighting on these four factors eliminates the over/under-weighting problem, since changes in stock price are only slightly related to changes in the fundamental value of a company, certainly over the short term. So, price changes do not directly affect the weighting and overvalued stocks do not increase in importance, nor do undervalued stocks decrease in importance in the index. As with cap-weighted indexes, fundamental indexing does not involve any security analysis of a stock's fundamental data.

Arnott did a lot of back-testing as he was developing the fundamental indexing concept. On that basis, he believes that it can potentially outperform cap-weighted indexes by as much as 200 basis points (2 percent) in the United States and by more than 250 basis points (2.5 percent) overseas over a period of many years.

Fundamental Weighting Doesn't Win Every Time

In fact fundamental weighting failed its first big test in the real world. In 2008 one popular fundamentally weighted fund, PowerShares FTSE RAFI US 1000 (PRF), declined 9 percent more than the Spider's ETF (SPY), which invests in the cap-weighted S&P 500 (–40.6 to –36.9 percent).

But since then, the story's been different. PRF outperformed SPY by 59 percent in 2009, (41.7 to 26.3 percent), and by 30 percent in 2010 (19.7 to 15.1 percent).

What went wrong in 2008? Part of the reason the indexes produce different results over time is that fundamental weighting gives these funds a value bias. Cap-weighted indexes are in the blend category. This means that if growth stocks do better than value stocks, as they did in 2007, 2008, and the first quarter of 2009, investors would be better off with cap-weighting, which has a comparative growth bias. The underlying reason for these trends is that tech stocks usually fall in the growth category, whereas financials are an important component of value investing. Financial stocks got killed in 2008. AIG lost 99 percent of its value. They came back in 2009, however.

Which Is Best Over the Long Run?

Whether fundamental indexing will dominate cap-weighted indexing in the future depends on whether growth or value is better over the long run. Although the research on this score is inconclusive, a major indexer, the Frank Russell Co., has continuous data from 1979 that gives value the nod. The Russell 3000 Index tracks about 99 percent of all stocks as determined by market capitalization. In the 32 years through the end of 2010, the Russell 3000 *Growth* Index has had an average annual total return of 10.6 percent, whereas the Russell 3000 *Value* Index has had an annualized return of 12.3 percent, a 17 percent performance advantage for value over growth. This advantage adds up significantly over time.

Traditional indexers sometimes argue for a third way. They say cap-weighted value index funds may outperform fundamental funds (also with a value bias) because they are cheaper, that is, the cap-weighted funds often have lower expense ratios. The proponents of cap-weighted value index funds note that over the long run, the lower expenses will give them a performance edge. This is true, but it ignores the reason we are moving away from cap-weighting to begin with. Remember: All cap-weighted portfolios suffer from the same limitation. They can overweight overvalued stocks and underweight undervalued stocks. So the argument is really about preferring value to growth. It's not an argument for preferring cap-weighted value to fundamental indexing.

And, in the following table you can see how three representative ETFs have performed over the past three and five years.

Annualized Gain

	Ticker	Type	Three years	Five years
PowerShares FTSE RAFI US 1000	PRF	Fundamental	8.3%	4.3%
SPDR S&P 500	SPY	Cap-weighted	3.1	2.7
IShares Russell 1000 Value Index	IWD	Value	2.2	1.0

Years ending June, 2011.
Source: Morningstar.

I think that value will do as well as, or better than, growth in the coming decade. If you agree, you can add cap-weighted value funds to the cap-weighted portion of your portfolio.

Also be aware that fundamental indexing does not produce equal weights. In fact PRF's top 10 holdings account for about 19 percent of assets, the same as for a cap-weighted S&P 500 fund. An equal weighted 500 fund would have 2 percent of assets in the top 10 holdings.

Both cap and fundamentally weighted index funds have a place in your portfolios. However, I recommend you replace any S&P 500 Index funds with total stock market index funds or a fundamentally weighted fund or both (unless there are significant tax consequences).

Some Fundamental Index Fund Choices

The first fundamentally weighted index funds distributed to retail investors have been the ETFs, which have some advantages over mutual funds. Three companies are sponsoring fundamentally weighted ETFs as this book is being written.

PowerShares Capital Management (an investment advisory firm now owned by Invesco) manages 90 ETFs (five of them broad-based domestic ETFs) is using Research Affiliates' methodology. Two that you should consider are PowerShares FTSE RAFI US 1000 (PRF), which owns approximately 1,000 stocks, and PowerShares FTSE RAFI US 1500 Small-Mid portfolio (PRFZ). See www.powershares .com (or Invescopowershares) for details.

Another company that sponsors fundamental funds is Wisdom Tree, headed by three of the biggest names in the business: Professor Jeremy Siegel (author Stocks for the Long Run), Michael Steinhardt, a famous hedge fund operator, and Arthur Levitt, a former SEC chairman.

WisdomTree contends that weighting by cash dividends provides you with the advantage of getting an objective measure of a company's value. The firms point out that earnings can be manipulated by depreciation schedules, sales of assets, and other hidden factors. But dividends don't lie, nor are they subject to interpretation or restatement. Their motto is "show me the cash!" Volatility is lowered when non-dividend paying stocks are excluded, and there is also some bear market protection since dividend-paying stocks tend to decline less during market declines.

WisdomTree says that their "earnings" family benefits from the exclusion of stocks without earnings. (Unless we are in another mania, I can buy that.) See www.WisdomTree.com.

At this writing, the only retail mutual fund group offering fundamentally weighted index funds using the Research Affiliates weightings is Charles Schwab. They have five: a U.S. Large Co. (SFLNX), U.S. Small-Mid Co. (SFSNX), Int'l Large Co. (SFNNX), Int'l Small-Mid Co. (SFILX), and Emerging Markets (SFENX). Schwab's U.S. Large Co. Fund essentially replicates PRF, and with lower expenses.

Consider both of these ETF groups, and Schwab's mutual funds.

Important Lessons in This Chapter

- Don't put all your indexed assets in cap-weighted funds. They may be a more "academically correct" representation of the market, but so what.
- Diversify your indexed assets among capitalization weighted, fundamentally weighted, and perhaps equal weighted funds for diversity and better risk-adjusted returns.

CHAPTER 9

How to Survive Bear Markets

Since the long bull market of the 1980s and 1990s ended in early 2000, there have been three major downturns. The worst was the Great Recession, which began in October 2007 and finally ended in March 2009. It is not likely to be repeated soon. But no doubt there will be other bear markets. The lessons I offer in this chapter cover both severe and normal bear markets.

Here's a thought. Why not just avoid equities altogether? That would solve the problem. The answer is that a few very rich people indeed can and perhaps should stay away from stocks and the periodic heartache that they cause. But all the rest of us have to take equity risks because we can't save enough to have a comfortable retirement without the growth that stocks can provide. If you need equity size profits, you are going to have to take equity size risks.

Therefore, it is a virtual certainty that somewhere down the road your investments are going to be under water. To avoid any losses at all is impractical; the goal should be to avoid the catastrophic loss that would change your lifestyle.

Too Little, Too Late

As befitting their mandates, throughout 2008 many financial publications offered advice to their readers on how to limit losses. They offered sound practical and psychological advice, but unfortunately much of the advice was of little help because it was offered far too late. And don't expect the advice to come earlier the next time around.

Heed the oft-repeated advice, "Plan ahead. It wasn't raining when Noah built the Ark."

The critical advice—the advice that will be most helpful—is that the best time, and for some, the only time, to prepare for the next bear market is well beforehand. Once you're in a bear market, it becomes far more difficult to take money-saving steps. For some there is a powerful urge to hang in hoping it's only a normal correction, not a bear market. Other investors panic and sell at what may be a low. They incur huge losses and will probably never get back into the market, certainly not at the right time.

I'll try to draw some practical and psychological lessons for the next bear market that, hopefully, won't be anything like the perfect storm we saw in 2007 to 2009.

First of all, you basically have two alternatives: (1) Keep your risk level under control at all times by adopting a conservative asset allocation; and (2) Market time. Let's analyze both.

Adopt a Conservative Asset Allocation

Plan ahead. It wasn't raining when Noah built the Ark.

By far the best way to prepare for a bear market is to have proper asset allocation and diversification to begin with. That's the key. If you're not overweighted in equities at the outset, you probably will not suffer an irredeemable loss. Do this when you determine your asset allocations. Assume unfavorable market conditions at the outset.

Asset allocation is usually a good technique for limiting losses. Unfortunately, it didn't work in 2008 because virtually every asset class except a few types of bonds declined. Gold futures, continuing an eight-year run, gained 5.5 percent, but it was the smallest gain since 2004. Most gold mining stocks suffered losses.

Don't let the anomalies of 2008 fool you. Proper allocation and diversification is basic in both bull and bear markets. In a more normal bear, some asset classes will rise, offsetting losses. In the kinds of difficult markets I foresee, some cash will never be trash. In fact, most advisors recommend you always keep some money in cash—for an unlikely reason: Having some cash in reserve may give you the courage to invest at precisely those times when it's hardest.

How to Protect Yourself from the Next Crash

Here are some specific hints for negotiating a future bear market. Try very hard to implement the strategies when the markets are still high.

- Have you *leveraged* any of your investments? If so, close out the leverage at the first whiff of a downdraft. Assets shrink; liabilities never shrink. I would consider sky-high valuations or even the maturing of a bull market as reasons to get off leverage. You need to think carefully about this. Not all leverage is obvious. Besides the leverage you employ in margin accounts, some mutual funds, ETFs, and closed-end bond funds borrow to enhance their investments. Similarly, get out of high-volatility risky investments, if you have any. Take the money from their sales and put it into safer investments like money funds or FDIC-insured bank accounts.
- *Know market cycle parameters.* They can provide useful guidelines.

Bull markets typically last about twice as long as bear markets. That's fairly common knowledge. Less known is how long it takes to recoup after a bear market ends. The following table lists the time it took to return to the previous highs from the four most severe bear markets since the Great Depression.

Months to Recoup Losses: Worst Bear Markets Since the Great Depression

Bear Market	% Decline S&P 500	75% Recovery in Months	100% Recovery in Months	Years/ Months
1973–1974	–48%	20*	64	5/4
2000–2003	–47%	43	50	4/2
1968–1970	–37%	9	22	1/10
1987	–34%	18	23	1/11
2007–2009	–57%	25	†?	?

*50% recovery in 5 months.
†Old high was 1565.15 on Oct. 9, 2007.

What I read from this table is that it may take the market several more years to come back to the October 2007 highs. That assumes a multi-year rally will follow the bottom and that governments will do a lot of things correctly along the way. Neither are givens. Use the table as a basis for your planning.

What's the worst-case scenario for a calendar year? The following table provides some benchmarks.

Biggest One-Year Drops Ever (Based on the S&P 500)

Before 1945	
1931	–47.1%
1937	–38.6%
1930	–29.6%
Since 1945	
2008	–38.5%
1974	–29.6%
2002	–23.4%

Note: In 1987, famed for its October Black Monday, the S&P actually gained 2.0% for the year.

- Consider buying *convertible bond* funds if you believe a bear market is nearing its end. They are almost as volatile as equities, meaning they have a lot of upside potential, yet in case you are premature, they provide a significant yield while you are waiting for a new bull market to begin.
- *Don't throw good money after bad.* Even the worst bear market years will feature short rallies. Be patient. Bear markets have a way of lasting longer than you think.
- If you're looking for the *sharpest gains* off a bear market bottom, buy the stock funds that have declined the most.
- If you have *unrealized losses* because of a bear market, sell to *realize a tax loss.* Losses should be harvested to offset anything sold at a profit. Tax loss selling is particularly beneficial for mutual fund investors who can be socked with late year capital gains distributions, even in a severe bear market, as a result of funds selling securities at a profit for market reasons or to meet redemptions.
- *Have sufficient cash on hand.* There are two reasons for having cash. The first is a normal reserve for emergencies, such as illness or losing a job. The second is to have money to invest when stocks are cheap.

Let's get the first reason out of the way. The conventional wisdom imparted by financial planners is that cash for six months' living expenses is normally sufficient. I guess the reason for this is that it would give you a half-year to sell investments (mainly bonds) at acceptable prices.

I never thought much about it, so the conventional wisdom seemed okay to me. Then, during 2008, a lot of advisors, including me, suddenly realized that figure might be low and needed redefining, partly because like a lot of guidelines in the financial services arena, one size didn't fit all.

Six months may be fine for a worker with a dependable income who is in no danger of getting laid off. But many people don't fall into that category. At the other extreme, retirees, who can't recoup stock market losses by working, need far greater cash and short-term bond reserves. Consequently, advisors started recommending keeping up to five years expenses in cash and short-term bonds. That's clearly excessive for emergencies. And, staying that liquid can defeat long-term goals.

So I say keep any money needed for the next 12 months in liquid, relatively safe investments like money funds or ultra short-term bond funds. Keep another two to five years' worth of spending in laddered short- and intermediate-term bonds as part of your portfolio's fixed income allocation

The second reason (having money to invest when stocks are cheap) turned out to be the most relevant in 2009. Having a large cash allocation is very advantageous when bargains abound, as they did in March 2009. Putting money into riskier investments can produce big profits at those times. You can dollar cost-average or even market time, which I explain later, to determine entry points.

If you have cash on hand, do some buying when the market is low. But be cautious. Don't bet the ranch. People who never bet the ranch, never lose the ranch. Bet the chicken coop instead.

- *Sell to your sleeping point.* This means that you shouldn't have so much in stocks that you are beside yourself with worry when they decline. But like a lot of good advice it can be hard to implement. One of the problems is knowing your "sleeping point." That's because during bull markets most people are not sleeping at all, they're wide awake—and happy. The anxious insomnia comes only after stocks have lost considerable value.

Over the years I have talked to many investors who, during good times, assured me they had the intestinal fortitude to handle a 25 percent loss. But when the market went down 25 percent, it turned out that they didn't! Most investors know that instinctively. They find that having peace of mind becomes very important. This produces an urgent desire to sell at what may be exactly the wrong time.

The solution in most cases is to adjust your asset allocation to the point where you are comfortable in the worst situation. If percentages aren't meaningful to you, then deal in dollars. Let's say you have $800,000 in the market. A 25 percent haircut means a dollar drop of $200,000. Would you be all right with only $600,000? Would you be able to console yourself with the knowledge that the missing $200,000 is only gone temporarily, not forever—unless you panicked and sold?

Keep this in mind. If you want to maximize your returns, well and good. But nowhere is it written that you must. I think too many of us have been brainwashed into trying to do so. Success has been defined as a higher returning investment. (And I'm one of the culprits; I brag about my high returns. It's human nature—and good business.) That wouldn't be so bad if risk was always mentioned alongside returns. Which it isn't! Note that the long-term record I mention in this book is risk-adjusted. My newsletter picks never came close to being number one on a raw score basis.

It's very important to be comfortable with the risk level of your investments. In the last week of December 2009, I brought my equity allocation down from 40 to 35 percent, a rare move for me. It wasn't a market timing move. It was an enhance-my-comfort-zone move. It was a lock-in-some-of-my-2009-profits move. Thirty-five percent was my sleeping point. The fact that 2010 turned out to be an excellent year for stocks didn't bother me. Achieving my sleeping point was more important to me than a few extra gains.

When a commentator on CNBC was asked to give advice to viewers as to what were the best positions to be in to ride out the market storm, he answered "cash and fetal."

—Reported by Thomas Friedman in
The New York Times on October 1, 2008

Here are some observations on when to sell. All refer to diversified stock market investments. The rules are different for individual stocks.

Market declines of up to 10 percent are termed "corrections," a nice, soothing label, not necessitating any action. So most people only consider selling when the losses begin to exceed 10 percent. But this is a very tricky decision. Nobody wants to sell and then have to buy back in at a higher price.

When does a correction turn into a full-fledged bear market? In 2008, the press declared that a 20 percent decline made it an *official* bear market. Wow! I never knew there was an *official* point. One reason is because over the years I have seen industry studies that used a 15 percent standard. However, whether it's 20 or 15 percent, the decline has to take place over a number of months. If the market sold off 15 percent for a week because of a news event, that wouldn't be a bear market.

Is either figure helpful in planning your strategy? Let's look at history for guidance. Since World War II the S&P 500 has had declines of 20 percent or more 10 times. If most of these declines ended just below the 20 percent figure, then it wouldn't make any sense to sell at –20 percent.

Here's what actually happened: The declines that exceeded 20 percent had a total decline that went from –21.6 to –48.2 percent. The median decline was –33.7 percent. So it can make sense to sell when the averages are off 20 percent. Based on history, you would have saved anywhere from a minimal 1.6 percent to a substantial 28.2 percent.

But that's not all profit for investors who wish to maintain their long-term equity allocations. They would have to reinvest at some point, and it's unlikely that most people could catch a market bottom, either practically or emotionally. So obviously there are no clear-cut answers.

What about a 15 percent cutoff? In the post-war period there were three additional bear markets that ended with the 500 declining from 19.3 to 19.9 percent. No bear markets ended with averages down from 15 to 19.3 percent. So as a practical matter, using the 15 percent cutoff wouldn't have been particularly advantageous.

If you don't sell at that 20 percent point, you then have two options: The first is to remain a buy-and-holder. The best way to do this is to put your head in the sand. Don't check your portfolio. Put your monthly statements in a drawer, unopened. Or as *The Times*'

James B. Stewart put it, "Be in a statement of denial." This is a fine option if you are still in the asset accumulation phase of your life. Less so if you are retired.

Actually, younger investors should welcome bear markets. They provide an unparalleled opportunity to accumulate assets cheaply.

Some people sell at or near bear market bottoms because they have a psychological need to exercise a *sense of control*. And for them that's what it's all about. Squelch this need. Not selling *is* doing something. Here's a possible way to do it: If the market is trending down, say to yourself, "if the market declines 8 percent or more, then I'll call that a buying opportunity." Perhaps that attitude will keep you from selling.

Finally, *stay alert for signs of a bottom*. Market recoveries typically start strong. The average return for stocks in the 12 months following the end of a bear market is 45 percent, but if you sat out the first six months of the rally in cash, that 12-month return becomes just 12.5 percent, according to a Charles Schwab & Co. study. Here's another way to look at it: If you were to separate the average bull market into quarters, 45 percent of the entire bull profits would come in the first quarter, according to a study by Birinyi Associates. Gains in the remaining three are far choppier.

Important Lessons in This Chapter

- Prepare for bear markets in advance. Don't wait until the market is off 10 percent or more.
- Understand bear market parameters.

10

The Case for Market Timing

I f you agree that the benefit of owning a diversified stock portfolio is the best way to grow your money in the long run, you have to choose between two basic strategies: buy-and-hold or market timing.

Because I think that stock markets are going to be volatile for the foreseeable future, I prefer the latter.

Buy and Hold—Not What It Used to Be

On December 31, 1999, the S&P 500 Index stood at 1,469.25. On December 31, 2009, 10 years later, it was 1,115.10. In other words, it was 24.1 percent lower. In between, the market was all over the place, but overall it was a decade from hell. *This is not a great recommendation for buy-and-hold.*

Of course, there was a great rebound in 2009 and 2010. But even with this comeback, at the end of 2010 the S&P 500 was still 211 points (14 percent) below its end of the century peak. The next table shows a shocking coincidence.

S&P 500

October 3, 2008	1099.23
October 3, 2011	1099.23

With stocks in a secular bear market, I believe market timing has an advantage over buy-and-hold. Buy-and-hold is far less effective in the up and down markets we are experiencing this decade, and which I believe will continue for quite some time.

How good an alternative is market timing? Well, one thing is certain: Short-term market timing is so difficult that for all practical purposes, it is not worth trying.

But what about long-term timing? Or what about just getting a sense of where the market is going, so you have some sort of framework for making allocation decisions instead of going by your emotions? It seems to me that here market timing has advantages. Even the Bible advises, "To everything there is a season," and "A time to get, and a time to lose; a time to keep, and a time to cast away." (Ecclesiastes 3:1, 3:6.)

Market Timing Doesn't Work, So Why Do So Many People Listen to Market Timers?

The standard advice found in virtually every investing book, and the vast majority of periodicals, is that market timing doesn't work. And this conclusion is backed up by tons of research. It's impossible to find an academic who believes in it.

And yet market timing advice abounds. Many newsletters offer market timing advice and their subscribers pay big bucks for their forecasts. Brokerage firms employ well-paid technical analysts to guide the firms' own trading as well as to offer market timing advice to clients. (The institutions don't call these forecasters market timers any more. They're *market strategists* or *strategists*.) Some mutual funds employ timers. At Fidelity, Jurrien Timmer, Director of Investment Research and Co-Portfolio Manager of the Fidelity Dynamic Strategies Fund, is a thoughtful timer. Also, Fidelity has offered market timing seminars to their shareholders. One such seminar was titled, "Getting Started with Technical Analysis."

The general media are not immune. Although they don't portray themselves as savants, they interview market timers, economists, professors, and Wall Streeters, and report their forecasts. Year-end "outlook" stories are a tradition. Or, with obvious intent, they print studies of past market patterns. Or they have teaser headlines that imply market timing. There's not a lot of difference between pretty explicit forecasts and timing calls. Both are essentially predictions of the future. Here are some examples:

"Overextended Rally Seen Ripe for Downturn; Look Out 6547.05, Says Mr. Roth." *The Wall Street Journal* headline, June 22, 2009.

"When To Get Back in the Market, Five Signs of a Long-Term Rally." *Smart Money* cover, July 2009 issue.

"Is This Bull Cyclical or Secular? Signs Suggest Stocks' Surge Is Blip Within a Bear; Still, There's Opportunity." *The Wall Street Journal*, June 15, 2009.

"As Dow Nears 10,000, Some See Bears Ahead." *The Wall Street Journal*, September 21, 2009.

"History Suggests That a Retesting of Market Lows Is Near." This was a call-out box in an article published in *The New York Times* on May 31, 2009, which suggested that after the big April 2009 run up, a correction was near. (A call-out box is a phrase or quote from an article set in very large, bold type usually within the body of an article. It's designed to catch the reader's interest.)

With only minor modifications, you can find all these articles in market timing letters.

And a Dow Jones, Inc. subsidiary, MarketWatch, publishes a market timing newsletter, *The Technical Indicator,* which contains market trading ranges, entry and exit points, breakout signals, "and more," as the promotional copy says.

Similarly, among *Forbes* magazine's stable of newsletters are *Professional Timing Service* and *InvesTech Research* which also focus on market timing.

I know this is a cheap shot but. . . .

[T]he investor who purchases securities at this time with the discrimination that as always is a condition of prudent investing may do so with utmost confidence. —*The New York Times,* October 29, 1929

And on August 20, 1929, *The Wall Street Journal* wrote "the outlook for the fall months seems brighter than at any time in recent years."

Notwithstanding the naysayers, market timing advice is ubiquitous; it's mainstream.

Obviously an appetite for this advice must exist. And it is a serious market. There are many people who pay anywhere from $150 to $1,000 or more a year for this advice. Why? They can't all be fools. They must be getting something for their money.

The market timers' advice has to be fulfilling some sort of need. I've never seen any studies, but I have read market timing newsletters, so I am pretty certain it's not huge profits. Market timing advisors don't promote their services the same way stock pickers do. Market timing is more about risk reduction. After all, if you are out of stocks part of the time, you have lowered your risk. (You may also have lowered your rewards, but that's the tradeoff.) Specifically, market timing seems to:

- Offer reassurance and comfort.
- Give hope that the timer will get you out at the top or in at the bottom, which could make economic sense if you have even one or two successes.
- Give the illusion of control. Don't underestimate the importance of that illusion. Statistics show that airplane travel is safer than auto travel, but many people act as if the reverse were true. That's because driving a car gives an illusion of control that you don't have when someone else is flying the plane.

I tend to listen to market timers. In my case, the market timers give me a framework for long-term planning that I find helpful. They assist me in determining when to dollar-cost average. They are a psychological crutch for me.

Where Are We in the Cycle?

A number of indicators can give you a sense of where we are in a market cycle.

- Stock valuations: These can tell us, broadly speaking, whether the market is cheap or expensive. Although these measures can't pinpoint entry or exit points, they are a useful part of the overall picture. The two most common measures are dividend yields and price/earnings ratios. (Warning: When evaluating P/Es, a forecast of future earnings is far more useful than a backward look at historical earnings.)
- Economic outlook: GDP growth, possibility of recessions, inflation, job growth, and, very important, the growth of corporate earnings.

- Federal Reserve monetary policy: Is it accommodative or restrictive?
- Sentiment indicators: Most common are bullish/bearish opinions of professionals, a contrary indicator (meaning that usually sentiment is the opposite of the true picture).
- A few long-term cycles, such as the presidential cycle.

Keeping track of all the preceding statistics is a full-time job. Few readers will want to do it themselves. It's better to seek professional assistance, which can come from many sources: market timing newsletters, brokerage house, and financial advisory forecasts. The biggest problem with most of them is that it seems like every time you start to rely on their signals, that's just the time their indicators fail. This probably happens for several reasons.

Timers are only as good as their indicators, which are measures of past market patterns. Unfortunately, what may be frequently true is almost never universally true. Sometimes the patterns repeat, sometimes they don't. And you don't know when they will or won't.

Moreover, there are hundreds of indicators. Most timers follow several. Many times they give contradictory messages. (For example, as this book is being written in 2011, corporate earnings are robust; however, the economy is sluggish and unemployment is high. Moreover, it's the third year of the presidential cycle, which has a history of favoring stocks.) A timer has to make a judgment call as to which indicators to follow, which to ignore, and which to give the greatest weight.

Remember that just because the pattern repeats it doesn't make the timer a genius, and the failure of a pattern to repeat doesn't make him a fool.

Market timing strategies tend to self-destruct when they become too well known or too successful. Take the case of Joe Granville in the 1970s. His record was so superlative that his every utterance made headlines. (Joe loved that. He uttered often; it sold a lot of subscriptions.) I always felt that Joe hurt his work by writing a book that detailed his methodology. That burst of candor, although good for business, enabled other market timers to "front-run" him. They could see when his indicators were close to giving a signal. His downfall came in August of 1982 when he remained bearish while

> Just because the pattern repeats doesn't make the timer a genius, and the failure of a pattern to repeat doesn't make him a fool.

the secular bull market was taking off. Just when you really needed them, his indicators failed.

How to Use a Timer

No timer bats 1,000, that's for sure. The question is how often do they have to be right in order to beat a buy-and-hold strategy? I think the answer to that question depends on how you use timers.

My recommendation is to use timers for their market wisdom and not for their asset allocation. The latter is, in too many cases, an all-or-nothing type of advice. Timers tend to recommend going from 100 percent invested in equities to 100 percent cash and, ultimately, back. (Timers develop egos that make them do this. Without egos they may become paralyzed at critical moments, like the top or bottom.)

I believe that if you don't let their advice supersede your long-term asset allocation parameters at both ends of the range, timers can prove useful.

Obviously, if you go all-or-nothing, as a timer might recommend, and the advice turns out to be wrong, you are dead—or, anyway, broke.

I suggest setting up an asset allocation band within which to operate. Let's say that on a long-term basis you want to be 50 percent invested in equities. If you also want to follow a timer, you might increase your equity allocation to 55 to 60 percent, if the timer is bullish, and reduce it to 25 to 45 percent, if he is bearish. If I were 100 percent invested, I might reduce it to 50 percent. If the timer is right even half to two-thirds of the time, this system could increase profits or reduce losses.

Another reliable method is to combine the timer's advice with dollar-cost averaging (DCA). Skip purchases after a sell signal, or heavy-up your purchases a bit or begin a dollar-cost averaging program on a buy signal. A DCA can build long-term profits if the bear market has a shallow bottom (meaning that it takes months to form a base before the new bull market starts).

In any case, there is a lot to be said for making all your investing moves incrementally. All-or-nothing maximizes risk. You can dollar-cost average *out* of the market just as easily as DCAing *in*.

Criteria for Hiring a Market Timer

Here's what to look for when considering a timer: I prefer timers who take into account a great many indicators—including all of the ones previously cited. I place less credence in those timers who seem to rely on just one or two indicators, say, technical indicators like moving averages or charts.

- The timer should have a well-honed ability to ignore most short-term news or market movements.
- Listen only to market timers who know their limits, who don't try to predict beyond their data. When you think about it, being able to call market turns is all you need. The ability to call the length and size of a run (like the index will be 1,000 points higher a year from now) is totally unnecessary, even if it were possible.
- Do not listen to two or more timers. That's only going to confuse you. Instead, find one market timer who seems solid and consider his or her advice.
- Listen only to timers whose records can be tracked. And their records should be in real time, not just hypothetical successes based on back-testing.
- You need a market timer with integrity. He must admit his mistakes, and try to explain what threw him off.
- Institutions account for 70 percent of stock market activity. You need a timer who understands the institutional mindsets, which can be radically different from those of lay investors.
- Avoid market timers who become so well known that they have the potential to move markets. This is one crowd you don't want to be a part of. (At this writing, I know of no timer who has caught the imagination of the press enough to move markets.)
- The fewer the timer's calls, the better. I prefer long-term timers who give no more than one buy or sell signal every couple of years, and frequently go even longer between signals. Done well, this kind of timer's greatest service is to keep you in the market when short-term corrections might frighten many investors away.

In summary, while timers are going to be terribly wrong on occasions, I would rather have imperfect advice than no advice. If you don't share my view, then you should buy-and-hold and hope for a good market. (Or maybe hope for an advisor who is really good at stock picking.)

Rebalancing: A Form of Market Timing

I can tell you two things about rebalancing: (1) Most investment advisors will recommend rebalancing, and (2) Most investors won't do it on their own. Here's what rebalancing is really about.

"Rebalancing" means periodically adjusting a portfolio to eliminate any changes in weightings created by market fluctuations. The goal is to move the current asset allocation (and thus the risk level) back in line with the originally planned asset allocation. Securities that have become overweighted are reduced; those that have become underweighted are increased.

You can rebalance within asset classes or between asset classes. An example of rebalancing within an asset class is when an S&P 500 equal-weight fund rebalances in order to bring each holding back to an equal weight. This discussion does not concern itself with rebalancing within an asset class, a strategy that makes sense if you are seriously overweighted in a particular stock. My comments are directed toward the more common rebalancing between asset classes.

Here's why I don't think much of that tactic. When you rebalance, you are selling your winners and replacing them with losers, the theory being that eventually everything reverts to the mean. That's decent advice in down markets, but it may be terrible advice in a strong bull market. In that case, you are more likely to do better riding with your winners, or even reverse rebalancing by selling your losers and using the freed up money to add to the winners. Sometimes you want to sell your winners and buy more of your losers; sometimes you may want to do the reverse.

A basic question is how much rebalancing adds to portfolio performance over the long haul? That can vary depending on the criteria you use and the volatility of the individual assets. If you've started with a 5 percent allocation to gold and gold's superior performance drives it to 20 percent, then rebalancing may make a major difference if gold tops out about that time and then trends lower. If gold continues higher, rebalancing will have cost you profits (though it will reduce your risk). Studies show that rebalancing can improve results among the three major asset classes: stocks, bonds, and cash.

However other studies have found that it doesn't make all that much difference. In one study conducted by Vanguard's John Bogle in 2007, it clearly didn't make much difference. Bogle wrote:

> [A] 48 percent S&P 500, 16 percent small cap, 16 percent international, and 20 percent bond index, over the past 20 years, earned a 9.49 percent annual return without rebalancing and a 9.71 percent return if rebalanced annually.

Bogle called the difference "noise," and thought it demonstrated that rebalancing is unnecessary. If one assumed 1 percent transaction costs were needed to rebalance, then the strategy couldn't possibly have added value.

Bogle isn't the only one with this point of view. In 2008, Chuck Jaffe, in his MarketWatch.com column, documents two other studies that are equally skeptical of rebalancing.

In addition, the Investment Strategy Group at Vanguard did a comprehensive study covering the years from 1926 to 2009 (reported in the *AAII Journal*), and found that risk-adjusted returns were not meaningfully different if you rebalanced monthly, quarterly, or annually. Nevertheless, more frequent rebalancing significantly increased costs, commissions, and taxes.

I believe that while traditional rebalancing can result in some improvement, for most people it isn't worth the effort. I'm aware of four different ways to rebalance:

1. Rebalance on a regular schedule—quarterly, semiannually, annually, or every 15 months. I do not favor the regular schedule approach. Even if your asset mix changes only slightly during a given time period, there are always costs to making the changes. If you do choose the regular schedule approach, I would not do this type of rebalancing more frequently than once a year.

2. Rebalance only if your asset mix has strayed from its target by more than 5 percentage points. You will vastly reduce your work, and in taxable accounts, your costs. After all, how much difference can being, say, 47 percent in equities instead of 50 percent make when the future is uncertain anyway? Note also that professionals sometimes rebalance when certain valuation measures move above or below their historic norms.

3. Rebalance in conjunction with market timing. Decide to rebalance back to your original allocation when stocks are very high or very low. Buying the laggards, or exiting the leaders at that time, can have significant profit potential.

Furthermore, it can be more advantageous to rebalance when the market is high rather than when it is low. Rebalancing at the top reduces risk, a good thing. Rebalancing at the bottom adds risk, which may not be as smart. Some simplified numbers demonstrate this.

Let's say you begin with 50 percent of your portfolio in a stock fund and the other 50 percent in a bond fund. A bear market ensues. The equity losses reduce that allocation to 40 percent. Bonds now have a 60 percent allocation.

If you then sell off 10 percent of the bond fund and reallocate the proceeds to the stock fund to keep the 50/50 allocation, you have significantly increased the portfolio's risk. If you have correctly bought when the market was bottoming, you will make much more money in the next bull market by taking on an additional 10 percent equity risk. However, if the bear continues, you will suffer greater losses as did people who rebalanced into Japanese stocks in 1990.

Now here's the important consideration: If you do nothing, the next bull market will likely reverse the allocation back toward equities anyway. By the time the bear market equity losses are recouped, you would be back to the 50/50 allocation. If you had rebalanced, your equity allocation would then exceed 50 percent.

4. Rebalance when necessary. Rebalance when you want more or less risk for any reason.

Here are some additional suggestions for rebalancing:

- I think a younger person probably should rebalance. A worker nearing retirement age might be better off just riding with the smaller equity allocation when the market is down (but still rebalance when the market is high).
- If you are engaging in a dollar-cost averaging program, use your periodic purchases to buy underweighted securities.
- Rebalance with new money to save the expense of selling existing holdings with possible tax consequences.

- Be more willing to rebalance in a tax-sheltered account.
- Give priority to rebalancing high volatility securities.
- Exclude illiquid assets such as art, or concentrated assets such as homes from your rebalancing.
- You can use fund distributions to rebalance by taking the capital gains and dividend distributions in cash, and recycling them to where you are underweighted (including cash). This method, while producing modest results, eliminates extra transaction expenses and taxes, and is a quick, no-brainer phone call. It is best implemented in December when the funds are making their annual capital gains distributions.

In summary, rebalance if you want to, but don't go overboard. Much of it is of little consequence, particularly if you have to pay transaction costs.

I would love to know exactly how common is rebalancing. In 25 years of working with individual investors not once did one ever tell me he or she rebalanced. Nor did a subscriber ever write me to ask for rebalancing information.

Tactical Asset Allocation: Another Form of Market Timing

You may also run across the term "tactical asset allocation," also called dynamic asset allocation. These are strategies requiring frequent changes in asset allocations, and are a form of market timing. I don't recommend short-term timing, but if you're doing that, then your primary concern should be your most volatile investments.

The mutual fund industry, which knows how to market products, may be tip-toeing back into market timing via tactical asset allocation funds. Interested investors should look for funds with "dynamic" or "tactical allocation" in their names. Read their prospectuses carefully.

What about "Trading"?

"Trading," which is usually considered fast in and out buying and selling, often in less than a day, is quite different than market timing. During the late 1990s, when stocks were in a mania, a lot of people "traded" and some made big bucks. You don't hear about trading any more (except by real professionals), and for good reason. Trading works best when there is a large supply of greater fools, which was the case during the mania. Today, greater fools are scarce or broke. Enough said.

Strategizing Fund Distributions

You might not think that how you handle your funds' cash distributions is a "strategy," but it is. That's because there are three ways to take distributions, and the differences between the three are greater than you might suppose.

Here are your three options.

1. You can have both your income and capital gains distributions reinvested in additional shares.
2. You can have income distributions paid in cash while capital gains distributions are reinvested in additional shares.
3. You can have both income and capital gains distributions paid in cash.

If you don't express a preference, the funds will usually give you the first option, reinvestment of both. That is the usual default option because the funds make more money when you reinvest, and that's okay. Reinvestment is fine in most situations, but consider all three of these options to find the one best suited for you.

And it's not all-or-nothing. You can have some funds on reinvestment, while others pay cash distributions.

For most investors, and particularly young people building an estate, the first option—reinvestment of all distributions—is best. Your investment compounds, and in a rising market, will grow faster.

The logic behind the second option is that you are gaining immediate benefits from the income dividend distributions, but are not eating into your capital. It is important to maintain your capital in real (inflation-adjusted) terms. Secondly, as a practical matter, an investor looking for steady income might prefer the second option so he or she does not receive occasional, large distributions that would only have to be reinvested. This is a good option for most retired investors living on their incomes.

Or you can take the third option, receiving all distributions in cash. This option can be used to restrict the size of your investment or obtain liquidity without incurring additional tax consequences by selling shares. There are a number of reasons to consider this option:

- You feel overweighted in equities, either for lifestyle purposes or because of market concerns.
- The fund has grown in value over the years to the point at which it is overweighted in your portfolio.
- You need cash, but don't want to sell anything.
- And, of course, for rebalancing.

This advice is more relevant for taxable accounts. With tax-sheltered retirement plans, you have complete freedom to sell without taxation. Also, note that the tax treatment of mutual fund income and capital gain distributions remains the same, regardless whether they are taken in cash or reinvested.

When my father turned 80, I noticed that he was still reinvesting his mutual fund distributions. I asked him why, reassuring him that he could spend more without fear of going broke. He replied that he was saving his money for his old age.

Mutual Funds Don't Market Time

Back in the 1970s, a number of funds practiced market timing. In June 1973, the Janus Fund was 88.6 percent in cash. The great secular bull market of the 1980s and 1990s killed that strategy. No mutual fund could afford to go to cash in anticipation of a bear market. The consequences of being wrong were simply too great.

In addition, funds were smaller back then. It's one thing to cash out your stocks when you have $100 million under management. It's quite different when you're managing $50 billion (although it's possible using derivatives, but they are not without costs). In any case, funds now leave the market timing to their shareholders.

Of course, they don't say that these are the reasons. Here's Vanguard's rationale as described in an e-mail to shareholders:

Vanguard stock funds don't cash out in a downturn [because] allocation decisions belong with the individual investor

We believe that one of the most important decisions an investor can make is determining the mix of assets—stocks, bonds, and cash investments—for his or her portfolio.

Informed investors know how each investment fits into their plans and why they own that particular asset. If an investor purchases shares in a stock fund and the fund advisor later decides to sell all the holdings because cash seems more attractive, the investor's personal asset allocation will change.

The letter goes on to say their fund managers "add value by focusing on the mandate (like large cap stocks)" and "while Vanguard's managers certainly have opinions about the market and its direction, they add value by focusing primarily on security selection."

The truth and the rationale are both valid.

Charts, Schmarts; You Have Facts

While I see the advantages of long-term market timing, I don't believe in charting.

The late Lou Ehrenkranz, the co-owner of a small Wall Street brokerage firm, related the following story to me.

Lou said that when he was a young broker, he was having lunch in a Wall Street café. Since he was alone, he began to listen to the conversation of two gentlemen seated at the next table. He heard one fellow say to the other that their firm would be cutting the dividend in half the next day, and it was going to be a terrible shock to investors, as nobody knew it was coming.

Lou jumped up, went to the headwaiter and asked if he could identify the two men. "Yes," replied the headwaiter, "They work for ABC Corporation."

Lou quickly finished his lunch. As soon as he got back to his firm, he went to see the senior partner, who was considered an outstanding chartist.

"What do you think of ABC Corporation?" Lou asked.

The partner pulled out his charts, studied them and concluded they looked quite favorable. The stock might even be a buy.

Lou then related the conversation he had just overheard at lunch. The partner's response was immediate: "Sell 10,000 shares short."

"Wait a minute," said Lou, "You just told me the charts were favorable."

"Charts, schmarts," said the partner, "You have facts."

In this case the chartist wasn't fooled by his own noise. You shouldn't be either.

I realized that technical analysis didn't work when I turned the chart upside-down and didn't get a different answer.

—Warren Buffett

Stop-Lossing Stocks and Mutual Funds

"Stop-lossing" is a strategy that sets a fixed point to sell in order to minimize losses. For example, a trader might put in a limit order to sell if a stock's price drops 10 percent. Stop-lossing may make sense for in-and-out traders but in my opinion it's a poor strategy for long-term investors.

A long time ago after a speech, a listener asked me my opinion on stop-lossing a stock. I thought for several seconds (a long time in front of a crowd) and realized I had never heard a mutual fund manager say he stop-lossed stocks.

What most fund managers do is continually review the fundamentals of their stocks, particularly the earnings estimates, and make their sell decisions on this basis. If a stock drops in the absence of an earnings decline or without a change in the fundamentals, the professionals might buy more. They would most likely sell if analysts reduced their earnings estimates or if reported earnings fell short of Wall Street's consensus estimate.

But these are professionals. On the other hand, I have rarely met nonprofessionals who developed earnings estimates for the stocks they own, let alone compared them to consensus forecasts.

Professionals are professionals for a reason. If you ask Ron Baron (head of the Baron funds) why he owns a stock, he will often take 15 minutes or more to describe the stats and the potential of the company. In the process he will throw out a dozen numbers—off the top of his head. He can do this for all his major holdings. I doubt if many nonprofessionals could spend even one minute describing their companies accurately, or articulating specifically why they like them.

Still, for psychological reasons I can understand using a stop-loss on stocks. They can go to zero, if the company goes bankrupt.

What about stop-lossing mutual funds? Yes, some advisors have followed this practice.

In the early 1970s there was a multi-fund, Fundpack, which adopted this strategy after conducting a number of theoretical studies that showed that stop-lossing would produce far better results than a buy-and-hold strategy. Fundpack selected a rigid 10 percent guidepost based on its hypothetical studies. It would sell any funds in its portfolio that declined more than 10 percent from any point, and would buy back after a 10 percent rise or unusually positive newsbreak.

Fundpack achieved some success in 1971, but did very poorly in 1972, 1973, and 1974. In a mid-1973 special report to shareholders, Fundpack noted: "But in the neurotic current market decline, Fundpack's prices declined 26 percent before Fundpack solidified itself. What happened?" They went on to explain that "In whipsaw actions of the market, some of our buybacks declined a second 10 percent, and as the 10 percent rule operated, this investment pool shed the mutual fund shares in its portfolio separately, the most volatile first, which was not always advantageous."

If you can have a 26 percent loss with a 10 percent stop-lossing rule, you've got problems, to say the least. Fundpack discontinued its strategy in 1975. After adding a money market fund they became the first fund group to offer telephone switching (selling long-term holdings over the phone with the money going to and from a money fund—the normal practice today).

I do not recommend stop-lossing mutual funds. Diversified portfolios don't normally fall as much as individual stocks. Then there is the practical problem that you cannot put in a standing order to stop-loss a mutual fund and have it automatically executed. Your stop-loss point must be mental, which means you have to check the fund's price each day (and also worry about not recognizing dividend and capital gains distribution, which lower the price). That's really impractical.

However, if stop-lossing makes you feel more secure, confine the tactic to exchange-traded funds. At least with ETFs you can put in a limit order and go about your business. If there is a huge sell off, you are protected.

Important Lessons in This Chapter

- The goal of market timing is not to avoid all losses, or to get you in at the bottom and out at the top. *It's to beat a buy-and-hold strategy.*
- If you are going to market time, make your moves incrementally.

CHAPTER

11

The No-Work Way to a Comfortable Retirement . . . Maybe

In the course of talking to our newsletter subscribers and advising our managed investment account clients, I found that their involvement in the day-to-day details of the investing process varied widely. At one extreme, some investors are as involved and knowledgeable as professionals. At the other extreme are people who are not interested in the details of investing and generally want to hand off the decisions to a professional.

The latter are not dumbbells, nor are they necessarily beginners. More commonly, they are busy people who believe it's more productive for them to invest their energies elsewhere. Although they want their money working for them as productively as possible, they just don't want to think about it very much. They have careers in other fields, and don't want to learn about investing.

If they have enough money, most of these people simply give professional advisors discretionary power and hope for the best. Most of the time, this works out quite well, but the fees for personal service can be steep.

So, smart investors look for other ways. I ran across one such investor back in the 1990s when I received a phone call from a doctor.

"Jacobs," he said, "I hear you have a fine newsletter, and I'm interested in subscribing. But only on one condition."

"What's that?" I asked.

"That I don't have to read it," he replied.

My response was easy. "No problem, doctor. You don't have to read the *Investor.* All you have to do is turn to its back page and follow a model portfolio. If we make a change one month, you make the change in your own portfolio. If we don't make any changes, just drop the newsletter into the waste basket."

The result: one happy subscriber, one successful publisher.

How to Invest without Paying Attention

If my five essentials are more than you want, several investment vehicles are appropriate for the uninvolved investor who doesn't want to, or can't, meet the minimums of professional advisors.

One solution is to buy a target date fund (TDF). These funds are designed to provide you with a lifetime asset allocation strategy. They do this by gradually decreasing their risk levels as you age, typically by decreasing their exposure to stocks and increasing their percentage of bonds as the years go by.

They almost always have a target date, which is normally the date you stop making new investments in the fund, generally your retirement age. For example, if you plan on retiring at age 65 in 2035, you would buy a fund whose target date is 2035. This is not the date at which the entire fund would be cashed out; these funds are designed to be held in retirement.

Target date funds are designed to provide you with a lifetime asset allocation strategy by gradually decreasing their risk levels as you age.

What to Look for in a Target Fund

Target funds would seem to be the simplest of no-brainers, but they are decidedly not. If you are going to invest in one, knowledge is paramount. Basically, you need to be certain that their risk levels parallel yours; and you need to understand what the fund is going to do when the target date is reached. The usual assumption is that the shareholder will withdraw the money gradually in retirement, which means that the fund needs to continue owning stocks.

The most significant feature of target funds is the fund's "glide path." This is the rate at which the equity allocation declines.

The glide paths for five major no-load groups appear in the following table. The groups are: Vanguard Target Retirement Funds,

Fidelity Freedom Funds, T. Rowe Price Retirement Funds, Schwab Target Funds, and American Century LIVESTRONG Funds (so named because American Century has an agreement with the Lance Armstrong Foundation for the rights to use that trademarked name).

When the target date is far off, the funds typically allocate 80 to 90 percent of assets to equities. The stock allocation decreases as you age, so that as you approach retirement, the equity allocation reduces to 45 to 55 percent.

Look at the 2010 target date funds in the following table. Presumably that's the year the shareholder had planned to retire. Still, the equity allocations ranged from 40 to 55 percent.

Next, look at the first line in the table, *Income.* These are portfolios whose target dates have passed, which can be as many as 10 to 15 years ago. People might assume that the target year is the year the fund becomes an income fund, emphasizing safety of principal. But this is not always the case. Fidelity, for example, doesn't merge its target-date funds into the Freedom Income Fund (with just 21 percent in stocks) until 10 or 15 years after the retirement date has passed. Until then, equity allocations can run as high as 44 percent. Fidelity's philosophy is that growth is necessary far into retirement in order to keep up with inflation. That growth is generated by stocks.

Target Date Fund Asset Allocations (Percent Equities)

Year	Vanguard	Fidelity	T. Rowe Price	Schwab	American Century
Income	30%	21%	42%	—%	44%
2005	35	44	47	—	—
2010	49	52	55	38	—
2015	59	53	64	52	48
2020	66	62	72	63	53
2025	74	71	78	70	58
2030	82	75	83	78	64
2035	89	83	88	84	70
2040	90	84	88	88	76
2045	90	86	89	—	79
2050	90	89	88	—	82
2055	90*	—	87	—	—

*Begins annually reducing stocks and increasing bonds around 2031.

Note: Data are through December 2010. These figures reflect post-2008 adjustments made by the funds to ward off severe future declines.

With equity allocations this high, there is obviously risk, which became painfully obvious in 2008.

Target Date Funds Crashed in 2008

Although it's certainly understandable that a fund with a target 30 years or more in the future will suffer substantial losses in a bear market, it's a lot harder to understand why funds whose target dates are imminent should suffer more than minimal losses. The concept of glide path was to prevent large losses, which turned out not to be the case in 2008. Because their stock allocations were never significantly reduced, many funds with 2010 targets—only two years later—lost about a quarter of their assets in 2008 and early 2009, a real shocker at the time.

The reason the funds kept their equity allocations high is that target fund owners could be in retirement for as many as 30 years, and equity investments would be needed to outpace inflation. Although this is certainly a consideration, it doesn't obviate the fact that there is clearly a trade off between risk and performance, and most retirees would consider 25 percent loss in what they believed to be a prudent investment is unacceptable.

In my opinion, the fund companies put too much emphasis on performance, perhaps for competitive reasons. Their shareholders got nailed in 2008. On the other hand, the funds that declined the most in 2008 bounced back the strongest in 2009 and 2010. The standard rule for volatility held.

Nevertheless, I think this is more an indictment of the investing concept than the fund managers. Their planning for a long retirement had much logic. Your time horizon doesn't end when you retire. It doesn't even end when you die, if you are married. And even when both spouses are gone, the money lives on for heirs.

Other Factors

In addition to risk and glide paths, consider several other factors.

- Costs. All are reasonably cost efficient, but Vanguard (no surprise) was the lowest. Vanguard's expense ratios ranged from 18 to 20 basis points (bp), Fidelity from 50 to 84 bp, Rowe Price from 60 to 79 bp, Schwab from 70 to 89 bp, and American

Century from 80 to 96 bp. As I explained in Chapter 4, the longer you hold a fund, the more important costs become.

- These target funds are very popular for 401(k) plans where they may be the default option. Some fund groups have a special series with far lower expenses for these retirement plans. For example, Fidelity's 401(k) target funds cost about 19 bp annually. Unlike the regular funds, this series invests in index funds.

- What do these funds invest in? *Vanguard* invests in other index funds; *Fidelity*, primarily in actively managed Fidelity funds; *Rowe Price*, actively managed Price funds; *Schwab*, primarily actively managed funds; *American Century*, actively managed American Century funds.

- How much cash do they keep? A check at the end of the first quarter 2011 showed wide variations, ranging from virtually nothing (*Vanguard*), to over 10 percent (*Fidelity* and *American Century*). I would take this into account in establishing your overall portfolio allocations.

- Performance. Considering the wide variations in investing styles there can be significant performance differences among TDF's. These are not passive investments. These are not idiot-proof investments. You need to review performance.

Should You Buy a Target Date Fund?

If these funds meet a personal need, they are worth considering, particularly if they are offered in a 401(k) plan with limited alternatives. On the positive side, an investment in them discourages frequent trading.

On the negative side, they can be volatile, losing ground during plunging stock markets. TDF funds primarily base their asset allocation decisions on one factor—age. As I explained in Chapter 3, there are other, possibly more important, reasons to determine allocations. For one, TDF fund managers fail to adjust their portfolios for market conditions. It's possible that there might be times when these funds will pull money out of stocks and put them in bonds when market conditions call for doing the reverse, and vice versa. In addition, they don't consider your personal risk tolerance at all (although you can adjust for that by buying different target dates).

I'm not opposed to buying target date funds, but in many, or even most cases, I think there are better alternatives.

TDF Alternatives

Target funds gradually reduce equity exposure as you age. Given my long-term market forecast, I think most of them are too risky when the investor nears retirement age, or when stocks are richly priced. That's why it can pay you to consider some other low-work alternatives to target funds.

One alternative is an asset allocation fund. These funds own both stocks and bonds, but vary their allocations depending on market conditions. That makes more sense to me than what the TDF funds are doing.

- A prime example of a fund that might be a suitable alternative is the Fidelity *Four-in-One Index* Fund (FFNOX). It owns four Fidelity Index Funds. Its minimum investment is $10,000. Its expense ratio is 0.23 percent. Its turnover ratio is a low 26 percent.
- At Vanguard, check their four *LifeStrategy* Funds (VSCGX, VASGX, VSMGX, VASIX). These invest in Vanguard index funds and the Vanguard *Asset Allocation* Fund (VAAPX). Their minimum investment is $3,000.
- At Schwab consider the Schwab *Market Track All-Equity Investor* (SWEGX). It owns three Schwab index funds. Minimum investment is $100.
- American Century offers five *One Choice* Funds (AOGIX, AOCIX, AOMIX, AOVIX, AONIX). They invest in American Century actively managed funds. Minimum is $2,500.

Another fine way to achieve balance is to simply own a broad-based stock index fund and an intermediate term bond fund in whatever proportions are right for you. *I prefer this alternative to both target and asset allocation funds for many taxable accounts where the holder's tax bracket requires tax-free bonds.* Asset allocation and target funds tend to own taxable fixed-income securities. The strategy I'm proposing lets you invest the fixed-income portion in munis, if you are not in a tax-sheltered investment like an IRA or 401(k). Also, you have the advantage of being able to sell from one basket (perhaps to take tax losses), but not the other.

In this case I would keep the same asset allocation between stocks and bonds until you feel there is a need to change, which in some cases might be well after you retire. You could then reallocate to suit your new circumstances. After all, the target date funds don't make any significant allocation adjustments for their first 35 years or so.

To reiterate, the recommendations in this chapter are for uninvolved investors. You can no doubt do better if you involve yourself in the investing process. On the other hand, there is something to be said for being uninvolved—especially if your time or interest is in short supply. Investing isn't everything.

> To achieve balance, simply own a broad-based stock index fund and an intermediate term bond fund in whatever proportions are right for you.

Important Lessons in This Chapter

- If investing is not your thing, turn the job over to a target fund, an asset allocation fund, or a stock index and bond index fund of your own choosing. It will cost a lot less than expensive personal advice. And depending on how good the expensive advice is, you could do as well, or maybe even better. This doesn't mean you should be sublimely ignorant.
- In all cases, it is critical to look behind the fund names. Research all these funds carefully before you invest!

CHAPTER 12

Dealing with Professionals

There are many fine securities salespeople. I don't want to say much about them because they don't teach any lessons. On the other hand, we know that the financial services industry employs more scoundrels than are strictly necessary. And because you never know when you are going to encounter one, it's worthwhile talking briefly about the bad apples. Knowing about the miscreants can protect your wealth.

Because I never have had a problem with a bad salesperson, I am going to tell you the experiences of someone who did—my father.

Bert Jacobs' Story

My father Bert Jacobs was an astute, very successful businessman, but a horrible investor. He could never get it through his head that the investment business worked differently than the clothing business he knew so well.

When a clothing manufacturer's rep came in his store and said, "Bert, I have a deal for you," it *was* a deal, because all the salesmen knew my father was a real pro. They knew that they had no chance of putting anything over on him. Also, he was a consummate salesman who loved other salesmen. He really felt at home with them.

Unfortunately, this made him a sucker for stockbrokers. He never understood that some stockbrokers always had a deal. No matter how treacherous the market or inferior the merchandise, there was always a broker willing to sell him something. If he liked the broker enough, he bought. He seldom understood the investment merits.

Once he was sold some very high yielding (around 11 percent, I think) California muni sewer bonds that were secured solely by the individual lot owner. One particular lot owner never paid the semiannual interest until he was sued. Consequently, my father had to sue him twice a year. Thank goodness that the property was worth more than the bond, so he always got paid. But what a pain!

Like most investors, dad couldn't stand losses. But unlike most, he also had a problem with profits. Back in 1982, when Federal Reserve Chairman Volcker was squeezing inflation out of the economy, bonds were yielding as much as 17 percent. A broker sold my father several just before the tightening ended. Three months later my dad had a huge paper profit and he was scared to death he was going to lose it. "Sell," he implored me. I didn't want him to. The bonds were decent quality, and whatever else he bought with the proceeds would have been a wash. He couldn't quite understand that. So I finally told him that he had to hold for six months to get the long-term capital gains rate. He did that, but the day after the six months was up, he sold.

After my parents retired to spend winters in Sun City, Arizona, they went to one of those suppers sponsored by brokerage houses. They met a very personable salesperson, who in short order became their best friend. I kept getting calls from dad telling me what a wonderful person he was.

Payoff time came. My dad phoned to tell me the broker had sold him some muni bond trusts (the kind that pay a salesman a nice commission). I knew trouble was brewing. I asked Dad what else was happening and was told the broker was developing a plan to restructure his entire portfolio.

"Send me the plan. And don't do anything until I read it" I commanded. I got the plan and found out the broker was just about to churn my dad's entire portfolio. Everything, good and bad, was to be sold, and replaced by new securities, not too dissimilar from the old ones. There would be double commissions for the broker.

I immediately called the broker's boss, the manager of the branch. I told him I was an RIA, a registered investment advisor, and that if this broker didn't disappear immediately from my dad's life, I was going to file a complaint with the NASD, the industry's regulatory body (now FINRA). He took me seriously, as he should have. The broker never called my dad again.

A free supper doesn't mean a free lunch.

If my dad, whom I loved dearly, were still alive, I would never have written this.

Too Early and Too Late

I come from a family of unsuccessful (or unlucky) investors. There was my dad's uncle, Marcus Jacobs, who lived in Dallas, Texas. He spent much of his life investing in oil drilling ventures—without success. Then when he was 82, one of his ventures finally paid off. It was too late for him to enjoy it; he died about a year later.

Then there was a distant relative whose name has been lost in the mists of time. He once owned an acre of land on Nob Hill in San Francisco. Unfortunately, he sold it before it became valuable.

Closer to home, there were my great grandparents, Simon and Dora Jacobs, who, between 1902 and 1915, purchased shares in at least five gold mines in and around Deadwood. I'm pretty sure none produced a profit, but the stock certificates, which are gorgeous, now enhance my home office.

Cold-Calling Brokers

In the old days, cold-calling brokers were only expert at cold calling. (With the advent of the FTC's national do-not-call registry a few years ago, this species has become rare.) I've had any number of ludicrous conversations with them, but the one that took the cake was the cold call from a broker selling an Internet gambling stock.

I didn't have the slightest interest in actually buying the stock, but from my professional point of view I was curious to see the prospectus. So, I asked him to send me one.

"What's a prospectus?" he asked.

I replied by asking, "When did you stop selling used cars?"

"Two months ago," he answered.

I no longer have any trouble with cold-calling brokers. When they ask me what I do, I tell them I'm writing a book on investing, and this conversation might be used in the book. They can't wait to get off the line.

I've had a number of brokers over the years, and worked well with all of them. I think that was due in large part to the type of relationship I enforced on them. I have a firm rule in dealing with brokers: Don't call me; I'll call you. Some absorbed my message more slowly than others. But they all got it eventually.

Nowadays I do virtually all of my trading online. (I buy no-load, closed-end, and exchange-traded funds, and individual muni bonds.) I only call my broker to solve administrative problems.

There was a time when I thought that brokers were the font of all wisdom. Working on Wall Street, they surely knew which stocks were going to be the winners. Then my brother became a stockbroker. A year went by and he never once called me with a tip. I finally asked him why, and he replied, "I'm doing you a favor." My brother was not long for the brokerage business.

Later on, I had a broker who was a distant relative. He was very good, and we had an honest relationship. One day I asked him what he invested in personally, and he told me mutual funds. That was the final blow. If the presumed font of all wisdom put his own money in funds, why in the world was I buying stocks?

I never bought a loaded fund, but when I found out about no-loads, they became my choice for life.

Lessons from the Madoff Mayhem

The only thing worse than investing in stocks in 2008 was investing with Bernard L. Madoff Investment Securities. Bernard Madoff perpetrated the largest security fraud in history, a massive Ponzi scheme that cost 13,555 investors, mostly wealthy people and charitable institutions, $64.8 billion. That number, somewhat controversial, includes "phantom" profits, in other words, nonexistent profits.

The list of victims who invested directly or through 15 third-party "feeder" funds (who provided Madoff with a total of $11 billion) was a who's who of boldface names. The biggest individual loser appeared to be a 95-year-old Boston clothing tycoon, Carl Shapiro, who was out more than $545 million. Shapiro had made his fortune by founding Kay Windsor, a now defunct women's wear label that is still known in vintage fashion circles for its classic dresses. The biggest corporate loser was the Fairfield Greenwich Group, out $7.5 billion of their own and their clients' money.

Other boldface names who lost money with Madoff include the media billionaire Mort Zuckerman, former New York Attorney General and Governor Eliot Spitzer, former Salomon Brothers chief economist Henry Kaufman, Senator Frank Lautenberg, CNN host

Larry King, actors Kevin Bacon and his wife Kyra Sedgwick, almost half the membership of the Palm Beach Country Club, as well as charities connected to the film director Steven Spielberg and the Holocaust survivor and Nobel Peace Prize winner Elie Wiesel. The most unusual victim may have been Stephen Greenspan, emeritus professor of educational psychology at the University of Connecticut and author of the 2008 book, *Annals of Gullibility: Why We Get Duped and How to Avoid It.* There's a lesson there, somewhere.

This scam also had many of the earmarks of an affinity fraud, because both Madoff and a preponderance of his victims were Jews.

Although most Ponzi schemes disintegrate in less than a year, Madoff's scam went on for nearly 20 years, fooling sophisticated hedge fund managers, and banks, as well as the SEC, which had investigated him many times during a 16-year period. Six days after the fraud was exposed, the SEC issued a mea culpa admitting it had received "credible and specific" allegations about the scheme at least nine years earlier. This tells you it's not wise to rely on the SEC to safeguard your money.

It was not until nine and a half weeks after the scam was exposed that investigators admitted they found no evidence of Madoff having purchased any securities whatsoever at least since 1995.

The Original Ponzi Scheme

Carlo (Charles) Ponzi was an Italian immigrant, who in 1919 and 1920 defrauded investors through a pyramid scheme (now often called a Ponzi scheme). Ponzi promised clients a 50 percent profit within 45 days, or 100 percent profit within 90 days, saying he would buy discounted postal reply coupons in other countries and redeem them at face value in the United States as a form of arbitrage. Early investors were paid profits—not through legitimate earnings because there were none, but through the entry money of new victims. The scheme worked on the "rob-Peter-to-pay-Paul" principle. Ponzi swindles usually end when the supply of new investors is exhausted. Carlo Ponzi's scheme ended when his own publicist, William McMasters, exposed the fraud to the *Boston Post.*

Although Madoff enticed a large number of high-profile people and institutions into investing with him, many knowledgeable institutional investors passed. Either they were expert in options trading strategies and realized Madoff's numbers didn't add up, or they were turned off by Madoff's lack of transparency. Denied the opportunity to perform a detailed due diligence review and Madoff's refusal to answer many questions, they declined to invest with him.

Unfortunately, most laymen wouldn't know how to conduct the necessary due diligence even if they were afforded the access to do so. So it is very difficult to avoid being scammed by a real confidence artist.

These people know how to get away with confidence games. Recall the case of Frank Abagnale whose exploits were made into a 2002 movie, *Catch Me If You Can* with Leonardo DiCaprio and Tom Hanks. In the 1960s, Abagnale, while still in his teens, posed as an airline pilot, a doctor, and a lawyer while using at least eight aliases over the course of five years. He passed bad checks in 26 countries. The checks amounted to about $2.5 million. The truth is that Abagnale's story is not all that unusual.

How to Reduce the Chances of Being Scammed

Here are the steps you can take to reduce the chances of being scammed.

Transparency

First of all, don't buy any investments that lack transparency. If what the advisor is doing is opaque, keep him and your money separate.

Surprisingly, it's fairly easy to tell whether your investments are legitimate. First, are you receiving regular statements from the custodian? It can be a bank, brokerage firm, insurance or mutual fund company. In Madoff's case, many of his clients received "statements" that were printed by one of his colleagues.

Next, look at the investments on the statement. In general, they should be publicly traded securities—stocks, bonds, mutual funds, ETFs. Legitimate firms generally put a ticker symbol next to the investment, which makes it easy for the investor to go online and check the current market value at any time.

Monthly statements should accurately detail all holdings and transactions. They should come from the broker-dealer through which securities are cleared. They should *not* come from the accountant, the advisor, or an offshore bank. When I had the BJ Group, our clients received quarterly statements from us, and monthly statements directly from the custodian, Charles Schwab. Your account should be in your name.

Also, if you're invested in mutual funds or ETFs, the fact that you can obtain a fund's net asset value daily provides a further measure of safety.

When you receive your monthly statement the first thing you should check is whether any money has been moved out of the account. Sick, elderly, or otherwise busy investors should have family members or trusted friends read their statements each month.

Independent Custodian

Second, make sure your advisor keeps your money with an *independent custodian*. Madoff Investment Securities did not. That's the biggest warning sign of all. An independent custodian proves the existence of the assets. If you send your check made out to a broker like Charles Schwab or J. P. Morgan, you know that you have an independent custodian. And never give the custodian authority to make cash withdrawals.

Mutual funds are required to have independent custodians, which is one reason to prefer them. Note that mutual funds may turn your money over to sub-advisors, but there is nothing wrong with that because it is disclosed in the prospectus. If you don't like the sub-advisor, don't buy.

Middlemen

Many advisors and hedge funds are middlemen who turn the actual investing over to third parties such as Madoff. If you have money with an advisor or hedge fund, find out whether they are doing the investing or passing it on to someone else. If it is "someone else" try to get the basic facts about them. In Madoff's case, some of these feeder fund middlemen told prospective clients that Madoff never lost money; others never informed their clients they were using Madoff or other third parties.

In any case, don't give up personal responsibility, no matter how honest and competent your advisor seems to be. In the Madoff case, these middlemen were fooled along with their clients. On the other hand, they were drawing sizeable fees for their sales representative services of finding Madoff and recommending him. When fees get too large, they weaken the desire to perform proper due diligence.

Send your money to an institution, not an individual. If an advisor wants the check to be made out to him personally, walk away.

Diversify

Third, the bottom line remains that scams are low frequency occurrences. To use today's catch phrase they are "black swan" events. Unless you become senile, you may be scammed only once in your lifetime, if then. That makes it very difficult to be alert enough to avoid being taken. Your real protection is that old standby: diversification, always your best insurance against unforeseeable losses.

In the Madoff case what was needed was diversification among advisors, not individual holdings. Madoff himself was the original toxic asset.

The problem here is that for most people there is a trade off between diversification and the level of service you get from an advisor. In the case of mutual funds, which are transparent and well-regulated, I would choose concentration. Large groups like Fidelity and Vanguard have different levels of service depending on how much you have with them.

In the case of the less transparent hedge funds and managed accounts, put the accent on diversification. I would not have so much money with one advisor that a fraud would wipe me out. As a general rule, I would not put more than 5 percent of my money with any advisor who lacks transparency, such as a hedge fund. I would also limit illiquid holdings to 10 percent. If 5 or 10 percent of your assets aren't sufficient to meet the investing minimums, then you are a small investor who shouldn't even be considering these investments.

Evaluating the Advisor

Generally speaking, *excessive returns* are a big red flag. In Madoff's case, the excessive returns took the unusual form of a barely credible consistency of performance, not eye-popping gains. Although his investments returned in the 10 to 12 percent range (one lawsuit alleges a 13.5 percent return), they generally notched about 1 percent a month, with only 13 losing months over a period of 15 years. His strategy seemed impervious to market fluctuations. Although 10 to 12 percent a year may not be unusual for hedge funds, making around 1 percent each and every month is. Markets fluctuate. The returns should have been a red flag. Moreover

Madoff offered investors unusual liquidity. Typically, hedge funds make it very difficult to redeem potions of your investment, requiring long notice periods.

To complicate matters, a few select potential clients were offered returns as high as 46 percent. Now that's far more than a red flag. Those people had to know there was something phony about Madoff's operation. They no doubt thought that Madoff was doing a little cheating, but it was for their benefit. They must have had some larceny in their hearts.

If a potential advisor gives you a hard sell pitch, that's a negative. In Madoff's case, he used the reverse strategy to good effect. He made it seem as though it was an honor to be allowed to invest with him. Often, he required a recommendation from an existing client, giving the investors a members-only feeling.

Madoff sometimes told investors his funds were closed. When mutual fund groups close a fund, they usually do it because it has grown unwieldy. In Madoff's case it was a psychological come-on.

Another piece of advice: Don't sign up with any advisor who tells you that his or her offer is only good that day. (The same advice goes for buying time-shares.)

Even though Madoff was selling exclusivity, I believe the fact that he didn't promote his money management record was in retrospect another tip-off. Even though he did make some media appearances in his other capacity as a broker-dealer, he never took the steps that would have made him a household name. The public never heard of him before the scandal. In the highly competitive investment advisory world it is standard procedure for any advisor with that kind of steady returns to quickly hire a public relations firm to promote it to the media. It never hurts that millions of people know you are very exclusive. Ask Tiffany. Or ask Warren Buffett, whose Berkshire Hathaway A shares sell for over $100,000 per share.

Recommendations

The usual commonsense rules apply. Just because an advisor has famous clients is no guarantee that everything is okay. These "stars" are often the most gullible of investors because they tend not to do their own due diligence, relying instead on friends or associates or word of mouth.

Do not accept or solicit advice from people who have no expertise other than knowing the scammer. It was not enough that many of them thought they knew, liked, and trusted Madoff personally. Nor did Madoff's sterling reputation mean anything in the final analysis.

It's fine to get recommendations, but still do your own due diligence. Here are a few simple steps that may pay off:

- Do a Google, Facebook, and Twitter search on the potential advisor. You never know what you may find.
- Check with the SEC or your state's regulatory body, whichever has jurisdiction.
- Ask if the advisor manages any institutional money, and whether you can check with the institution.
- Completely understand the advisor's investing strategies. If you don't, ask the advisor for clarification. He needs to answer all your questions, something Madoff didn't do. If you still don't understand it, ask a knowledgeable third party. If you are still up in the air after that, find another advisor.

Auditing

Madoff's auditor was Friehling & Horowitz, a three-person accounting firm based in New City, New York (about an hour north of New York City across the Tappan Zee Bridge). They occupied a 13-foot by 18-foot storefront space in an office plaza. How could such a tiny, unknown outfit handle a multibillion client like Madoff? The SEC wanted to know. On March 17, 2009, they charged David Friehling with securities fraud for conducting sham audits that enabled Madoff to perpetuate the scam. The firm, Friehling & Horowitz, was charged in a civil action.

If you are talking real serious money, try to find out how long the advisor has been with the accountant. If the answer is not long, it can pay to talk to the advisor's previous accountant. There are instances when an advisory firm has been asked to leave because the accounting firm is not comfortable with the financials.

If the money is being held by a brokerage firm, it's of some help to stay under the $500,000 maximum per customer for Securities Investor Protection Corporation coverage for stocks and bonds. The SIPC, a non-governmental agency, restores funds to investors with assets in the hands of bankrupt and otherwise financially troubled brokerage firms. It does not specifically provide any compensation for fraud. However, SIPC found $826 million in liquid assets at Madoff's brokerage firm, which was made available to qualified victims.

Finally, heed what they say in Deadwood: "Trust everyone, but cut the cards."

"Somebody Had to Get Lucky with Him"

Ralph Amendolaro, a Queens, New York, construction worker, explaining his rationale for playing Bernard Madoff's prison number in the New York Lottery. He won $1,500.

And for you lottery fans, the number is 61727–054.

Do You Fit the Victim Profile?

Anybody can be a victim, but contrary to the usual assumption, the typical Ponzi victim is not an over the hill senior citizen who thinks he has found a free lunch. Rather, it's a person aged 55 to 64, more literate than most, but more willing to take risks, and one who does insufficient due diligence.

Warning: Ponzi schemes tend to unravel in tough economic times. But that doesn't mean you can relax your vigilance during good times.

Advice for Those Who Have Been Taken

Usually there are no effective remedies for investors who have been scammed. But there is one thing you can do and that is put the whole sordid mess behind you. Now that may seem like obvious advice, but for some people it isn't. They refuse to believe they have been taken, or they believe that by some magic they will get their money back. It's called "buyer's denial."

Getting to admit to yourself that you are never going to get your money back is very difficult. But it's something that has to be done. For those who don't, the consequences can be severe. There are recorded instances where the sucker makes further investments in the scam even after it has been exposed. Far more commonly, these suckers are put on lists that are sold to other scammers who know they are prime prospects for their scams.

So if you are unfortunate enough to be cheated, put it behind you. Just learn the lesson so it doesn't happen again.

How One Professional Checked Out a Recommendation

This story was told to me by a mutual fund manager. Back in the bull market days of the 1990s, one of his fund's shareholders sent him a retail stock recommendation for his information. It was a typical one-paragraph write-up meant for individuals. (Recommendations meant to be read by professionals can easily run several pages.) The fund manager liked what he read, but noted that the stock had risen since the recommendation was published. Taking care, he called the research department of the large brokerage firm that had issued the recommendation, asking if the stock was still recommended. The research analyst he spoke to recoiled in horror. "No, no Jim," he exclaimed. "This recommendation is not for you!" He then explained that the purpose of the recommendation was to find buyers so that his institutional clients could unload their holdings.

Independent Financial Advisors

When I first started in the financial business, I thought no-load fund investing would ultimately dominate load funds, because you can clearly come out way ahead by avoiding onerous sales charges. But I never expected the degree to which people now lack the confidence to do it themselves.

So, clearly there is a market for personal advice and service. Although you should never deal with a broker simply to get securities recommendations, there are advisors who give personal service, determine asset allocations, manage money on a discretionary basis, and provide continual oversight. In addition, financial planners advise on insurance, health care issues, estate and retirement planning, and tax issues, and offer risk assessments and tax advice. Mutual fund managers generally do none of these things for their shareholders.

There are more than 175,000 advisors and planners working in the United States today. If you feel comfortable hiring one of them, then please, please heed the following advice:

What to Look for When Choosing an Advisor

- Make sure the advisor is a "fiduciary," a person who is legally required to work in your best interests. Not all advisors and planners are fiduciaries.

- The advisor must be honest and truthful.
- He should outline his fees at the first meeting, and then not add unexpected additional fees.
- He must know how to invest as tax efficiently as possible.
- He must have been in business at least five years. (Let other clients experience the inevitable growing pains.) He should be 35 years of age or older.
- He must learn your risk parameters, and not put you into investments that are too speculative for you.
- The advisor should inform you where your money is being held. The custodian-clearing firm must send you regular monthly or quarterly statements. These statements must be readable, understandable, and informative. They must come directly to you from the clearing firm.

Here are three websites that may help you find a Certified Financial Planner in your area:

- The Financial Planner Standards Council, (http://fpsccanada .org/directory-cfp-professionals-good-standing)
- The National Association of Personal Financial Advisors, a fee-only group, (www.napfa.org)
- The Garrett Planning Network, (www.garrettplanningnetwork .com), whose website states that it can locate a planner for a one-time consultation.

You're on your own with these websites. I have no personal experience with any of them. And always ask a planner you are considering for the names of several of his/her long time clients. Call the clients and ask about their experience with the planner.

In addition, there are certain rules of "etiquette" that would endear you to any advisor you would like to work with.

Don't Be a "Bad" Client

Every advisor dreads "bad clients." By that I mean clients who take up too much of the advisor's time. These are clients who call or visit the advisor too often and continually pester the advisor.

These clients don't accept the advisors' recommendations or they tediously ask the same questions time and time again. These are people who don't understand investing concepts but fail to appreciate their level of ignorance.

Particularly troubling to advisors are clients who keep suggesting investment recommendations heard elsewhere, adding "of course, I only want it if you approve." From the point of view of the advisor, the client is trying to have it both ways. If the recommendation is a winner, the client remembers that he was the one who found it—and that's whether or not it's added to his portfolio. On the other hand, if it's added to the portfolio and turns out to be a loser, it's the planner who agreed to it. Then it's his fault.

If a planner *who works on commission* advises a client *not* to buy or sell, he is giving his best and most honest advice. Accept it; he makes no money on this advice.

The absolute worst clients are those who annoy or abuse the advisors' staff.

Advisors will go to significant lengths to avoid "bad" clients. If they know in advance the client is going to be a problem, they will frequently just pass on the business. "Life is too short; I'm wealthy enough," they might say.

Here's what may happen to you if you're a "bad" client:

- The advisor may resign your account.
- The senior partner, who was the reason you went to the firm in the first place, will turn your account over to the most junior planner in the firm. This may very well impact your portfolio's performance.
- They may be slow to act on your complaints.
- They may be slow to return your phone calls. They may act like they didn't receive your messages.
- Many advisors prefer clients they seldom meet face to face. You will be very lucky to get more than one personal meeting a year from them.
- They will make certain you understand that they are there to manage your portfolio, not hold your hand.

Here's a practice that is seldom seen today, but used to be fairly common. Potential clients would avail themselves of an advisor's offer of a free initial consultation. At that appointment, this sort would try to pick the advisor's brain, and walk away with as much "free advice" as possible. These freeloaders never realized that free advice is worth just exactly what you pay for it.

On the positive side, advisors love clients who are always gracious and respectful of both of the advisor and his staff, and ones who co-operate. If a form needs to be signed and returned, they do so promptly. If a recommendation is made, a "good" client will ask intelligent questions and then follow good advice. If an appointment is needed, this type of client makes an effort to schedule—and keep—an appointment. This is all common courtesy, but you would be surprised how many "bad" clients don't know what constitutes good manners—and a good relationship.

Be Happy That You Are Not a Pro

The pros are better than you, but you have some advantages over them.

1. You can hire them for their expertise—or fire them for their lack of it.
2. Pros managing active portfolios are supposed to beat their benchmarks (often the market). You don't have to. You can buy low cost index funds that have a good chance of outperforming actively managed portfolios over the long run.
3. Pros are accountable to their often-impatient clients. You are accountable to no one. There's no pressure on you. Nobody cares if you underperform by getting out of stocks a year before the top. You can wait for your investments to work out, while professionals are measured as often as quarterly. This distinction is most important during bear markets when shareowner redemptions may force professional selling at distressed prices.
4. Bad investment decisions will cost you money, but not your job. You have no career risk; they do.
5. Unlike the pros, you will never have a conflict of interest between your clients and your career. Suppose you are a pro managing other people's money at the peak of a boom. Most of your direct competitors are buying securities that are riskier than you think prudent. What do you do? If you refuse to buy these risky securities and the market continues up, you are going to be an underperformer. Not good. On the other hand, if you do what your competitors are doing and these securities go bad, you will have lots of company. So, even though you lost more money this way, your job will be safer

than if you had followed the prudent course. This explains why thousands of money managers load up on the same "can't lose" blue chips. It's dangerous for pros to stand out.

6. You are smaller. Your purchases or sales won't affect the price. It may take weeks for an institutional fund to liquidate a large position.

7. You have more liquidity. Mutual funds always accommodate investor buy and sell transactions, and even with ETFs there will usually be sufficient shares available on the other side of the trade.

8. You don't have to sell a stock that changes its style. The T. Rowe Price New Horizons Fund, a committed small-cap fund, bought Wal-Mart when it first went public in 1970, and sold it in 1983 when it outgrew small cap status. They were forced to leave a lot of money on the table. T. Rowe Price estimates that that Wal-Mart holding is now worth twice the total value of the fund.

Relax, enjoy investing, and sleep better. Benefit from a pro's expertise without having the burdens of being one.

The Prospectus

First of all, the prospectus is far down the list of important stuff. But there are occasional times when you need it.

A prospectus is a legal document written by lawyers, and it has two purposes: to satisfy the SEC, which requires it; and, to inform you of every possible risk so that if things go wrong, it will be harder for you to win a lawsuit or arbitration hearing.

The original idea was for you to read the prospectus before you bought a security. But in recent years, investors who actually read prospectuses before buying seem to be the exception to the rule. In the case of mutual funds you're more likely to receive them in the mail after you have made the purchase, or you may have to view them online.

If you're at all typical, the odds that you'll ever read it thoroughly are nil, and the chances of you even glancing at it aren't very good, either.

But don't worry; you are doing the right thing. Consider the prospectus your personal instruction manual for operating an investment, similar to the instructional booklets you receive when you buy cell phones or electronic gadgets (and about as useful). Various sources suggest that probably 400,000 trees were cut down in 2010 to produce mutual fund literature. What a waste!

If you're buying a mutual fund from an established, well-known company, about the only thing you need to check is the table of fees and expenses to see how much you are paying. But if you are buying a more esoteric security, you should definitely read its prospectus *before you buy*. Do not rely on the sales person's word.

I once became curious about a type of "structured product" called Principal Protection Notes, which guarantee you can't lose money if you hold them for a predetermined number of years. I attended one meeting held by a reputable brokerage firm, at which a representative explained how these notes work. At the conclusion of the meeting I asked for a prospectus. They told me they didn't have one with them but would mail me one. They never did.

Several months later, I met a broker from another established firm and recounted my experience. He said he would get me a prospectus, as his firm sold structured notes too. A few weeks later I got an e-mail from him saying the prospectus would be in the mail as soon as I signed a release. I found that odd as I had never heard of having to sign a release to receive a prospectus. So, I ignored the e-mail. A few weeks later the second broker called to follow up. He never did explain why they needed the release, but said he would get me one without it, which he did. A 198-page prospectus soon arrived in the mail.

I read much of it and found it didn't really explain what they were doing, nor was there any clear description of the commissions and other costs.

I did learn a lot about the risks, though. The prospectus listed 66. Over and above the usual risks, here are some that concerned me: (2) There might not be a secondary market for the notes; (5) You must rely on your own evaluation of the merits of the investment. You are urged to consult your own advisor; (14) The calculation agent could be one of our affiliates, which could result in a conflict of interest; (16) Research reports and other transactions may create conflicts of interest between you and us.

Now, I am not saying there is anything wrong. These notes may very well be a good investment for exceptionally risk-averse people, and most of the top brokerage firms sell them (and pocket significant fees/commissions for doing so). This particular prospectus was issued by one of the largest brokers in America, a firm with a good reputation. In this particular case, I was thankful for the Securities Act of 1933, which mandated prospectuses whenever new securities are issued.

I wondered if perhaps the fault might be with me. I just didn't understand the prospectus. This concern was alleviated when I read an interview with financial planner Harold Evensky in *Barron's*, who made the following comment in response to a question about structured notes: "Intellectually, [they] might make sense, but what's available in the retail market to the average investor is very expensive, very second-rate, and very opaque."

There is now a new document available called a Summary Prospectus, which runs about five pages. If you are sent one, keep it. It's all you need.

Form ADV

There's a prospectus-like form that advisors have to maintain that you should be aware of, and may even find useful on occasion. The SEC calls it Form ADV.

If an investment advisor manages $100 million or more, he must register with the SEC using Form ADV. If the advisor has less than $100 million under management, he needs to use the Form ADV to register with his state securities regulator.

Form ADV has two parts. Part I contains information about the advisor's education, business, and disciplinary history within the last 10 years. Part II includes information on an advisor's services, fees, and investment strategies.

You can find a copy of an investment advisor's Form ADV, Part I, on the *Investment Adviser Public Disclosure* (IAPD) http://adviserinfo .sec.gov website. You can get Part II directly from the advisor; he must furnish it to you free, and must offer it to his clients annually.

In all the years I owned the BJ Group, only a few clients ever asked for copies of the ADV, so it's hardly necessary. It won't protect you against scams, but it will teach you quite a bit about the advisor.

If you just want to get a feel for the type of information in the ADV, I suggest you go to the IAPD website and search on a few large and small advisors. In the large category is Fisher Investments, owned by Forbes columnist Ken Fisher. In the small category are Stellar Capital Management in Phoenix and American Planning Group in Stamford, CT.

One thing you can learn from the ADV is approximately how many clients an advisor has. My gut feeling is to go to an advisor with fewer, and hopefully you will get more personalized service. Also noted is whether the advisor has an outside custodian. If you can't find the ADV it may be that the advisor has fewer than eight clients, or maybe you don't have the name quite right. A quick call to the advisor can confirm the latter.

Important Lessons in This Chapter

- Don't deal with advisors who work on commission. If you need personal help over and above what the fund company's reps can provide, go to an advisor who is basically compensated by assets under management, or by a flat fee.
- When it comes to your finances, never abdicate personal responsibility.
- Only a minute percentage of people are scammed. Nevertheless, learn to protect yourself from the scammers. There will be more Madoffs.

PART

III

BECOMING A WELL-ROUNDED MONEY MAVEN

13

For Clearer Thinking

I suppose you should always try to think clearly about everything. But it seems extra important when it comes to investing. We are awash in facts that hold various degrees of relevance and accuracy. The purpose of the next two chapters is to give you some insight into which facts are important, which to note, and which to ignore. These chapters focus on the need to be skeptical, to see through commonplace misconceptions, to consider the impact of other investors, to deal with the unknown, and to learn how to overcome weaknesses. How well you apply these "facts" to the task of investing will, to a great extent, determine your success. It is just as important to learn *how* to think, as it is to learn *what* to think. We'll begin with a quiz.

Clear Thinking Quiz

1. What product do television networks sell?
2. Cruise lines are in what business?
3. McDonald's is in what business?

If you know how to think, then you should be able to answer these questions without any trouble. If you can't, read on.

Answers are at the end of this chapter.

Correlation Is Not Causation

If you have never taken a course in statistics, here's one thing you should learn: Correlation is not causation. Just because two series move in tandem, it doesn't mean one series causes the other.

Investment lore includes any number of correlations that can be quite high, but may not mean a thing. Probably the best-known example is the Super Bowl indicator. It's bullish when the winner is a team from the old National Football League, and bearish when the winner is a team from the old American Football League.

Most people would say that there is no causation between the two series. However, the discoverer of the relationship, Wall Street legend, Bob Stovall, points out that the correlation "works" because the old NFL teams are generally stronger, coupled with the fact that stocks rise more often than they fall. That explains the correlation, but that doesn't mean that the sporting event *causes* the market action. Stovall calls the relationship "financial entertainment."

Financial analysts are constantly producing thousands of data series. With so much data floating around, some sets are bound to move together. Sometimes two series move together because they are both caused by a third series. Analysts who produce these correlations are called data miners, and it's a fitting description because they do try to exact a few valuable nuggets of information from massive amounts of fairly useless ore.

I recently ran across a new correlation, and it's a lulu: "Ninety percent of market gains are made when Congress is not in session." The back-up data was prepared by two economists working in academia. Their study, based on the 1965 to 2007 period, showed a 1.6 percent gain when Congress was in session; a 17.6 percent gain when out of session.

Even assuming the data are correct, the skeptic in me doesn't believe that Congress being on vacation should cause the market to move to that extent. I'm inclined to believe its just coincidence, or can be explained by other factors. Yes, I believe the authors are sincere in thinking Congressional actions are a negative force on the market, but I wouldn't bet money on the pattern continuing. And, as a matter of fact, the stock market had a terrible month in August 2011, with Congress off on its annual summer recess!

Amazingly, the authors of this study are so convinced of its validity that they launched a mutual fund in 2008 to implement a strategy of only being in the market when Congress is out of session. The fund switches in and out of stocks 15 to 20 times a year using derivatives. It's called the Congressional Effect Fund (CEFFX). It was down 4.4 percent in 2009, but then had an above average year in 2010, up 15.2 percent. The 2010 performance doesn't impress me.

There are too many coincidences in this business. At year-end 2010 the fund had $8.6 million in assets. In 2011, the fund lost 5.1 percent.

As a general rule, if you can't see obvious causation, just assume the relationship is coincidental.

I would be remiss if I didn't conclude this topic by recounting the story of Paul the Octopus, who in 2010 accurately predicted the result of every German soccer match as well as the World Cup final in

With so much data floating around, some sets are bound to move together.

South Africa. Paul made his predictions by choosing between two mussel-filled containers adorned with the flags of each team.

Sadly, in October 2010, Paul passed away from natural causes in his aquarium in the German city of Oberhausen. "Paul inspired people of all continents," said the aquarium's general manager in a statement to the press. Americans shouldn't feel superior to this German manager. After all we have Punxsutawney Phil.

Similarly, there are many times when you will run across relationships that appear to have some importance, but upon careful analysis turn out to be at best superficial. Here's one from a syndicated political columnist who shall remain nameless: "Since 1968, every Republican president with the exception of the accidental Gerald Ford has come from either California or Texas."

Does this pattern have any political implications? Not that I can see. It may just imply that California and Texas are big states.

Let me contrast that "fact" with this statement by political and media commentator, Bernard Goldberg: "Since 1936, 11 incumbent presidents have run for a second term and only three were defeated— Gerald Ford, Jimmy Carter, and George H.W. Bush." Now this statement is analyzable!

Are Patterns Projectable?

The pros love to find patterns and report them to the press, which at times accepts them rather credulously because our brains are hardwired to detect patterns, even when they don't exist. The reality is that some of these patterns never existed while others existed in the past, sometimes for many years, but won't necessarily continue in the future.

Until 1957 stocks always had higher yields than bonds. This made sense to everybody; after all, stocks were riskier. Then, beginning in

1957, stocks began to yield less than bonds. Professionals bet a lot of money that this pattern would reverse itself, that is, regress to the mean. So far, it hasn't.

Another indicator that gained popularity in 2004 was the "Years Ending in Five indicator." It postulates that the market will do extraordinarily well in years ending in five. The following table shows the record based on a period of 120 years that forms the basis for this belief.

Performance by Year Ending Digits

Years ending in	Average annual % change	Number of up years
1	–0.2	7
2	2.2	7
3	6.2	6
4	7.4	7
5	**30.7**	**12**
6	6.0	7
7	–3.2	6
8	18.5	8
9	9.2	9
0	–7.2	4

Source: DJIA, 12 decades, 1884–2003.

So, if you had bet on that indicator at the beginning of 2005, how would you have done? Not too well, I'm afraid. The Dow *lost* 0.6 percent in 2005.

I never paid any attention to this indicator, or wrote about it in a positive way, because I couldn't see any reason why years ending in five were any different than years ending in any other number.

There's an inexhaustible supply of these trivia. Here are some other correlations churned out by Wall Street:

- In years ending in eight, stocks have taken flight [in other words, gained] after March. This, of course, made the rounds in Wall Street just at the end of March 2008. Yeah, right. Stocks reached their lowest point in 12 years that November.
- The Philadelphia Phillies won the World Series in 2008 and took the first game in the 2009 Series. That's when Wall Street noted that the last time the Phillies had won the World Series

twice in a row was in 1929 and 1930. The implication, of course, is that if Philadelphia won the series in 2009, making two in a row again, that would be bearish. Luckily for the credulous, the Yankees won.

If history were a foolproof way to determine what the stock market is going to do next, the world's richest investors would be historians and data processors.

Keep in mind that when you use historical data to make forecasts, these data are always time period sensitive, meaning they were produced by past market and economic conditions that may or may not repeat.

Some Correlations Make Sense

In contrast to the years ending in five, there is the four-year presidential cycle, which I believe does have some predictive power in the third year. It postulates that we can expect a good market during pre-election years like 2011, and to a lesser extent during the election years. This is based on the fact that there has not been a losing pre-election year since Depression era (and war-torn) 1939 (see the following table).

Presidential Cycle, 1940–2010 (17½ Cycles Total)

	Number of losing years	Percentage of years down
Mid-term years (like 2010)	7	39%
Pre-election years (like 2011)	0	0%
Election years (like 2012)	6	33%
Post-election years (like 2013)	8	44%

Source: DJIA

This makes sense to me because politicians do have the ability to influence the economy, and they do want the economy to be buoyant when they are running for reelection. This is most evident in the pre-election years.

They also know that there are times when bitter medicine has to be taken, and from their point of view, those times are right after elections. Most bear markets take place in the first or second years after the elections.

As indicators go, the presidential year cycle is one of the more reliable because you can postulate cause and effect. Nevertheless, what happened in the most recent pre-presidential year, 2011, is instructive. With the market hostage to bad economic news and international tensions, it was touch and go the latter half of the year. Still, the Dow finished 2011 up 5.5 percent, although the S&P 500 was flat. I count that as a win for the indicator, but you should never consider it the only factor in making a forecast.

Why Averages Can Be Misleading

If you open a "Second Avenue Deli" on First Avenue and open another "Second Avenue Deli" on Third Avenue, are your delis, on average, located on Second Avenue? *The New York Times* published an in-depth discussion of this topic on January 14, 2009.

Three statisticians went deer hunting. They spotted a deer. The first statistician fired but the bullet went two feet to the left of the deer. The second statistician fired; his bullet went two feet to the right of the deer. The third statistician jumped up and down shouting, "We got him; we got him!"

Let's say you are flying from LAX to JFK and the pilot goes on the speaker to announce that, based on average weather conditions, airspeed and traffic, the flight should take 4 hours and 45 minutes, and you should assume the average. Would that satisfy you? I doubt it. I am pretty sure you would want more specificity.

Warren Buffett and I, both investors, have an average total net worth of $20 billion.

The Best Six Months

Here's a seasonal indicator that many investors find believable. It's called the Best Six Months, and was originated by Yale Hirsch, founder and Editor at Large of the *Stock Trader's Almanac*.

It says that your stock investments will do far better in the six months beginning in November and ending in April than in the other six months beginning in May and ending in October. As the Wall Street cliché says: "Sell in May and go away."

If you track the Dow Jones Industrial Average's winter half-year versus summer half-year performance since 1950, the difference, on average, is stunning. The average gain for the six winter months through 2009 is 7.4 percent. The average gain for the six summer months is 0.4 percent, in other words, virtually nothing. Over a period of 60 years, it appears that virtually all the market's gains have come in the winter.

Perhaps the reason for this disparity in performance is that big money investors really do "go away" in the summer, if not actually, then at least mentally.

With a study showing differences that great, should you sell all equities every May and stay in cash until November? No. Here's why that would not be a good idea.

Although the comparison appears to be valid, this knowledge is less useful than you might think. The reason is that sometimes averages can be very misleading. When you examine the individual year data, you will find wide disparities of performance. For the six summer months period, there were 36 up years, while 24 years were down. This probably reflects the long-term uptrend of the market

Now, let's look at the six winter months. Yes, winter is better; there were 46 up years and 14 down years in that part of the cycle. But so what? Even though the summers had almost twice as many down years, you still had a 60 percent chance of making gains in the worst part of the year, as the following table shows.

Best Six Months Indicator, 1950–2009

Number of years	Winter Nov.–Apr.	Summer May–Oct.
Up	46	36
Down	14	24
% years up	77%	60%
Average annual performance	7.4%	0.4%
Best performance	29.8	19.2
Worst performance	−12.5	−27.3

So even though there appears to be some validity to the cycle, you obviously should not routinely get out of the market each summer even if there are no tax consequences. After all, if you had made a practice of doing so, you would have missed one of the biggest run-ups in history in the summer of 2009.

I think it's good to be aware of seasonal indicators that seem to have some logic behind them, but they are at best just one of the several factors you should consider in timing stock purchases or sales. What's true on average over time very often has no bearing whatsoever the day you are making a specific investing decision.

There are many other seasonal and annual indicators similar to those mentioned before, Most were discovered by data mining. Use them only if the rationale, if any, for the correlations makes intuitive or economic sense to you, or is generally accepted by the "Street."

Sell on Rosh Hashanah; buy back on Yom Kippur.

—Old trading saw

The Fallacy of Missing the Best Days

Most studies meant to show that buy-and-hold is better than market timing are valid within their own methodology. But there is one glaring exception, and, obviously, it's the one you will see most often. It's usually referred to as "missing the best days."

Using various time periods, "missing the best days" studies "prove" that if you are out of the market for only a handful of days over a very long period of time—decades—your profits will shrink to a fraction of the market's return.

One such study I ran across in the course of researching this book showed that for the 2,516 market days between 1997 and 2006, the S&P 500 had an average gain of 8.4 percent per year. That's the benchmark.

Then the author of this study showed that if you were out of the market for only the 10 best days (mind you now, that's out of 10 years), your average gain would have declined to 2.2 percent per year. That's a huge drop. Even scarier, if you had missed the 15 best days your long-term overall profit would have been zero. The conclusion this author draws was that you should buy-and-hold for greater profits.

Why take issue with that? It's not that there is anything wrong with the calculations. The gains on the 10 best days out of a decade can be awesome. I have no doubt that removing them from the averages can cause such a dramatic decline in performance.

The problem is the concept is so hypothetical and so self-serving as to be meaningless hogwash. In real life it's not possible to be out of the market for just those 10 or 15 particular days. These days arrive randomly, without warning, and virtually never consecutively.

It's like a parent telling a child that if all his A grades were excluded, his overall grade point average would be lower. Duh! But you can't exclude the As just to obtain a desired or predetermined outcome.

Mark Hulbert once ran some numbers and determined that if you remove Warren Buffett's 15 best decisions from the hundreds of others, his long-term performance would be mediocre.

The reason people do these studies is to prove that buy-and-hold is better than market timing. But in order to do that, they have to ignore the flip side of their studies. That is, what would happen to performance if they were out of the market the 10 *worst* days? If you did that, your gains would zoom to incredible heights!

That would be a great argument for market timing, so the people who prepare these statistics don't show that.

Of course it's equally impossible to be out of the market the 10 worst days. Like the 10 best days, they arrive randomly, without warning, and virtually never consecutively.

It's still totally hypothetical, but there is an honest way to show these patterns: Exclude *both* the 10 best and the 10 worst days from the broad period. The result: If you remove both, the two exclusions tend to offset each other, and you usually end up with about the same return as the buy-and-hold average (although there may be a decrease in volatility).

This study is rarely done. However, [Laszlo] Birinyi Associates did do such research and found that missing the five worst days per year from 1966 through 2001 would improve return by a factor of 88 times! Another study reported in *The Wall Street Journal* found that if you had sidestepped the market's 10 worst days over a period of 109 years, you would have tripled the return on the Dow.

The real bottom line here is that "the 10 best (or worst) days" studies don't prove anything, one way or the other, in terms of investing strategy. If you are a buy-and-hold investor, you will get the market averages. If you are out of the market part of the time, for whatever reason, you will get a different number. In real life, that number may be higher, or it may be lower. You can't assume the number will be lower. Inevitably, the people who produce such studies usually have a vested interest. Often, they are mutual fund companies. Their interest is in keeping your money invested with them.

But don't misunderstand. A case can certainly be made for long-term buy-and-hold. The "10 best days" exercise is just not that case.

Do You Benchmark Your Performance?

Professional money managers and institutional investors routinely benchmark their performance, often to a broad-based index like the S&P 500. In fact, the SEC mandates that mutual funds benchmark to a relevant index in their prospectuses.

The purpose of benchmarking, of course, is to find out how well you are doing. After all, you may be making money in a bull market, but if you are lagging a benchmark, you are probably not doing as well as you should be doing. Similarly, a small loss in a bear market may be an exceptional performance. Most investing articles and books routinely advise benchmarking.

Nevertheless, I have never heard of an individual investor rigorously benchmarking his or her entire portfolio.

I must confess that even though I always meticulously benchmarked mutual fund performance in my newsletter (and considered it one of the newsletter's strengths), I have never done it for myself.

So, why don't we benchmark? Well, first of all it's a lot of work to do it properly. Benchmarking must be done on a risk-adjusted basis, taking into account transaction and advisory fees and, very importantly, cash additions or withdrawals during the measured period. It also means finding the most appropriate benchmark, a surprisingly difficult task.

Second, most of us aren't really going to use that information. Let's be honest. We really don't care how we do versus the market. We just want to make money. Mutual fund professionals are heartened by good *relative* returns, such as losing less than the indexes. If, in 2008, a fund declined 32 percent while the S&P 500 was off 38 percent, professionals would have considered that an excellent performance.

But that has never been the goal for nonprofessionals. We can't spend relative returns. We just want profits, or in Wall Street's lingo, we want absolute returns.

So, benchmark when you can, but don't lose sleep if you don't. Just be happy when you make money.

Finding the Appropriate Benchmark

You may want to benchmark the performance of a fund you own. Here's how to do it. Find the index whose performance correlates most closely with your fund.

An easy way is to go to the Morningstar website. Enter your existing fund's name or ticker, and then click on the Ratings and Risk tab. That screen has Best Fit Index data that will tell you the most comparable index.

If for any reason you want to replace an actively managed fund with its most closely comparable index fund, you can use the same procedure and data base.

Rules of Thumb

Investing has many rules of thumb. Here are some that I've heard:

- You can retire on 80 percent of salary.
- A stock that trades at a P/E ratio that is less than its expected growth rate is attractive for purchase.
- Save at least 10 percent of your gross income.
- Over time, the stock market should produce a 10 percent return.
- Retirees can safely spend 4 percent of their assets each year.
- The trend is your friend.
- Widows should wait one year from the death of their spouse before adjusting their portfolio.
- Your stock asset allocation percentage should be 100 minus your age. (This means that if you were 65, you would subtract that number from 100 and get 35. Your stock allocation would thus be 35 percent.)

My advice is to avoid taking such rules of thumb literally. At best, they are starting points for good planning. At worst, utter, distracting hogwash.

Take the asset allocation rule. Some advisors say stock holdings should be 115 or 120 minus age, not 100. Then there is a famous anecdote about Philip Carret, the founder of the Pioneer Fund. At the age of 97, he was still 100 percent invested in equities. (Carret died in 1997 at the age of 101. He was active to the end, so we will never know how he would have fared in the 2000 to 2002 and 2008 bear markets. I suspect he was wealthy enough to have easily weathered those storms.)

I never recommend 100 minus your age. This is what I tell some affluent people: Put enough into bonds so that you can live well off the interest. Then, it doesn't matter what you do with the rest.

The widow wait rule depends entirely on the late husband's investing acumen.

The trend is your friend. (Well, at least until the trend ends.)

Actually, the 4 percent rule is a pretty good rule of thumb. A retiree heeding this rule has a 90 percent chance of having his money last 30 years. But it makes a difference how well diversified he is, whether he invests speculatively or conservatively, and whether his gains come at regular intervals, or are bunched up at the beginning, middle, or end of the accumulation period.

The other rules have their own variations.

Know What You Don't Know

It's been my observation that too many investors select advisors on the basis of personality. And I don't just mean financial advisors. The same holds true when selecting all sorts of professionals including doctors, lawyers, and accountants. With doctors, it's called "bedside manner."

People who select advisors this way usually don't know what they don't know. On occasion, that can be hazardous to your health or wealth, or both.

Luckily, I've always had a pretty good sense of what I don't know. In 1989 I found out that I needed a heart bypass operation. At the time, I belonged to the Kaiser-Permanente HMO, and for this operation Kaiser had a relationship with Albert Einstein Hospital in the Bronx, New York. If I wanted Kaiser to pay for this costly operation, it had to take place there.

I called the hospital and learned that they had two surgeons who performed heart bypasses. One was an older doctor, department head and presumably the most experienced. The second was a younger, Italian doctor who had received his medical training at an Italian college. Those were my two choices.

How did I choose between them? Realizing that I had absolutely no competency in evaluating heart surgeons, I called two doctors who were personal friends and asked each to please check out these two doctors for me. One doctor was a hematologist who practiced at Mt. Sinai in Manhattan. The second was a Westchester pediatrician affiliated with Einstein.

A few days later, the first doctor called back and told me to go with the Italian. When I asked why, he said that he had called the blood bank at the hospital and asked whether either surgeon was in the habit of requisitioning emergency blood supplies. He learned that the older doctor frequently called for more blood during an operation, whereas the Italian never did.

The next day I heard from the second doctor. He had talked to several doctors at Einstein and found that the consensus among them was that the Italian was better.

The Italian doctor performed the operation, which went well. Five days later, when he dropped by my hospital room, I asked when I could go back to work. He told me, "It depends on how much you like your job." So I went back to work eight days after the operation. I had a newsletter to write.

Had I interviewed these two doctors myself, I would probably have asked them how many times each had performed the operation and how many of their patients had died. That would have been better than nothing. But tapping into the wisdom of real experts worked out better. I knew what I didn't know.

Recognizing that you cannot know the future does not mean you shouldn't have a view of the future. Rather, it means you recognize your view of the future might be wrong and knowing that will induce you to manage your investments so that you will survive the possibility of being wrong. You will find that you will be investing quite differently from those who crave certainty. The trick is to make money without knowing exactly what will happen.

A *Wall Street Journal* interview with billionaire speculator, George Soros, of June 21, 2008:

> **WSJ**: How is that you are rich despite your worldview having been wrong so far? (Soros had been predicting disaster for years.)
>
> **Soros**: I'm only rich because I know when I am wrong.

Here's another practical consequence of not knowing what you don't know: Studies have shown that investors who think they know what they don't know can be overconfident, trade more frequently, and take excessive risks—and have lower returns. Not surprisingly, this malady affects men more than women.

Ignorance more frequently begets confidence than does knowledge.
—Charles Darwin

What do we really know with some assurance? Well, we know that over the long run stocks will gain. We know that over the very long run, risky investments such as stocks will generally perform better than less risky investments such bonds, albeit with a greater possibility of loss over shorter intervals.

How do you make money with such limited knowledge? By investing sensibly using all that you do know. By being skeptical of the experts. And, by knowing that nobody is offering you a free lunch. If you know what you don't know, you'll do better in the market, and in life.

Know What Is Unknowable

Let's consider all the forecasts on global warming that have been discussed in recent years. Is it really possible to predict the earth's temperature a century from now? Here's an excerpt from *The New York Times* that made me wonder. It was in a column written by Paul Krugman, a Nobel Prize winning economist.

> . . . Thus researchers at MIT, who were previously predicting a temperature rise of a little more than 4 degrees by the end of this century, are now predicting a rise of more than 9 degrees.

Now, I have several questions. How can there be what may be a significant revision in their forecast in only a few years? Did the MIT researchers obtain new data? Did a trend fail to continue? Can we rely on the latest forecast, or will it be subject to revision too? In fact, are any of these forecasts accurate enough to be actionable?

I think the only valid conclusion you can draw from the data cited by Krugman, and much of climate change research, is *nobody knows*.

Here's the way I look at it: I am not a climatologist. I know nothing about global warming (now known as "climate change"). But I do know something about forecasting. Forecasting has been an important part of my job description for over 50 years. At the networks, I used to forecast audiences. At the newsletter, I forecast fund and market performance.

Now let's compare forecasting the climate 90 years out with a time series that I do know something about, the Dow Jones Industrial Average. The Dow and the climate are both determined by multiple variables, but you can make a case that the Dow has fewer. Some would say the Dow has only two variables—corporate earnings and the price/earnings ratios. Clearly, the climate has more than two variables. Nevertheless, there is no doubt that forecasting either the Dow or the climate over the long term is very difficult.

Now, is there anybody in the world who thinks that I, or anybody else for that matter, can predict the Dow's level in the year 2100. Of course not.

Top analysts have a tough time predicting the market just twelve months out. At the end of each year, *Barron's* asks a number of strategists for their market forecasts for the forthcoming year. At year-end 2009, 12 prominent strategists, who are as skilled at their craft as the climatologists are in theirs, predicted that in 2010 the S&P 500 could range from a 0.5 percent decline at one extreme to a 19.9 percent gain at the other extreme. That's an incredible range considering that all the analysts are essentially looking at the same facts. The reason for the wide scope of opinions is that the analysts place different emphases on each variable. They were a little better on average—a predicted gain of 10.0 percent, compared to an actual of 12.8 percent in 2010.

I don't know whether these same market strategists were chastened in 2010, but their forecasts for 2011 were quite different. Many panelists didn't make a market prediction at all. Those who did, with two exceptions, couched their forecasts in ranges, such as up 5 to 10 percent or (and here's a good one) between 10 percent up and 10 percent down. Now that certainly increases the odds of a correct forecast!

In forecasting 90 years out, other factors come into play. On one hand the regression to the mean phenomenon might make forecasting easier by narrowing results. But on the other hand, this will be offset by four other factors that come into play:

- Things change over time; they don't remain constant (think Egypt, Libya, Tiger Woods).
- There can be new variables in the future that are totally unknown now.
- Small differences become big differences over time.
- You just don't know how these variables will interact.

Now that you understand a little about forecasting, I'd like each reader to take a guess at the level of the Dow Jones Industrial Average on January 1, 2100. See if you can come within a country mile of a reasonable guess. And don't read further until you have a forecast in your mind. Caution: Zero is not an acceptable guess.

Okay, got it? Now here's my professional estimate for the Dow, 90 years from now: 1,700,000! I'll bet your guess was far less than that. Of course, this assumes Dow Jones index will never do a reverse split, and for that matter that there will even be a Dow index in 2100.

Now here are some practical conclusions. First, I am sure you will realize my 1.7 million forecast is not particularly useful. So let me hasten to add that there is a way to make sense out of this and other similar forecasts. Simply reduce the numbers to average annual gains. Those of you who are mathematically inclined can easily do this. If you're not, look to the forecaster for guidance.

Now we can make some informed guesses. In this simplified example, I merely projected the past (excluding dividends which are not reinvested in computing the index), but the upcoming 90 years will almost certainly be different. A more precise analysis might result in a somewhat better forecast, but the bottom line is that the accuracy of any long-term forecast, whether we are talking about climatology or the market, is far more luck than skill. The only reasonable conclusion is "The experts don't know." Now that's clear thinking.

According to Jairam Ramesh, India's Environment and Forests minister, the "climate world is divided into three: the climate atheists, the climate agnostics, and the climate evangelicals." Ramesh says he is a climate agnostic. So am I.

And Know What Your Advisors Don't Know

Sure, professionals know their stuff. But they can't predict the future any better than you can.

I'm going to quote an expert on this—Barbara Walters, from her memoir:

> Because people saw me and others on their TV screens, they automatically assumed we must have some sort of special wisdom. Otherwise we wouldn't be on the air. Television not only validated

our opinions, it made us all knowing. The truth is that while we may be more articulate, we may be just as confused about things as the people watching at home.

—*Audition* by Barbara Walters

You can say that about a lot of stock market seers.

The Difference between Investing and Speculating

In common usage most people define investing to mean buying conservative securities, often for the long term. They define speculating to mean making riskier purchases, often for quick profits. If borrowed money is used to finance the transaction, it would likely be termed a speculation, except, of course, for housing.

Here's a typical definition:

> [I]nvesting [is] a method of purchasing assets to gain profit in the form of reasonably predictable income (dividends, interest, or rentals) and/or appreciation over the long term. It is the definition of the time period for the investment return and the predictability of the returns that often distinguish an investment from a speculation. A speculator buys stocks hoping for a short-term gain over the next days or weeks. An investor buys stocks likely to produce a dependable future stream of cash returns and capital gains when measured over years or decades. —*A Random Walk Down Wall Street* by Burton Malkiel

I would disagree with the common definition. The root of the word *speculate* is simply to look. Remember, eyeglasses used to be called spectacles. The speculator is simply an investor who looks ahead. He is doing nothing more than betting on the future course of prices. He is taking a risk on what the future holds in hopes of making a profit. Investors also take risks, usually just more moderate ones. So, for all practical purposes the difference between a speculator and an investor is basically a matter of degree, not kind.

It'll never happen, but I would be happier if the word investing meant a positive-sum game like stocks, while speculating meant a zero-sum game like gambling or options.

Also consider this important distinction between gambling and speculating (or investing) to store in your mental database.

With gambling, you usually deal with a known risk. For example, an experienced gambler knows the exact odds of rolling a seven in craps, or drawing to an inside straight, and can plan accordingly. With investing or speculating you have only a very general idea of the amount of the risk you are taking. You are basically dealing with uncertainty. Each endeavor requires its own specific set of skills.

And the word evolves. In the summer of 2008, politicians and pundits tried to define speculation as manipulation, which it usually is not. These authorities frequently alleged that the high oil prices at that time were the fault of speculators, who were unjustifiably manipulating prices. The pundits and politicians were incorrect, as they often are. By year-end oil prices fell as market forces reasserted themselves.

You can avoid reality, but you cannot avoid the consequences of avoiding reality.

—Ayn Rand

Answers to the Clear Thinking Quiz

1. Many people would guess television networks sell programs; a few might say they sell advertising. But that would be incorrect. With rare exceptions, TV networks sell *eyeballs*—they sell the people who view the programs. That's the basis for collecting advertising dollars.
2. The first criterion for success is to understand what business you are in. Cruise lines used to be in the transportation business. With the advent of the jet airliner, that business disappeared. Cruise lines are now in the *entertainment* business. (Several synonyms would qualify as correct answers.)
3. Yes, McDonald's sells fast food. But its principal source of profits is the franchise revenue from 31,000 restaurants worldwide. (Only 15 percent of McDonald's restaurants are owned and operated by McDonald's Corporation directly. The remainders are operated by others through a variety of franchise agreements and joint ventures.) McDonald's is in the *franchise* business.

Important Lessons in This Chapter

- Your investing decisions and strategies will always be made under conditions of uncertainty. Learn to live with this restriction.
- How you think is just as important as what you think.
- Be perspicacious.

CHAPTER 14

The Psychology of Investing

Understanding the psychology of investing is on my "what's important" list. As Yogi Berra once put it, "Ninety-five percent of this game is 50 percent mental."

Your mental attitude toward investing is critical. Entire books have been written about its importance. Academic studies exploring the subject are now popular. So let me touch on some of the psychological topics that are relevant to your investing success.

Anchoring

Anchoring is a universal psychological phenomenon. We tend to base estimates and decisions on known *anchors* or familiar positions, with an adjustment relative to this starting point. Anchoring influences the way we intuitively assess probabilities. That's because we are better at relative thinking than absolute thinking.

Here are some familiar noninvestment examples of anchoring:

- Discounts off a list price. Stores routinely advertise 20 percent off, 50 percent off, and so on, not the absolute sale price.
- If the price of a house has been reduced, that's highlighted because many buyers may believe that makes it a good deal.
- "Used cars for less" or "dress for less." Now, that's anchoring at its best.

In all these cases, we are influenced by the anchor. We don't really know if anyone ever bought at the list price. We don't know if the discount price is a good value just because the asking price of a house has been reduced.

Anchoring has a number of applications to investing.

- Investors will tend to hang on to losing investments by waiting for the investment to break-even at the purchase price. Thus, they anchor the value of their investment to the value it once had, rather than to its present value. There is no guarantee that the investment will ever go back up to its purchase price, of course.
- It is very common for homeowners to be so anchored to their home's peak value that they refuse to reduce their selling price in any meaningful way.
- Some investors believe that they should liquidate a position after it has gone up in a series of trading sessions, because they don't believe that the position is likely to continue going up. Conversely, other investors might hold on or even buy more of a stock that has fallen in multiple sessions, because they view further declines as improbable. Just because a stock has gone up on six consecutive trading sessions does not mean that it is less likely to go up during the seventh session. And just because it has declined doesn't mean it can't decline further. History is replete with stocks that declined to zero, with some inexperienced investors continuing to buy all the way down. Brokers can get even more hung up on this because they don't want to admit that they made a mistake. Whether you buy a stock for 10 dollars or for one penny, if it goes to zero, you have lost 100 percent of your money.

Anchoring is unavoidable. We all do it. If you think about what you are doing, you can identify the times when it is inappropriate.

Here's a suggestion that will help make you a better investor. Most nonprofessionals and the media anchor their perception of the market to the Dow Jones Industrial Average. By that I mean it's the Dow's level that becomes the reference point in determining market levels. That's really old thinking. Professionals anchor to the S&P 500 Index. You would be better off doing the same.

There used to be a ready-to-wear store on 34th Street in New York City named Orbach's. Its founder, Nathan Orbach didn't believe in having sales. You never saw a price tag in Orbach's saying "originally $50, now only $30." That's because Nathan didn't believe in anchoring. If he had to mark an item down to $30, it was because he knew it was only worth $30 (or less). He believed that if it had been worth $50, it would have sold for $50. The store was a beloved retail institution for decades. Sadly, it's long gone.

Recency Bias

Investors often think that the market's recent trend will continue for a while. There is some truth to this, but you can't depend on it.

If bullishness is your default attitude, try to be more cautious. If bearishness resonates with you, make a special point of considering the bullish case.

Luck versus Skill

Much of what we think is skill is really luck. If you flip a coin long enough you will eventually have a run of a dozen heads in a row. In the case of coins, most people will recognize there was no skill involved; they just had a lucky run.

Though less obvious, it's no different in many other disciplines. People see patterns where none exist. Athletes frequently have long winning streaks; a number of baskets in a row, or getting a hit in a number of baseball games in a row. All could be within the laws of probability.

A real life corollary here is the common belief that a slot machine in a casino that hasn't had a big winner for quite some time is "due." Although slot machines do have a payback percentage programmed into them, each individual play is said to be random. According to the American Gaming Association, there is no such thing as a "hot" or "cold" slot machine, not even right after a jackpot, nor does the amount of the wager affect the outcome.

For those who are interested, the Gaming Association explains it on this website: www.americangaming.org/assets/files/regw/2010/Taking_the_Mystery_Out_of_the_Machine_Brochure_FINAL.pdf.

Without being an expert in this area, I wouldn't bet a lot of money on the belief that a certain machine is "due." After all, the same people who think slot machines run hot or cold also think that dice have a memory.

Randomness in the Markets

In 2009, efficient market theorists, Eugene Fama and Kenneth French completed a massive study covering 3,156 stock funds over a 22-year period. The study was titled "Luck versus Skill in a Cross Section of Mutual Fund Returns." The highlight: Outside of the top 3 percent of funds, active management lagged the results that an investor could have gotten purely by chance.

Let's examine one specific case, Bill Miller's winning streak when his Legg Mason Value Trust outperformed the market every year from 1991 to 2005. During the run, he was credited with great skill, but then starting in 2006 he began lagging badly. In 2008 he was down 55.1 percent, 17 points worse than the market. Miller also managed Legg Mason Opportunity Trust. It declined 65.5 percent for the year.

I don't dispute that Miller is a far above average money manager. However, it now appears that he simply fell afoul of the basic rule that if you take great risks, you will get great volatility on both the upside and downside. Both of his funds outperformed the averages in 2009; 2010 was mixed.

> On November 17, 2011, Bill Miller announced his 30-year stewardship of Legg Mason Value Trust was ending.

The point is: Most occurrences, in or out of investing, are within the laws of probability and luck may play a part. At a minimum, you should conclude that with most winning performances, luck overlaid great skill. Always think about this when you read about some guru's record.

I can be just as dumb as anybody else.

—Peter Lynch, September 2008

In September 2008, the great Peter Lynch had the dubious honor of holding both AIG and Fannie Mae in his personal portfolio. They dropped 82 percent and 76 percent, respectively, during that month.

Boldness

This is a tough one for me for two reasons. First, it's very difficult to give practical advice. Second, this is my own particular weakness. I am not bold enough. Sometimes, I am pretty sure an investment is right. But then I don't buy enough of it.

You should be bold—but not to the point of becoming foolhardy.

The top investors are, almost without exception, very bold. Hedge fund operators like George Soros are excellent examples. When they are certain, or even when they think the odds are just clearly in their favor, they will back up their beliefs to the tune of hundreds of millions, even billions of dollars. If they lose a billion or so, here or there, it doesn't change their attitude toward bold-ness. I strongly suspect bold investors are richer than timid ones. I also think that boldness—or timidity—is a character trait, and not something that anyone can easily change.

Where is the line between bold and foolhardy? I have only the vaguest answer. The dictionary tells me that to be bold is to be dar-ing, fearless, confident, and audacious. But how audacious? This sort of reminds me of the late S. I. Hayakawa's conjugation of verbs: I am prudent; you are stubborn; he is a pigheaded fool. The char-acterization is in the eye of the beholder.

You need to know yourself. Think about how you would describe your own outlook.

Procrastination

Lack of boldness also ties into procrastination. In my case, sometimes I am too busy with other work and I don't find the time to do the needed investigation before buying or selling. Are my priorities not right, or is it just procrastination, or maybe a little of both? Fight pro-crastination. When markets are moving swiftly, delay can be costly.

Indecision

It's easy to be indecisive in the face of uncertainty, particularly when it comes to making a sell decision. Perhaps this advice can help: When you are in doubt in a bull market, hold. When you are in doubt in a bear market, sell. But don't sell in a panic. The Wall Street cliché for this situation is: Let your gains run, but cut your losses short.

Don't Gravitate Toward Round Numbers

We humans love round numbers. We cheer when a round numbered sports record is achieved: the hallowed four-minute mile or Derek Jeter's 3,000th hit. We attach special significance to birthdays ending in zero. We'd like to be a *millionaire* (six zeros). And we carry that attitude into the market, paying special attention when market averages end in a string of zeros.

If you think about it, you will realize that the very roundness of the figures indicates a certain arbitrariness. So why should we give a round number greater importance?

In the strong bull market of the late 1990s, investors rejoiced whenever the Dow hit a new round number, 9,000, 10,000, 11,000. I still have, and occasionally wear, a Dow 10,000 tee shirt given me by a mutual fund group.

Yet, those achievements are far less meaningful than most investors believe. The fact is that toward the end of that bull market, fewer and fewer of the 30 Dow stocks were participating in the great rally, which of course ended in early 2000. In investing, don't credit round numbers with any special significance. A stock index or stock hitting a new round number is not a reason to buy or sell.

Being Too Comfortable

If you find it easy to make purchases when the market is way off, you may not be taking enough risk. As Jesse Livermore (1877–1940), a notable early twentieth-century stock trader, said:

> There are only two emotions in the market—hope and fear. The problem is, you hope when you should fear, and you fear when you should hope.

Myopia

We follow our equity investments too closely. Until the housing bubble burst, most people commonly made more money investing in their homes than investing in stocks. The reason is that stock prices are published daily; real estate is only priced when it is on the market, and even then, the asking prices are only optimistic approximations.

> **How the U.S. Army Improved My Investing Performance**
>
> In 1953 the Army ordered me to Korea. The day before I left, I took every cent I had—about $600—and bought odd-lot shares of what is now United Technologies and the Texas Oil Company, which became Texaco and is now part of Chevron. I didn't see a stock quote for a year. When I returned I found United Technologies had doubled. So I sold it, which was a mistake. It went on to triple. Texaco had gained about 50 percent, so I held it, and it, too, eventually doubled. I am certain that if I had stayed in the States and followed these stocks closely, I would have sold them far earlier than I did.

Because stocks have more volatility in the short run than in the long run, and thus more underwater periods in the short run, traders are more likely to sell out too soon.

Playing with the House's Money

This misconception is prevalent in gambling. Those of you who inhabit casinos know that sooner or later some gambler (usually at a slot machine) will explain to you that he can take greater risks because he is ahead. He no longer thinks he is playing with his own money. It's the house's money, and he doesn't have to be as careful with it. Wrong. Whether at a casino or in the equity market, think of what you are doing as one life-long venture. Today's gains will surely be needed to offset some future losses, or to recompense some long ago loss. Once you've won it, it's *your* money. It is no longer the house's.

Similarly, money is fungible and mentally segregating "baskets" of any nature can impair sound investing. For example, your regular investments and your IRA or 401(k) investments are both yours. Conceptually, they should be lumped together, certainly for purposes of determining risk.

Buying High and Selling Low

It's sometimes viewed as a beginner's mistake, but the truth is, buying high and selling low is a common occurrence. Many studies document that investors in a fund typically have smaller gains than the fund itself. These studies find that the higher the share price of the fund the more shares are bought, and the lower, the more shares are sold.

I used to follow this phenomenon in the Fidelity Sector funds. I found that many investors waited until there was a three-year positive performance record before investing. Unfortunately the growth cycle for many sectors is about three years, so most investors bought at or near the high.

The Fidelity Select Technology Fund had $491 million in assets in the beginning of 1997. In the raging bull market, investors poured money into tech stocks. By the end of 1999, the fund's assets had grown to $5.2 billion, with $1.8 billion of new money arriving in the final six months of the year. Even though the Dow peaked on January 14, 2000, new money continued to pour in for a few months, but unfortunately that was the last good year for some time. The fund lost 46.1 percent in the next three quarters while, incredibly, the fund's assets increased to $9.6 billion. Most investors failed to realize that the market had reached a turning point.

The lesson here is that in the difficult markets I foresee for the rest of this decade, the odds greatly favor investing primarily on weakness. By that I mean investing, preferably dollar-cost averaging, after a 5 to 10 percent correction. Conversely, you will be fighting the odds if you wait until after a significant run up to invest, even though that's emotionally far more comforting.

Take Your Emotional Outlook into Account

I once asked the president of a fund group his criteria for hiring portfolio managers. He told me that when he was hiring a manager for a growth fund, he looked for an optimist; and when he was hiring a value manager, he sought a pessimist.

Bull versus Bear Market Behavior

In a bull market, investors follow their stocks and funds avidly. Back in the 1990s at the height of the mania, many thousands of investors subscribed to several personal finance magazines and a dozen investment newsletters. As if that wasn't enough, they followed the markets closely on broadcast and the Internet.

To illustrate this preoccupation with the market during a mania, I want to tell you about the time that I was asked to speak at an adult education course at Iona, a small college in New Rochelle, New York. The small room in which I spoke was filled to capacity, including a few standees. About 30 people came to hear me. After my speech concluded, the program chairman enthusiastically congratulated me on the turnout. "Why, last week's speaker" she gushed, "drew only four people."

Mildly curious, I asked what his topic had been. I was told: "Sex after 60." You know you're in a mania when mutual funds outdraw sex seven to one.

In a bear market these same investors pull in their horns, cutting their informational intake to close to nothing and closing their eyes to ideas, new or old. This is a natural human inclination, especially during times of low confidence. I do it myself to some extent. In bad times, I tend not to be on the alert for new investments, in the same way that I am during a strong bull market. Yet, it's during bad times that the financial media can be of the most help. It may not be the same media that you listened to in good times. But it's a mistake to drop out completely. Even when stocks are doing poorly, there's almost always some other asset class that's performing well. The *Investor* did well with its large cash position between 2000 and 2002. But had we gone more into value funds as some other newsletters did, we might have done even better during this particular bear. Your portfolio doesn't drop to zero, and your interest in financial information shouldn't either. And to state the obvious: It's during *bad* times that you can find the most bargain investments.

Why Employees Overweight Their Own Company Shares

In an earlier chapter I commented on how employees frequently overweight their 401(k)s with their own company's stock. Unless you are lucky enough to work for the next Microsoft, Intel, or dot-com wonder, this is a serious mistake. The underlying reasons behind this error are usually psychological.

The following four points are adapted from an Internet article written by Elaine Scoggins, an investment advisor employed by Merriman, Inc., a Seattle-based wealth management firm.

For many people, selling company shares is the hardest investing decision they'll ever make. It's exceptionally hard because like so many aspects of investing, you can fall victim to mental and emotional traps. Here's what to watch out for:

1. **Rooting for the home team.** A company is like a sports team. Employees are proud believers who bring hard work and team spirit to a quest for winning. Not buying or selling company shares feels like betrayal and disloyalty. Being loyal to the company and the team is important. But so is being loyal to your own interests.

2. **Believing you know it all.** Longtime employees begin to believe that they can see the future of a company. They watch what goes on every day. They're the first to hear the marketing plans. They know the management team. They know whether revenue is growing or not. Most likely they fully believe in the product or service the company offers.

    Despite all that, nobody—not even the CEO—can be sure of accurately foreseeing the future of any company or industry. (Again, familiarity is not knowledge.)

3. **Believing stock analysts.** Employees may frequently exchange analyst reports about their company—especially those that predict that their stock will go through the roof. They might get so excited that they will calculate their future wealth, certain that the stock price will eventually hit the analysts' target. They began to feel richer than they are and start spending money they don't have. In all too many cases, the stock never comes close to the sky-high forecasts of the analysts, whose crystal balls turn out to be no better than those of the managers and executives.

4. **Looking in the rearview mirror.** For the employees who do sell their shares, there's another trap lying in wait. They may be in the habit of looking at the company's share price every day, and then continue doing that even after they sell. On days when the stock price falls, they feel brilliant. On days when it rises, they feel stupid for having sold. This is a guaranteed recipe for stress. Selling company stock isn't easy. But it's often necessary. When a single stock makes up a large part of your portfolio, selling even half of it can make a big difference to your future.

You Can Also Be Too Close to the Facts

Back when I was working for ABC, I owned about 50 shares of the stock. One day, a rumor swept through the company that ABC was about to lose its Proctor & Gamble business, which accounted for 10 percent of ABC's revenue at the time. I immediately sold my stock. The rumor turned out to be false; it never happened. What I should have done was immediately buy back the stock. I didn't do it, which was a huge mistake. Over the years the ABC stock did exceptionally well for the long-term investor.

Buying back a stock you have just sold is emotionally very difficult. But at times it should be done.

What Are Others Thinking?

In dealing with markets, it's not enough to know your own view; you have to consider what others are thinking. Here's an essay that is absolutely essential to absorb because in just a few words it gives you an essential insight into markets. It was written by John Maynard Keynes, the great English economist best known for his efforts to end the Great Depression. In addition, he was a very successful investor.

Keynes' Beauty Pageant Advice

Professional investment may be likened to those newspaper competitions in which the competitors have to pick out the six prettiest faces from a hundred photographs, the prize being awarded to the competitor whose choice most nearly corresponds to the average preferences of the competitors as a whole; so that each competitor has to pick, not those faces which he himself finds prettiest, but those which he thinks likeliest to catch the fancy of the other competitors, all of whom are looking at the problem from the same point of view. It is not a case of choosing those which, to the best of one's judgment, are really the prettiest, nor even those which average opinion genuinely thinks the prettiest. We have reached the third degree where we devote our intelligences to anticipating what average opinion expects the average opinion to be. And there are some, I believe, who practice the fourth, fifth, and higher degrees.

—*The General Theory of Employment, Interest, and Money,* John Maynard Keynes, 1936

This is sometimes called second level thinking. I've always believed that this is a basic insight into investing success, which the great portfolio managers of our time know in their guts.

Don't Let the Size of Your Portfolio Psych You

In talking to potential managed account clients I've noticed that many investors seem to be able to handle their investments with confidence as long as the size of their portfolio is under approximately $250,000. Over that amount many investors feel the responsibility is too great and seek professional guidance. I don't see the validity of this logic, although I do understand the psychology. If all an investor has is say $100,000, then that sum should be as important to him as a larger sum is to a wealthier investor. The reality is that the fundamentals of investing hold, no matter the size of the portfolio. The advice offered in this book applies equally to a $3,000 or a $3 million portfolio.

The standard line on Wall Street is that capital markets are so complicated and your financial circumstances so unique, you can't be trusted to manage your own money. You need a professional.

Do you really? With the education supplied by the media and a bit of discipline, you can run your portfolio yourself at a fraction of the cost of using a full-service broker.

And when you manage your own money, you don't have to worry about conflicts of interest, self-serving advice, or hidden fees and expenses. A broker has many clients but you have only one.

Greed

Greed has always been with us, but I think it's more harmful now because with today's media overload, the label has become much more common. The Oxford dictionary defines greed as an intense and selfish desire for something, especially wealth, power, or food. That's certainly true. As an investor I would suggest that you will gain valuable insights if you realize there are now two quite different uses of the word. First, there is greed as an emotion. Second, there is greed as a pejorative. The second meaning seems to be overwhelming the first.

Greed as an Emotion

As an emotion, greed makes people lose sight of risk, particularly during bubbles. It also lets them fall prey to crooks. In both cases, you begin to believe that you really can get something for nothing. You begin to invest irresponsibly.

Greed was certainly a major reason for the 2008 bear market. Professionals, including the people running Bear Sterns, Lehman Brothers, and Merrill Lynch, took on far more risk than was prudent. The riskier and riskier security products that they packaged were a major factor in creating the giant bubble. When this bubble finally burst, institutions and individuals alike suffered huge losses.

Greed lets you fall prey to crooks as the old saying, "You can't cheat an honest man" attests. There is a lot of truth to this old saw. Ponzi schemes wouldn't do as well as they do if this weren't true. But the classical definition of Greed is now being superseded.

Greed Clouds Your Thinking

The word greed is now mostly used as a pejorative and has become a handy whipping boy for all kinds of activities some think deplorable. The list of people and institutions that have been called greedy is long. Here's a sampling from my general reading over the last two-three years. Described as greedy are: Investment bankers, corporate executives, and bankers who took advantage of easy credit to grant mortgages that borrowers could not afford. The borrowers themselves. Wall Street executives who created dangerous financial derivatives. Big Oil (but only when prices are rising). Republicans when in office. Corporate self-interest. Capitalism. Governments. The SEC. AIG bonus recipients. Day-traders. Speculators. Business school graduates. House-flippers.

You get the idea. All these varied activities, some legal, a few illegal, have elicited charges of greed.

Greed on Wall Street

On March 27, 2008, then presidential candidate Barack Obama went to New York and blamed lobbyists, greedy businessmen, and complacent Washington politicians for creating "an ethic of greed" that led to the foreclosure crisis.

Yes, there are a lot of greedy people working on Wall Street. However, unlike the caring professions, a financial company endeavors to make as much money as possible for its executives, employees, shareholders, and even customers. The primary goal of financial firms has always been to maximize monetary profits.

Did Wall Street, lobbyists, and politicians become greedier in the 2000s? Are New York landlords, limited by rent control, greedier than small city landlords? No. Greed is a constant.

But clearly, something changed. What changed were the laws and regulations, and the invention of new financial products such as subprime mortgages and unregulated credit default swaps. It was the easier money made available by the Federal Reserve. It was the government-sponsored enterprises like Fannie Mae and Freddie Mac, which securitized mortgages that should never have been made in the first place. That's what changed.

If society changes the rules and morals to permit greater profits, people will strive for greater profits. The change is in the conditions and restraints under which society operates, not greed.

So, I must disagree with President Obama. Greed was not the cause of the 2008 financial implosion. The bankers' and financiers' desire for profits was just as intense in bygone days as it was in 2008. One might characterize this profiteering spirit as "greed." But, prior to the recent stock market bubble and economic meltdown, such greed was seldom an issue for the public.

Investors need to look for the real reasons. You wouldn't say that gravity was the cause of a plane crash, or the death of a person pushed out of a high window, although it certainly played a part.

I believe that investors feel better blaming the woes of the stock markets and the economy on greed. But that's not clear thinking. Blame it on bad policies that need to be understood and corrected, not excused. Realize that efforts to curb "greed," such as limiting corporate pay, are the wrong approach, and will never succeed. (That's because compensation specialists are smarter than politicians.) Ignore these solutions when you've made your investment decisions.

The point that the next box makes is that two of the three real life corporate raiders mentioned in the box went to jail because they broke the law, not because they were "greedy." All three probably could be characterized as greedy one way or another.

Wall Street's Real Life Role Models

In the 1987 movie, *Wall Street*, the lead character, Gordon Gekko (played by Michael Douglas), is claimed to be based loosely on arbitrageur Ivan Boesky, who mentioned greed in a commencement address at the University of California, Berkeley Business School in 1986. Another possible model is activist investor and corporate raider Carl Icahn. The film's producer also says that the character is partly based on junk bond king Michael Milken.

Boesky was investigated by the SEC for making investments based on tips received from corporate insiders. He received a prison sentence of 3.5 years and was fined $100 million. Although he was released after two years, he was barred from working in the securities business for the remainder of his life. Milken was indicted on 98 counts of racketeering and fraud in 1989. He was sentenced to 10 years in prison, but was released after less than two years, and also banned from the securities business.

For the record, here's what Boesky said at Berkeley: "I think greed is healthy. . . . You can be greedy and still feel good about yourself."

Now that we've dissected the deadly sin of greed, we should acknowledge that the other six deadly sins—lust, gluttony, sloth, wrath, envy, and pride—can also hamper your investing success. It's not easy to act dispassionately—but try.

Important Lessons in This Chapter

- Ignorance of yourself is more costly than ignorance of the markets.
- Understand the psychology underlying many of your investment decisions.
- Know your weaknesses and work around them.
- You may not agree with all of my advice. But if what I have written makes you step back and think, then this book will have served a useful purpose.
- Do something. Hope is not a strategy.

15

Integrity, or the Lack of It

Understanding the mechanics and strategies of investing is only part of what it takes to make a good investor. Knowing who to work with is vital.

Unfortunately, there are people who go into the investment business for the same reason that Willie Sutton is said to have robbed banks. *That's where the money is.* (Actually, this famous quote came from a reporter who put it in Sutton's mouth.)

The amount of money that can be made by financial executives is phenomenal. According to John Bogle, stock brokers, fund executives, money managers, hedge fund proprietors, plus their lawyers, accountants, marketers, and advertisers are collectively paid about $530 billion a year for moving capital around. If you are lucky enough to work for one of the most lucrative firms, you can do very well as an average employee. Goldman Sachs, at the top of the list, has 36,000 employees. Their *average* total compensation in 2010 was $232,000. With this kind of remuneration, there should be no excuse whatsoever for investment professionals putting their own profit motives ahead of their customers' interests.

Sadly, too many people working on Wall Street did not put their small customers first during the recent heady days. And that includes such major firms as Merrill Lynch, Citigroup, and Bank of America.

If you're a client of any investment advisor, whether it is a personal financial advisor, a publication, or a mutual fund, you have a right to be treated with absolute integrity. I'm not talking about being involved with financial executives who are obvious crooks. You should obviously stay miles away from that sort of person.

I mean it's important to deal with people who conduct their businesses with honesty and who put the welfare of their customers first. And that includes not extracting the last buck from them. It also means dealing with advisors who put the interests of their current clients ahead of acquiring new ones.

Of course it's easy to advise investors to deal only with honest companies and individuals, but that's not exactly practical advice. There's no easy and foolproof way to identify unsavory people. Fortunately, the vast majority of those in the financial business are reasonably honest. Then, there are a few that are at the extremes—either exceptionally honest or outright dishonest. Their stories can give you a feel for the type of advisor you should work with.

I believe that mutual funds put their shareholders' interests up front more than any other kind of financial firm—for three reasons. One is that funds are closely regulated under the Investment Company Act of 1940, a law that carefully details what funds can or cannot do.

Second, the industry, which appeals to small investors more than do other kinds of financial firms, realizes it's in the companies' best interest to treat small investors as well as possible. Complaints or lawsuits can ruin reputations. Referrals from satisfied clients can help to grow great and valuable brands like Vanguard, Fidelity, American Century, T. Rowe Price, Gabelli, Baron, Royce, Ariel, and many others.

Finally, the industry is blessed to have a trade organization, the Investment Company Institute (ICI), that believes looking out for Mom and Pop shareholders is simply good business. The ICI has said that it actually enjoys being regulated by the SEC because that helps to insure the mutual fund industry's reputation for integrity.

How the ICI Fought the Banks—and Won

Here's a story of how the ICI came to the rescue of small investors.

Money market mutual funds were invented in 1971 at a time when money market rates topped 8 percent. Banks, limited by law, then paid only 4 percent. As a result, the banks were bleeding massive amounts of money, which was going to the brand new money funds. The banks fought ferociously to retain these assets, inducing their allies in many state legislators to propose laws limiting the amount of interest that money funds could pay. The ICI met the banks head on. Wherever hearings on the money fund rates were held, the ICI lawyers brought their own witnesses to the hearings to rebut the banks' attempts to reduce competition.

In one case, in the Utah legislature, one of ICI's witnesses was a retired teacher. She was one of those teachers that we all pray we have when we (or our children) are in school. The kind you write heartwarming books and movies about. As this particular former teacher sat on the witness stand, she looked out over the sea of Utah legislators and recognized a half-dozen that had once been her pupils. She testified that the 8 percent interest she was getting from a money fund made a crucial difference to her well-being— real food versus dog food, so to speak. The banks' monopoly proposal was defeated.

The same thing happened in 23 other states. The ICI never lost once! And because of this long ago battle, to this day money funds pay market rates, minus modest expenses—and there are no longer any caps on the rates banks can pay. Savers: Thank the ICI for that.

The Mutual Fund "Market Timing" Scandal

In 2003, there was a rare scandal in the fund industry when several fund groups were found guilty of what was called "market timing" (a misnomer in my opinion). In essence, they were letting hedge funds place big daily orders to buy or sell (often on preferential terms) that were detrimental and costly to long-term investors in the same funds. The offenders were severely punished with fines and exposed to terrible publicity. For the most part, shareholder losses in the affected funds were small. The affected shareholders at Janus (one of the two major no-load groups affected; the other being Strong) had an average loss of $4 and pursuant to an SEC Distribution Plan were reimbursed $20. In terms of modern financial scandals (for example, Enron or the subprime mortgage meltdown) that is very small potatoes. An unscrupulous broker or advisor can easily take a client for hundreds of thousands of dollars. They've done it many times.

A Personal Reimbursement

On November 19, 2010, out of the blue, I received a check in the amount of $299.11 from something called the "Fair Fund," which had been established by the SEC in connection with Strong Capital Management market timing activity. I had been identified as a Strong shareholder between 1998 and 2000. This came as a total surprise to me: I had sold the fund at a profit in early 2000. I had no idea the profit should have been a few hundred larger.

In order to explain what you should look for when seeking honest people, I'd like to profile four exceptionally honest men.

John Bogle

John Bogle, the founder of Vanguard, is renowned in the mutual fund industry for his integrity. In fact, some call him "Saint John." He has earned this reputation, in part, by championing the rights of the mutual fund shareholder for 60 years—and he's still at it.

Unique among all mutual fund groups, Bogle organized Vanguard as a mutual company owned by its shareholders. Consequently, his salary is a fraction of what it would be if he were a true owner like his peers at other major mutual funds. He has proven that integrity can be profitable. Vanguard is now the largest fund group in the industry.

In 2007, Bogle was interviewed by an analyst from Morningstar. Here's how he responded to two of the questions submitted by the analyst. His answers offer real insight into what you should look for when investing in a mutual fund.

Q: **What other fund companies do you admire, and why?**

Bogle: The Vanguard competitors I most admire are TIAA-CREF, Dodge and Cox, Nicholas, and the Capital Group (but own only if you can sharply minimize the impact of their sales loads). Why do I admire them?

1. Management character and integrity. For me, that's where everything begins.
2. Intelligent long-term investment strategies.
3. Clearly defined fund objectives and policies.
4. Consistent returns vs. their peers.
5. Low portfolio turnover.
6. High tax-efficiency.
7. Reasonable expense ratios (mostly below 0.75 percent . . . but I hope they're working to get them lower!)

    It's sort of discouraging that, with some 100-plus competitors out there, I can only think of four that meet these standards. But more will come forth as investors become more discriminating.

Q: **What is the biggest challenge facing the fund industry right now?**

Bogle: The biggest challenges are:
1. Getting our own house in order. We've failed to deliver to our shareholders a fair participation in market returns, largely because of excessive costs, insane (and tax-devastating) rates of portfolio turnover, and an inadequate corporate governance system.
2. Deflating investor expectations, borne of the Great Bull Market, of high future returns.
3. Returning to our roots as investment managers and stewards of our shareholders, and abandoning our self-appointed mission as product marketers and opportunists.

For the record, Bogle is harsher on the fund industry than I am.

I would add one thing to Bogle's comments. Read the letters from management in the annual reports and note their clarity and candor. If a fund has had a bad year, is management candid about it? Or do they try to whitewash poor performance with platitudes?

Now, I'd like to switch gears and talk about a man who revolutionized the financial newsletter industry.

Mark Hulbert

When I first started publishing *The No-Load Fund Investor* newsletter in 1979, I was somewhat ashamed to be in the newsletter industry. Back then, the standards were pretty low. The direct mail advertising, upon which the industry relies for subscribers, was filled with misrepresentations. A lot of the editorial content wasn't much better.

I will always remember one newsletter editor who would write something like this one month: "The market will go up unless it goes down." The next month, his lead paragraph invariably started like this: "As I correctly predicted last month . . ."

Back then newsletter editors quite commonly boasted about their winning recommendations and ignored their losing ones. Sell recommendations were often obscure.

All this began to change in 1980 when a new force came on the newsletter scene: Mark Hulbert. He launched a newsletter called the *Hulbert Financial Digest*, whose mission was to rate the performance of other newsletters. He set up exacting standards to calculate the performance of all the major financial newsletters. He encouraged newsletter editors to make their recommendations in easy-to-follow model portfolios rather than just in text.

Why did he do this? When recommendations are made in copy, there is a tendency to make a big splash about them initially. But then, if the recommendation doesn't pan out, the newsletter can conveniently forget about it, rather than issuing a clearly defined sell recommendation. When recommendations are published in a continuously updated model portfolio, it's impossible to bury them.

Hulbert also established clear guidelines for rating those newsletters that made their recommendations in copy. Generally he constructed model portfolios of just those recommendations the newsletter rated most highly.

Hulbert had two ways to force his standards on the industry:

1. He paid for a subscription to every newsletter that he rated, and furthermore, he put these subscriptions in blind names so poorly performing newsletters couldn't cancel them to deny him data.
2. He wrote a regular column in *Forbes* magazine for many years sometimes using his column to expose newsletters that engaged in false advertising. His income comes from investor subscriptions for the HFD newsletter. He takes no money from the industry.

Needless to say, Hulbert made a lot of enemies in the industry. The bad apples complained loudly about his rules and standards, but even upright newsletters had differences of opinions regarding his methodology. For example, if a newsletter downgraded an in-copy buy recommendation to a lesser category (like hold), Hulbert might have considered that a sell recommendation. The newsletter might not have.

I had occasional differences with Hulbert, but I respected him because his points of view were honestly held. He is not a vindictive person and never used the power of his *Forbes* columns to unscrupulously attack anyone.

In part because of Hulbert's leadership, the newsletter industry now is nothing at all like it was 30 years ago. Miscreants are rare today.

Very few people can come into an established industry as an outsider, write their own rules for the industry, and then enforce those rules to substantially improve it. Hulbert did. As a result, I can say that I am now proud to have been a newsletter publisher.

Thank you, Mark.

Chuck Schwab

One sign of integrity is keeping your word—even if it costs you big bucks.

In November of 1981 Charles Schwab negotiated the sale of his company, Charles Schwab and Co., Inc., to Bank of America. Payment to the privately held Schwab brokerage house was 2.2 million shares of Bank of America stock, then worth $53 million.

It took quite some time to complete the deal, partly because Federal Reserve approval was required for a bank to buy a brokerage firm. By the fall of 1982, the deal still had not closed, yet the situation was quite different. Bank of America's stock had dropped from 26½ to 19½ because of the tight-money period engineered by Fed Chairman Paul Volcker. As a result, the value of the B of A stock to be received by Schwab at closure had declined to $43 million.

At the same time, Schwab's business was booming because a new secular bull market had begun a few months earlier. So, Chuck Schwab was a substantial loser big time on both ends of his deal, and the Federal Reserve still hadn't approved the merger.

It was in this climate that a Schwab executive went to Chuck Schwab and told him that he felt there was a clause in the contract that would allow Schwab to get out of the deal. But Chuck would have none of it. He told this employee that a deal was a deal, and he would not back out of it. And he didn't.

Finally, in January 1983, the Federal Reserve approved the merger, and Charles Schwab became part of Bank of America. The only bright spot in the deal was that Bank of America made an adjustment in the purchase price, giving Schwab an additional 400,000 shares, thus bringing the value back to approximately the one that was originally negotiated.

But it was still a very bad deal for Schwab. The firm's value had soared in the now ongoing bull market. Matters came to a head four years later, when in July of 1987, Schwab repurchased his company from Bank of America, paying $280 million in a management-led buyout. Sticking to the deal had cost the company $227 million. That was the price of integrity. (Chuck Schwab was not the sole owner. Other executives and institutions also owned shares, but he was the largest shareholder.)

I know some readers are going to think, what's the big deal about living up to the terms of an agreement? Don't most businessmen abide by the contracts they negotiate? Well, maybe. But remember that this writer spent a quarter of a century in the entertainment business. Integrity was certainly not always in evidence there—particularly in Hollywood.

In show business, it wasn't unusual for contracts to be rewritten if circumstances had changed. For example, if a TV show bombed, it was cancelled. Whether the network compensated the production studio for the episodes contracted for but never produced depended to a great extent on "leverage," that is, who needed whom the most, and not the terms of the original contract. Similarly, if an unknown actor suddenly became a big star and asked for a raise, the producers were open to negotiations, no matter what the contract said. Back in 1983 and again in 2010, Jay Leno said "NBC stands for Never Believe your Contract."

These were written contracts. If the contract was verbal, it meant even less than it did in Hollywood's heyday when Samuel Goldwyn was reputed to have said, "A verbal contract isn't worth the paper it's written on."

Another reason I respect Charles Schwab is for an article he wrote for *The Wall Street Journal's* Op-Ed page in March 2010, which criticized the Federal Reserve's policy of maintaining excessively low interest rates. He rightly pointed out that these low rates were starving seniors living on fixed-income investments. Yes, everybody knew and still knows that, but Chuck made the case.

I was very impressed with Chuck Schwab's integrity.

One thing I've noticed about corporations, even the very largest ones, is that the values of the founder set the tone for the entire organization—even when he has gone.

A number of years later, I chose Charles Schwab to administer my BJ Group's $600 million in client assets. We were always treated fairly.

In 2010, Charles Schwab had over $600 *billion* in custody for more than 6,000 independent advisors.

Robert L. Rodriguez

I've never had the pleasure of meeting Robert Rodriquez, and given that he is associated with a load fund group, he works in another world from me. Nevertheless I was greatly impressed by some comments he made during a speech he delivered at the annual Morningstar conference in 2009. He exemplifies the kind of integrity you like to see in a money manager. Here's part of his speech:

> I have always maintained my professional and personal integrity. I have never wavered, despite having paid some very high prices. It seems as though it was a lifetime ago in 1986, when I had few assets under management, and the consultant to my largest account insisted that, if I wanted to continue the relationship, I had to pay to play. I was shocked, dismayed, and speechless. Though this would probably have never become public, if I had agreed, how would I have ever lived with myself? By not agreeing, it meant that I would lose nearly 40 percent of my business. When I was fired shortly thereafter, this termination compromised my efforts in the raising of new money for nearly six years because I could not say why. Despite the pain and humiliation, there was no price high enough for me to compromise my integrity. With the subsequent disclosures of improprieties at this municipal pension plan, the cloud of suspicion over me ultimately lifted. I not only survived, I prospered.

Robert Rodriguez, with 39 years in the investment business, was the long-time manager of the FPA Capital and FPA New Income funds. He spent 2010 on a sabbatical, and is now back at FPA in a supervisory position.

Integrity in the Media

I think the need for integrity is even greater in the media than in other fields. Yes, it's a very competitive industry, and success is measured by the ability to find an audience, but there is a distinction between enlightening an audience and pandering to it to enhance profits. The job of a journalist is to report news and information with accuracy and integrity, not to promote private agendas.

I realize my view of media integrity will strike many of my colleagues as unrealistic. But it's what I've tried to do throughout my career.

I've always practiced what I preach. I have never overemphasized recommendations even though I know that's what sells investment publications. I have always hewed to no-loads, avoiding higher cost investments that might deliver greater profits, at least temporarily. My advertising never promised more than I could deliver. When I managed money, I never accepted the totally legitimate 12b-1 fees from the mutual funds because I thought they might bias our recommendations. That policy cost me a tidy sum.

This book has no get-rich quick schemes. It is light on recommendations and offers no novel investment strategies to excite you. I simply tried to make my advice as sound as I could. That's always been my way. In 25 years I've never had to apologize to a subscriber for anything I wrote.

A writer's job is to tell the truth.

—Andy Rooney, in his final
appearance on CBS's *60 Minutes*

How to Go from Best to Worst in Five Years

On the opposite end of the spectrum from Bogle, Hulbert, and Schwab is the saga of the 44 Wall Street Fund, whose rise and decline is unparalleled in mutual fund history.

From 1975 to 1980, it was the top-performing fund in America. The next five years it became the worst performing fund in America, experiencing a cumulative loss of 52 percent. In 1984 alone it lost 59.6 percent. That was a year in which the average stock fund lost 0.7 percent and the S&P 500 gained 1.3 percent. And still its losses continued. Over the entire decade of the 1980s, the fund's cumulative loss grew to 73 percent.

How could this have happened? The fund had the same portfolio manager, David H. Baker, Jr., for the whole period. How could Baker, who did so well in the 1970s, totally lose it in the 1980s?

I searched for the answer for years. Then one day by accident I ran across a woman who may have had at least a partial answer. I met her at a business cocktail party. In talking to her, I discovered she had once been David Baker's personal secretary. I immediately asked what had happened.

Her response was that Baker had become attached to four different women, and was spending all his time with them. To complicate matters, the four were in four different cities: New York, Washington, DC, the Bahamas, and either Boston or Miami. That didn't leave a lot of time for managing the 44 Wall Street Fund. She went on tell me that, in addition, whichever one he was with, he, and she too, then had to spend additional time mollifying the other three. There may be more to the story, but I doubt if any outsider will uncover it.

Was that the primary reason for the abysmal performance? I'll never know for sure, but in my opinion David Baker exhibited a total lack of integrity. He badly hurt his shareholders, who had entrusted their money to him in good faith on the basis of his 1970s track record.

Sometime in the late 1980s, *Barron's* did an article on Baker that generated some of the most heartrending letters to the editor I have ever read. One in particular said he saw the money he had put aside for his child's college education go down the drain. He plaintively asked why he didn't have any recourse.

The fund is no longer in existence. It was merged into another fund in 1993.

I Don't Know

Have you ever noticed how unusual it is for somebody in the public eye to say, "I don't know"? It's almost unheard of. The reason is that people seem to believe that if you want to present yourself as an expert you need to be all knowing. That's particularly true of a guru who is asked for forecasts.

Unfortunately, there is much truth to this belief. Gurus who are able to convince their audience that they are omniscient will generally make more money than those who don't claim to be all knowing, at least for a while.

I will always remember that a number of years ago, there was a very self-confident economist who said, on TV no less, "I'm often in error, but seldom in doubt." He knew exactly what he was saying, and the media constantly sought him out. They knew he made mistakes, but they loved his forceful tone.

I've never been afraid to say I don't know. There have been many occasions when, in the course of being interviewed or simply taking questions at the conclusion of a speech, I was asked something I didn't know.

If I don't know, I say it. Has it hurt me? Probably. But that's the way I am.

In my case, most of my I-don't-knows are in response to questions about specific sector funds. There are more than 40 different industry sectors that can be bought through mutual funds. Why anybody would expect me (or anybody else) to be knowledgeable about that many industries is beyond me. Big research organizations employ large numbers of analysts, many of whom focus exclusively on the market's narrowest niches. Fidelity Investments has more than 500 analysts. Morningstar, best known for its fund research, employs 120 *stock* analysts.

I am just one person, and I've always worked hardest at trying to understand the big picture, not the pieces.

I think saying "I don't know" has added to my credibility, particularly when I was being interviewed by the press, which happened frequently during the bull market years. I also thought that not admitting what you don't know can lead to suspicions about what you do know.

How do you find an honest advisor? One test is whether he admits not knowing.

Moreover, if you don't know what somebody is saying, don't be afraid to ask. There have been numerous times when I was in an audience and didn't understand the speaker's point. Even though I am sure many others in the audience had understood, I would stand up and ask for clarification. I believed it was more important for me to understand than to appear smart. And I have never cared what others in the audience thought of me.

I Was Wrong

The step beyond admitting you don't know is admitting you were wrong. Pros are good. But there is a pronounced tendency for them to do a lot of fancy tap dancing when forced to own up to a poor forecast or recommendation.

One of the most grievous forecasts ever—in a book title no less—was the 1999 book, *Dow 36,000: The New Strategy for Profiting from the Coming Rise in the Stock Market* by James K. Glassman and Kevin A. Hassett.

On February 24, 2011, James K. Glassman wrote an article for *The Wall Street Journal* titled "Why I Was Wrong About 'Dow 36,000.'" I've met James Glassman. I like James Glassman. I read his column in *Kiplinger's* regularly.

September 2008 addendum: Kevin Hassett, co-author of *Dow 36,000*, later became an economics advisor to the Republican presidential candidate, Senator John McCain.

Important Lessons in This Chapter

- It's your money. Safeguard it to the best of your ability by dealing only with people or institutions you are certain are honest. Give the fast talkers, cold callers and tall taletellers short shrift.

CHAPTER 16

Women Aren't Different; They Just Live Longer

Here's a diehard truth: It's more important for women to be good investors than men. That's because women live longer, typically earn less, and spend fewer years in the workforce. A surprising 80 percent of men die married whereas 80 percent of women die single.

So women have the greater need for investment income. Yet, all too often, they are significantly poorer at investing than men. Consequently, women over the age of 65 are a whopping twice as likely to live out their golden years in poverty than men.

In this chapter I am going to try to get behind the averages. That's because some women are among the best investors and financial pros you will ever see, and others are the worst.

Let's talk about the best. A number of women are (or were) outstanding financial writers. A few who come quickly to mind are Jane Bryant Quinn, Terry Savage, Nancy Dunnan, Mary Rowland, Grace Weinstein, and the late Sylvia Porter. Successful newsletter editors and publishers include Janet Brown, Chloe Lutts, and Mary Anne and Pamela Aden.

Among women who have made successful careers discussing money and financial topics on TV, Suze Orman, Consuelo Mack, Maria Bartiromo, and Sue Herera are on CNBC; Gerri Willis on Fox Business, who covers business news in terms of how it affects viewers' finances, and many others. All of the personal finance magazines and many newspapers employ outstanding female writers.

> 80 percent of men die married whereas 80 percent of women die single.

Barron's publishes an annual list of top 100 women financial advisors. The rankings are culled by *Barron's* from more than 400 nominations. In 2011, the women advisors, mostly hailing from large brokerage houses, managed big accounts that averaged about $14 million. Their clients had a typical net worth of $50 million. And they do a good job. Proof: They retained 98 percent of their clients from the previous year.

Women have held executive positions on Wall Street as far back as the 1920s. Muriel Siebert had her own firm and her own seat on the NYSE. Julia Walsh had her own company, a seat on the Exchange, was on the Board of Directors of AMEX, and was a regular panelist on Wall Street Week. Abby Joseph Cohen is the market face of Goldman Sachs. Mary Callahan Erdoes is the chief executive of JP Morgan Asset Management, the fifth biggest asset management company in the world.

When Bob Brinker and I started the BJ Group to manage money for clients, I was initially the chief investment officer. Over time, the company grew too large for me to handle this demanding job and still do justice to my newsletter.

At that time, we had four account executives reporting to Bob and me, three men and one woman. We wanted to promote one of them to my job and of the four, the woman, Joan Guccione, was the best. She merited the job and did it well for many years. Clients loved her intelligent handling of their portfolios.

One academic study found that on average there is no detectable difference in performance between mutual funds run by men and funds managed by women. Another study conducted in 2001 found that women investors did a third less trading than their male counterparts, and consequently performed 1.4 percent better.

There is, unfortunately, the other side. Women can also be some of the worst and unknowledgeable of investors. I have known women who refuse to learn the difference between stocks and bonds. It has nothing to do with brains. To a great extent, I think it's because most women were not brought up on the fundamentals of personal finance. In a 2006 survey commissioned by Allianz Insurance, 90 percent of women who participated rated themselves as feeling insecure when it came to their finances. Thus, perhaps they are more likely to trust "experts" and let themselves be taken advantage of by the unscrupulous ones.

Profiles in Success

I am going to profile five people, one man and four women, to illustrate that there is no reason why women can't invest as competently as men.

Michael Levy

I had a firsthand look at how women invest courtesy of a remarkable man, Michael Levy, who decided to enrich his retirement years by teaching women about money. Michael, a former insurance company executive, taught an adult education course of his own creation in Tenafly, New Jersey, a suburb of New York City.

He called the course "Women and Money." In the course of a semester, he covered everything from stocks and mutual funds to insurance, wills, and divorce. He became a father confessor to many of the women in the class, and spent hours helping them with their financial problems, and in a few cases, their divorces.

Mike subscribed to more than 50 financial publications in order to prepare himself for the class. That's how he found me. He then prevailed upon me to teach his class once a semester, on mutual funds night.

When I taught in Tenafly, Mike was always telling me stories about how this or that woman had been cheated by a broker or advisor. One woman in the class had been cheated so badly that her story was profiled in a major *New York Times* article.

So, when I taught Mike's class, I really got down to basics. It was frightening how little some of the women knew. But these women had a thirst for knowledge and diligently attended class every week without fail. They learned a lot. Gradually, over the semester, their questions became sharper, their knowledge deeper, and they began to understand the psychological underpinnings of investing.

Michael passed away in 2006 at age 92. He had continued to teach the class until he was 91. He never received a cent for his many years of work, and he regularly went in the hole buying instructional materials for the class out of his own pocket. But he always told me that the joy he felt from teaching these women added years to his life.

Unfortunately, there are many women investors like those in Mike's classes. I run across them every day. When a woman asks me what I do with my time, I tell her I am writing a book on investing. All too often, the response is that this is a subject she doesn't understand. (Men never respond that way.) These women aren't kidding. Some don't even have the foggiest notion of the interest rates on their credit card debt. Many have husbands who take care of bill-paying, investing, and all household financial affairs. Not knowing any of this, they just aren't wary enough of financial advisors, particularly those who are glib and personable. As a result, they get taken, frequently. If they handled their own financial affairs, or understood basic personal finance, they could stand up to these people. They don't have to be brilliant about money they just need to know the basics. Come on, women, you can do it.

Let me conclude with stories about four women who had real financial savvy. The first woman apparently acquired it when she was about to come into money, the second learned it at a very early age, the third developed it out of necessity later in life, and the fourth learned it on the job.

Not Taking Good Advice, or How I Really Blew It

We all have a story about the stock we should have bought, but didn't. My story is better than yours.

Back in the mid-1960s, I went back to Deadwood to visit my parents. At the end of the trip, my father drove me to the Rapid City airport for the trip back to New York.

At the airport, my dad spotted a woman on the other side of the small waiting room. He told me she was into something very big, and I should meet her. Dad took me over, introduced us, and we boarded the plane together.

As soon as we had taken off, I asked her what she was into, and learned that she and her husband owned the McDonald's franchise in Rapid City, South Dakota. For one solid hour, all the way from Rapid City to Minneapolis, this woman raved about McDonald's and explained very knowledgeably how successful the company was and how terrific their franchise operation was. It wasn't only the arches that were golden, she said.

For reasons I no longer remember, I never bought the stock. As the years went by, I realized the enormity of my mistake. (McDonald's went public in 1965. A hundred shares of stock costing $2,250 that day would have multiplied into 74,360 shares, worth approximately $3.3 million, by December of 2006.)

Perhaps a decade later, I mentioned this encounter to my father, saying how sorry I was to have ignored the woman's advice.

Dad gave me a very quizzical look, and asked if I knew what had happened to that woman. I told him that I had no idea, and in fact didn't even remember her name.

"Well," he informed me, "That woman divorced her husband and married Ray Kroc."

Joan Kroc, who had married the architect of the McDonald's empire in 1969, went on to become one of America's greatest philanthropists. She died in 2003, a multi-billionaire. She owned the San Diego Padres among other properties. In her will, her bequests included $1.6 billion to the Salvation Army and more than $200 million to National Public Radio.

I had to admire her. She knew hamburgers, business, and she certainly knew how to go for the gold.

And me? All I got out of it was this story, which I must say has been a mainstay of my speeches for many years now.

One final note: Being a two-career person myself, I found it most interesting to learn that her first career was music. She was playing piano in a bar in Saint Paul, Minnesota when she first met Ray Kroc. She apparently acquired her business savvy when she and her first husband ran the McDonald's franchise.

Surmounting Adversity

Connie Austin wasn't a celebrity like Joan Kroc, but in her own way her story is just as important. Connie was a dear personal friend of long standing. I first met her when she was an infant in a baby carriage. I mean this literally.

She grew up in Deadwood, moved to Orlando, Florida, married, had one child and adopted another. Because her husband commuted to work by private plane, he protected his family with a large life insurance policy.

Tragically, the worst happened, and Connie found herself widowed with young children. But thanks to the insurance, she didn't have money worries. She took the insurance money, invested it wisely in commercial real estate and stocks, and also bought a wholesale battery company to run herself.

Within the space of about four years, she had tripled her wealth, even after her considerable living expenses.

I asked her how she had done it. First, she told me she had bought the battery company because "dirty businesses make money." But, she explained, the real reason was her upbringing. She was the older of two girls. Her father, the owner of a Ben Franklin five-and-dime store in Deadwood (and a Harvard MBA), didn't have any sons. So he talked business with her, as he would have done with a son.

I think the lesson in Connie's story is that it's never too early for parents to begin discussing money matters with their daughters, who will need this knowledge in the modern world every bit as much as their sons will.

Westchester County, an affluent suburb of New York City, where I have lived a good part of my life, is filled with women who have rich husbands. Once their children are grown, they need a way to occupy their time, so many own "life-style" businesses, like a village cheese store, a knick-knack store, or a consulting firm, that sort of thing. Most don't make much money, but they aren't in it for the money. They are happy with their "clean" businesses. They get some prestige, nobody knows how much money they make or don't make, their husbands may get a tax write-off, and they get out of the house in the daytime.

They should all take a cue from Connie.

Make the Effort

A number of years ago I received a letter from the widow of a close friend. She wrote in part:

> Well Sheldon, it is almost six years since Harry died. As a result of his death I had to become a real adult and take charge of my life. It has been a long journey, but I am proud of myself, and more self-confident. In the process of growing up, I discovered that I had to take full responsibility for my estate, so I began to read the business sections of the newspapers and to study the language. My son Andrew was my coach. After a lot of patiently explaining the concepts to me, I finally understand why bonds go down in price when interest rates go up, or . . . is it the other way around?
>
> —*Lucy*

My friend was joking. She's a smart person who now lives a well-ordered life. But she is typical of many women who only relate to money when they are forced to.

Lucy's story shows that it's never too late for women to learn business and financial acumen, if given a chance.

Maria Bartiromo—A Self-Taught Pro

Maria Bartiromo has been a star on-air anchor on CNBC since 1993. Before that she spent five years working for the now defunct CNN Business News network. Nicknamed the "Money Honey" due to her striking looks, she was the first woman to report live from the floor of the New York Stock Exchange. She has written three books on financial topics. I am including her in this chapter because she is essentially self-taught. Here's how she related her path to financial expertise in her book, *Use the News* (HarperBusiness 2001, 2002).

> Learning how the market works isn't brain surgery. I'm living proof of that. I'm hardly a mathematics whiz. In fact a couple years ago, I ran into my high school math teacher and she said, "I can't believe you cover finance."
>
> I never took any classes in Wall Street 101, either. I learned it from the ground up. Okay, in my sophomore year at New York University, I took an introductory course in economics . . . where I learned about the relationship between supply and demand and the difference between macroeconomics and microeconomics. Big deal. You don't learn how markets move in school. You learn that by following the markets and watching trends. In my case I learned it on the job.
>
> Some people think they need to learn million-dollar theories and use fancy jargon to understand investing. They think there's a special club with a secret handshake that they have to be a member of to understand the significance of earnings expectations and price-to-earnings (P/E) ratios.
>
> I taught myself about the financial markets, and in my experience it really comes down to common sense and doing your homework . . .
>
> I know what you're going to say. You're going to say, "But, Maria, this is your job. It's different for you." I'll admit, it's different because I do this every day. That means that I've got access to contacts who might not be available to ordinary investors. I know where to go to dig up the information I need . . .

But much of that information is now available to you. Today individual investors can access much of the same information that professionals do.

If Maria could learn stocks, pretty much on her own, you can learn the far simpler tasks of investing in professionally assembled portfolios.

These four women all became financially adept. Don't ever think you can't do it. When you take charge of your money, you're in the driver's seat for life.

I've touched on the incredibly important psychological aspects of how women invest. A far better discussion of this can be found in the first five chapters of Suze Orman's bestseller, *Women & Money*. If you are a woman who has trouble relating to investing and finances, I urge you to read those chapters.

Important Lessons in This Chapter

- Managing finances is a trait anybody can learn; all you need is a "can-do" attitude.

17

Adventures in Collectibles

The most important point to understand about collectibles is that, no surprise, the law of supply and demand governs their prices. In this respect, they are no different than any other commodity or investment. In my earlier description of the five levels of risk, I noted that collectibles fell in the riskiest category. They are only worth what a buyer will pay for them. That's why the baseball hit by Barry Bonds in his all-time home run record sold for $752,467, and why John F. Kennedy's rocking chair went for $415,000. The demand for this particular baseball, or this particular rocking chair, was great. Supply was limited to "one."

Even when the supply is greater than one, there can be huge differences in the selling prices. In December of 2007, one of the most famously flawed stamps in U.S. history—the 1918 airmail depicting an upside-down Curtis JN-4 biplane—was sold for $825,000. A month earlier, another "Jenny," as it is known, sold for $977,500. Condition was not a factor in explaining the whopping $152,500 difference. The probable reason for the disparity: The first stamp was sold at auction; the second stamp was sold privately.

The bad news is that supply often exceeds demand. There are many collectibles not demanded by anybody, in which case they have no market value. They may even be hard to give away.

A lot of collectors lose sight of this. Some tend to collect what is in the public eye at the moment. That's not the way to make money because it's a cliché that when everyone knows it's a "collectible," the game is over. In 2006, I read that space mission memorabilia, vintage compacts, and Nouveau & Art Deco table lamps were hot, and that collecting postcards has become the third most popular hobby in the United States after stamps and coins. (I've heard nothing about them since.)

Collecting what is in the public eye may enhance your pleasure but it is usually not the way to make a profit. Without knowing anything about the above collectibles, my first impulse would be to avoid them. Barack Obama inaugural memorabilia may be a meaningful souvenir, but it will be decades before it will have any significant resale value.

If you're interested in pursuing collectibles for profit, you should answer three hard questions:

1. Will your collectibles appreciate over time?
2. Will there be a resale market?
3. How transparent is that resale market?

Take transparency: For a number of years now, there have been auctions of rare, costly, and ancient watches. They have sold for astronomical prices; some for over a million dollars. But it turns out that in some cases, it was the watchmakers themselves, such as Patek Philippe, that were buying back their own watches at top dollar. This "secondary market" buying helped their watches gain reputations as things of great value, which tended to raise retail prices in general, and allowed them to introduce pricier models.

It's usually better to forget about making money at all. Just collect things you love. If they become valuable later on, consider that a nice, albeit unanticipated, bonus.

However, some collectibles are so ingrained in our culture that they will never become completely worthless. Stamps, coins, and art come to mind. But even for these standards, which develop new collectors each year, profitability is still governed by the law of supply and demand.

When investing in collectibles, collect things you love. If they become valuable later on, consider that a nice bonus.

Why I No Longer Collect Stamps

Take stamps. Like a lot of kids, I started a stamp collection while still in grade school. But back in those days, the government wasn't trying to make a profit on collectors the way it does now. By and large, the Post Office only printed enough stamps to meet demand.

That's not true today. In 2011 the U.S. Post Office issued 116 different stamps including stamps honoring Gregory Peck and Helen Hayes. The print runs for these commemoratives ran from 40 to 100 million stamps.

But that's nothing. The Elvis Presley stamp, which came out in 1992, had a print run of 500 million. Only 124 million were sold. And since many were put away in the hope of future profits, they will *never* become valuable. Supply will always exceed demand. And it's going to get worse. Desperate for additional revenue, the post office has changed its historic policy of only honoring dead people on stamps. Beginning in 2012, live people are eligible to appear on stamps.

Here's how the post office manages the supply. First, the stamps are available in post offices for about a year. After that, they still can be purchased online for another six months to a year. Only then, are any unsold stamps destroyed. Consequently, stamp dealers have plenty of time to gage demand and stock up.

Many years ago, I had a first-hand experience with the stamp market. In December of 1968, I decided to send out some holiday cards with the Mount Rushmore stamp on the envelopes. Growing up in the Black Hills as I did, the Rushmore stamp was very meaning-ful to me.

In 1968, it cost six cents to mail a letter first-class. At that time, the Rushmore stamp was 16 years old, and had a face value of three cents. This would work out well. All I would have to do was just put two Rushmore stamps on the envelope and it would meet postal requirements.

I went down to Nassau Street in lower Manhattan, walked into a stamp store, and asked for two unused sheets of the Rushmore stamps. They had them in stock and sold them to me for *face value.*

Now, I grew up in retailing, and knew damn well this dealer wasn't in business for his health. So I asked him how much he had paid for the stamps. He told me he bought them at a 15 percent discount from face value.

"Why would anybody sell at that price?" I asked.

He explained. "There are people who collect U.S. stamps all their lives, buying a sheet or more of each new issue. By the time they reach old age, their collection could have a face value of as much as $40,000. Now they are ready to cash in. They are looking for a nice profit. So they come to me and ask how much I will pay for their collection. I offer 85 percent of face. 'That's highway robbery,' they say in horror. 'Why, I could get face value by just using them on the letters I mail.' So, I tell them to go right ahead and do just that. That's when they sell to me for less than face."

That's when I quit collecting stamps.

I now have three groups of collectibles without apparent value: a swizzle stick collection and two separate coffee mug collections.

My swizzle stick collection includes ones from the Stork Club, Lou Walter's Latin Quarter (Barbara's father), and the original Copacabana. Someday I'll try to sell it on eBay.

One mug collection consists of mugs sold in the lobbies of Broadway musicals. This collection includes *Annie Get Your Gun, Les Miserables, Cats, Phantom,* and 24 others. (I also collect the *Playbills* from these shows.)

The other mug collection consists of mugs commemorating U.S. presidents. The ones of the earlier presidents were obtained from their historic homes, the more recent presidents from their libraries. I never pay more than $10 for a mug. The point of these collections is to give me joy.

However, I also have one other collection that has become very valuable.

I Love Art

It's my art collection that has become worth something. Although I had bought some art in the late 1990s, in 2000 I made a conscious decision to invest in art using part of the proceeds I had received from selling most of my equity mutual funds that January.

My primary reason was I love living with art, but I also thought it would be a good asset class for diversification. I reckoned that stocks weren't going to do much in the next several years. I anticipated that many other stock investors would think the same as I did.

At the time, I had no idea that so many hedge fund managers and investment bankers, far wealthier than I, would shovel their bonus money into art, driving up prices. Nor did I realize the extent to which new wealth in Russia, China, India, and the Middle East would find its way into the art market. Art has a two-fold attraction for these people—investment potential, combined with the social cachet of owning important works.

As a result, art has outpaced equities in recent years. For the 10 years ending 2010, the authoritative Mei Moses All Art Index gained 4.86 percent per year, beating the S&P 500 return of 1.35 percent per year. For the most recent five-year period, art won over stocks 3.59 percent vs. 2.28 percent per year. Even better, the correlation between the All Art Index and the S&P 500 is low.

I don't routinely appraise my art collection so I don't know its exact performance, but I am pretty sure it has appreciated by far more than my equity funds.

If you want to put some real money in art, I would make four suggestions. First, work with an art consultant. They get nice commissions, but they are worth it because the art market is vast and complicated, not a friendly place to go uneducated and unescorted. I work with Barbara Schwartz, a Manhattan consultant who favors modern art for her own home. She is constantly shopping the art galleries with clients and has an eye for quality and appreciation. Her website is www.BarbaraSchwartzArtAdvisor.com.

Second, make sure there is a market for the particular artist you like, in case you ever want to sell. You can check this by calling the auction houses, Christie's or Sotheby's, or by asking a local consultant or gallery. Example: I once bought western art. However, when I wanted to sell it, I found that Christie's would only accept on consignment Indian art that was more than 50 years old.

Third, you can't "day trade" art. Commissions are too high. For example, the auction houses charge 25 percent of the first $50,000, 20 percent from $50,000 to $1 million, and 12 percent over a million. That's not all. Uncle Sam levies a 28 percent capital gains rate on profits realized by collectors, regardless of holding period. Then there are insurance costs, and there can be substantial transportation costs if you can't carry your art into the auction house. Needless to say, art is an illiquid asset.

With art, the main driver is the satisfaction of buying, holding, and enjoying. According to several studies, collectors hold an average piece of valuable art for 30 years, far longer than other assets. In fact the main reasons for selling are the three D's: death, debt, and divorce. Not profit-taking.

Fourth, there is a question of whether you should buy the best you can afford. My answer is a resounding "Yes." It will give you far more enjoyment, and there is a good possibility that the pricier art will be more likely to hold its value or appreciate. Go for museum quality if you can afford it.

A word of caution: Be aware that correlations between many asset classes tend to rise during bear markets, and that certainly includes art. A rule of thumb is that the art market trails the Dow Jones Industrial Average by about 6 to 18 months. When the bull market in art ended in November 2008, much art sold for far less than its pre-sale estimates, or went unsold at the fall auctions. Prices declined 30 percent between January and September 2009, and then began to come back.

Important Lessons in This Chapter

- You may make good money investing in collectibles. But that should not be your primary purpose. Collect for the love of collecting. Don't *assume* your collection will have any resale value. The value of your collectibles depends totally on demand. Collectibles have no inherent worth.

CHAPTER 18

Vanity Investments

A vanity investment is one in which making money isn't the primary motive or, sometimes, even a motive at all. It's a bit like the vanity press, which caters to authors who are willing to pay the full cost of publishing and promoting their own books, just to see their names in print. For these authors, the goal is to have books in their hands to give to friends or customers. Bookstore sales are unimportant.

You can occasionally make money with a vanity investment, although it's rare to make big money. Take, for example, my experience with a show-stopping vanity investment.

Ever since I came to New York, I have wanted to invest in a Broadway show. Now that's a vanity investment if there ever was one. I know perfectly well that the odds of a Broadway "angel" making money are slim. Fewer than one out of four shows recoup their investments. But I'm an inveterate theatergoer, and I really wanted to be a part of the Broadway scene. Knowing the odds, though, I was never prepared to commit any large sum to satisfy this longing.

How to Invest in a Broadway Show without Having to Mortgage Your House

Suddenly, an opportunity opened up for me. I found a producer who would accept small investments and pool them, like limited partnerships in real estate or oil and gas drilling. The minimum investment was usually $10,000. I passed on the first show they offered me, the *Producers*. Big mistake; it became a huge hit.

But they next offered an investment in *Hairspray*. I had seen the 1988 movie, and they sent me a CD of the music. Deciding this was my opportunity, I took a chance and made my first Broadway show investment.

I picked a winner! Let me tell you just how big a winner I picked. *Hairspray* opened in August 2002 and ran until January 2009. Of 35 Broadway productions that opened in 2002, *Hairspray* performed the best. It went on to log 2,462 performances, making it the 20th longest-running Broadway show of all time, going back more than 100 years.

I made big money, right? Unfortunately, not right. From opening night through August 2011, my profit was 117 percent. And that's total profit over six plus years, not annualized profit. That's just slightly more than a double. This includes occasional small checks I continue to receive even though the show has closed.

On a risk-adjusted basis, which is the only way to look at any investment, I did terribly. Let me give you a comparison to make the point. Two months after *Hairspray* opened, Wynn Resorts (WYNN), the Las Vegas and Asian hotel and casino operator, went public at $13. You could have bought it the next day for $21 to $23. In 2007, WYNN achieved a bull market high of $176. That's about a 700 percent paper profit, and it would have been achieved with less risk, even considering the beating that the stock took in 2008.

But of course, with a vanity investment, making money is only part of it. There were peripheral benefits galore. First of all, I got two free tickets to opening night. My wife and I got to walk the red carpet with crowds and TV cameras panning on us. After the show, we went to the celebrity-laden cast party held at Roseland, also free. Another perk was the right to buy two house seats a month on short notice. (House seats are full-priced tickets that are set aside by the production and held for the producers and other insiders, usually until several days before the performance date, and then released for public sale. They're always excellent seats and are very limited in number.) I impressed a lot of friends when they found out I could get them tickets at face value for a hit show without months of waiting. Finally, I received a framed poster of the show's ad.

But I think the best perk of all is what is generally called "cocktail chatter." You can casually mention you are an investor in a Broadway show. That has vastly more cachet than saying you bought a top-ranked mutual fund, or even a high-tech stock.

Once, when I was out with an old friend who is a sophisticated Manhattanite, I casually mentioned I had invested in a show.

"What show?" he immediately asked.

Watching his face, I could see he was getting ready to commiserate with me on my loss.

"*Hairspray*," I replied.

His expression changed completely. Without enthusiasm, he said only "that's nice" and changed the subject. That, by itself, almost made the investment worthwhile.

Given my success on Broadway, I decided to accept an offer to invest in the *Hairspray* road show company. Road show companies are separate productions with separate investors and funding. I made some money on the road show investment, but not as much as I should have made, for a strange reason. Every time the road show moved to another state, it generated a new limited partnership K-1 tax reporting form. My accountant filed income tax returns for me in seven states. He made more money than I did.

If you're interested in making a vanity investment in a Broadway show, the production company I invested with is called Scorpio Entertainment. It's dangerous to invest in Hollywood movies because of the possibility of being victimized by sleazy accounting. But as near as I can tell, Scorpio is on the up and up. They have been in business for 26 years. They send me comprehensive financial statements at frequent intervals. I've broken bread with their president. Their phone is 914-948-1300. Incidentally, Scorpio has two other productions in the all-time top quarter of shows: *The Producers* and *Smokey Joe's Café*. Scorpio productions have won six Tony awards.

Let me explain the specifics of my deal, so you'll understand why I didn't make more money. The limited partners (like me) get 100 percent of net profits until they recoup their investment. Then they are cut back to 50 percent, so the show's creative and producing team can participate in half of the remaining profits. I can't fault that.

Then another factor comes into play. During the first year, a hit show is a sellout at premium prices. *Hairspray* grossed an average of $900,000 a week during its first year. But as the years go by, grosses ease off. By the fifth year, *Hairspray* was grossing in the $600,000 range per week. A lot of tickets were sold at discount. Costs remained the same.

Actually, in the case of *Hairspray*, the show got an unanticipated boost in the summer of 2007 from the highly successful movie version of the Broadway show, which temporarily raised the Broadway grosses back above $900,000 again.

On the other hand, I discovered another risk factor that I had not anticipated. In November 2007, the theatrical stagehands struck Broadway, putting *Hairspray* and 26 other shows out of business for 19 days. That offset the movie bonanza.

You can make your investment back relatively quickly if you have a hit. *Hairspray*'s limited partners recouped in nine months. But after break-even the cash flow slows.

Please, dear reader, don't take any of this as a complaint. My lifelong dream was fulfilled without costing me a penny. This is easily my most memorable investment.

I am sure most readers will think my successful investment in *Hairspray* was just beginner's luck. But I'm not so sure.

Aside from the element of luck that is present in any investment, I knew going in that achieving investment success in the arts is chancy, even for the most knowledgeable insiders. (That's why they offered me the opportunity to invest in the first place.) But even though it was my first such investment, I would not call it beginner's luck.

Because of my TV job, I have followed movie and Broadway grosses for more than 40 years. I still subscribe to *Variety* to get the details on these grosses beyond what is covered by the popular media. That background knowledge was a big help in enabling me to pick a winner. My *Hairspray* profits will at least pay for my *Variety* subscription for the rest of my life.

The All-Time Winner! 24,000 Percent Profit over 50 Years

On May 30, 1960, a small, low budget musical called *The Fantasticks* opened at the Sullivan Street Playhouse, a small off-Broadway theater in New York City's Greenwich Village. At a time when major Broadway shows were budgeted at $250,000, *The Fantasticks* was budgeted at $16,500. The show's 52 original backers, mostly small investors whose main motivation for investing was to support friends and neighbors, had no idea they would be investing in what would become the longest running musical and the longest-running uninterrupted show of any kind in the world. The original production continued for 42 years, closing on January 13, 2002 after a record-shattering 17,162 performances.

Profits were immense, and are continuing until this day because the original limited partnership agreements stipulated that they would receive remuneration from revivals for another 18 years after the original run ended. By the show's 50th anniversary, gross profits amounted to 24,000 percent or about 11.6 percent a year annualized.

Notable actors who appeared in the off-Broadway and touring productions throughout its long run, include Jerry Orbach (who was in the original cast), Liza Minnelli, Elliott Gould, F. Murray Abraham, Glenn Close, Kristin Chenoweth, Bert Convy, and Dick Latessa (who years later had a featured role [the father] in *Hairspray*).

Source of profit statistics: The New York Times.

Don't Invest in Anything That Eats

I have no personal experience with this, but I'm told that investing in thoroughbred racehorses is another vanity investment. Most investors probably lose, but a few do make it big. Perks include free admission, parking at the track, and (maybe) inside tips on whether your horse is sick or rarin' to race. I'm told the operative phrase here is "don't invest in anything that eats."

In trying to track this down for the book, I went on the Internet and found a mare for sale. Her name was Vanity's Investment. Her sire was Investment Creditor. Her grand sire was The Big Investment. The asking price was only $22,500.

Hmmm.

Important Lesson in This Chapter

- Vanity investing can be a great way to enjoy your money. However, before you take the plunge, always assume you will lose 100 percent of your money.

CHAPTER

19

Increasing Your Workplace Income

This book is about making money, so there is no need to restrict it to the most common types of investing. I've already discussed collectibles, which have made fortunes for a knowledgeable (or lucky) few. Now I want to discuss a few of the ways that both employers and workers can enhance their incomes.

To get truly rich. . . .

Own Your Own Business

The best way to become wealthy is to be an entrepreneur and own your own business. You will recall that earlier I noted that in an article in Kiplinger's, 9 of the 11 millionaires profiled had made it by starting their own businesses.

Conversely, employees, excepting some CEOs, and key presidents of the largest corporations, seldom get really rich. And once you get beyond Warren Buffett, how many people can you name who made billions investing passively in other people's businesses? I can't name any offhand. And even Buffett's investing is only partially passive.

Entrepreneurship Is Not for Everybody

It's risky. According to some business experts, over 80 percent of all new enterprises fail.

You have to work very hard. In the beginning you will find yourself doing menial jobs that in a large corporation would be handed off to lower level employees. As Eitan Wertheimer, the CEO of

Iscar, an Israeli high-tech company, put it, "If you sleep on the floor, you never have to worry about falling out of bed."

Forget about diversification. You need to put all your eggs in one basket—yours.

You can't be afraid of failure. I once knew a man who had started 14 businesses in his lifetime. The first 13 failed; the 14th, launched when he was middle aged, was a huge success.

You need to be a generalist. You can't specialize like an employee would. The best-selling book *Rich Dad, Poor Dad* by Robert Kiyosaki lists several areas an entrepreneur needs to know:

- The markets (supply and demand)
- Accounting
- Investing
- The law

You will never achieve more than the goal you establish for yourself. So set your sights as high as you can within your capabilities. The best example of this is Frederick Smith, who conceived the idea for FedEx Corp. while he was still in college.

Small business requires different talents than big business. The pathway to success in big business is the ability to be a leader, to get along with and to motivate people. Loners don't make it in big business. Not true of small business, particularly start-ups. There, the concept, the business plan, the ability to be a generalist, and drive are all-important.

As with investing, you need to have savings in order to have seed money to start your business.

A comprehensive discussion of entrepreneurship is well beyond the scope of this book. For people who are, or might someday want to be their own boss and enjoy the benefits of ownership, here are some suggestions that come from my own personal experiences as an entrepreneur. I successfully made the transition from a large corporate environment, where everybody was a specialist, to owning a small business. (Watching my father run a small business many years ago was a key factor in helping me make this transition.)

> Don't let the noise of other's opinions drown out your own inner voice. And most important, have the courage to follow your heart and intuition.
>
> —Steve Jobs

Don't Give Away Stock in Your Company

In Silicon Valley, companies hand out stock or stock options to middle management and even secretaries. That may be a good business plan if you are a budding Google. But few entrepreneurs are going to be in that league.

When you start your own company, you may find that many capable, prospective employees will ask for stock as the price of joining your new venture. *Don't give it to them.* Don't consider it, even if you are hiring for a key job. You can always find someone else who won't demand stock. Your cousin or your wife's brother-in-law wants to join your new venture? Fine. Just don't give him any stock. Be hardnosed about it. When demands come up, don't even discuss it. Just say *no!*

You will find your job of running the company is much easier. If you are successful and decide to sell years later, or turn the business over to your children, you will be very thankful that you own 100 percent of the stock.

There is one exception to this rule. If a prospective employee or partner can bring in a substantial amount of business, it may be wise to make him or her part owner. Without an equity stake in the enterprise, this person may decide to leave, taking part of your business with him.

Tip

When launching a new company, keep your day job as long as you can.

It'll make it easier to say no to people who want to buy into your company, your family will eat better, and you won't go as deeply into debt. (I kept mine for three years, before I went full-time with the newsletter.)

The Customer Is Always Right

If you are going to be a successful businessman, you break one fundamental rule at your peril: "The customer is always right." These are the five most important words in business. Tattoo them on your forehead. Make them an everyday part of your business. Make sure all your employees understand the concept as well as you do.

Getting my employees to understand that the customer is always right was one of the hardest things I had to do. It was the first thing I explained to every new employee.

It was not unusual for subscribers to fail to get their newsletters on time. Sometimes it was the fault of the post office. Occasionally, computer errors were responsible. Knowing delivery wasn't perfect, some subscribers tried to get free copies, or their subscriptions extended. In some cases, we knew for a fact that a subscriber was lying to us. It didn't matter. My rule was that the customer was always right. Give them whatever they ask for. It will pay off in the long run. I would never let any of my employees challenge a customer, whatever the facts. It's no different with major newspapers that distribute by carrier. If you say you never got your paper, they never question it.

Let me tell you how I came to this policy. Back in the late 1950s, when I was single, I had a roommate who was a buyer at Gimbels department store in New York. One day he told me about Gimbels' return policy: If a customer was upset enough, or complained loudly enough, he was authorized to take back anything and make a cash refund. He told me that it didn't matter how long ago the purchase had been made, what condition the merchandise was in when it was returned, or even whether it had been bought at Gimbels or somewhere else. Of course, this policy was never publicly announced, and low-level employees didn't have this discretion. Surely this attitude contributed to Gimbels success. For 99 years (from 1887 to 1986) Gimbels was one of the premiere department stores in America. They had major stores in New York City, Milwaukee, and Philadelphia and also owned the Saks Fifth Avenue department store chain.

Some corporations don't get this religion until they are in deep trouble.

> Wednesday, the top 300 executives at Chrysler are expected to turn off their BlackBerrys and begin three days of in-house management seminars aimed at putting customers first in all of Chrysler's operations.
>
> —*The Wall Street Journal,* June 18, 2008

Oh well, better late than never.

The most important business lesson I've learned is "Always make your business about your customer and never about yourself." I learned that when I invested in a sports paraphernalia store. I was also the buyer, so I bought everything I liked and didn't buy anything that the customers liked. I ended up losing a lot of money because of that.

—Magic Johnson, interviewed by *Time* magazine

Investment advisors have a fiduciary relationship with their clients. All businesses should have a fiduciary relationship with their customers.

Never Forget Your Customers

This holds even when you are selling your business. Sometimes it's not possible. But certainly you should look for a buyer who will treat your customers as well as you did.

After 25 great years, the time came for me to sell *The No-Load Fund Investor*. When I put the newsletter on the market, I received two cash offers. The highest bid came from an ex-stockbroker who seemed like a fine person. However, he didn't have much writing or fund experience. Backed by family money, he offered 10 percent more than the other bidder, Mark Salzinger, an experienced newsletter editor. I chose to sell to Salzinger. My subscribers had been good to me all those years; I had to be good to them. I couldn't put them in untested hands.

We Hired You to Make Money

The purpose of a corporation is to make goods and/or provide services that can be sold at a profit. All the top executives, probably down to the department head level, and certainly all the sales executives, understand that. But it's very doubtful that many employees below this level understand that their real function is to "make money" for the corporation.

Ask a typical employee what his or her job is, and they'll reply that it's to administer, file, process, or whatever. They virtually never see the big picture. I suggest that CEOs of corporations, put a sign in the employee cafeteria: "Your Job Is to Make Money for Our Company, so Our Company Can Make Money for You."

Return Your Telephone Calls

I developed a rule in the days when I worked for the networks: The more important a person was, the more likely that he or she would return your phone calls. And conversely, the less important he was, the less likely your calls would be returned. There were, of course, many exceptions. Generally it was a valid theory, though. I always found it easier to reach a senior vice president or president, than some junior executive.

Some examples: During my broadcasting days, I found that Ed Bleier, first at ABC, and then as an important president at Warner Brothers, would always return my calls. Ed was an extremely busy executive. He routinely kept two secretaries working long hours. It frequently took him two to three days to return calls, but he always did.

Another top executive who returned calls was Leonard Goldenson, the long-time chairman of ABC. He returned my calls even though I was just a youthful researcher who had no direct working relationship with him.

The exception to my rule was Roone Arledge, the president of ABC News and Sports. Roone was notorious for never returning calls. I was once offered a job at ABC Sports, a plumb job that many people would have given a lot to get. I turned it down for several reasons. One was that I didn't want to work for anybody I couldn't reach on the phone.

Many years later, in 2000 to be exact, I was invited to attend a memorial service in New York for Leonard, who had died in Florida a few weeks earlier. Even though I had left ABC 30 years earlier, I accepted the invitation, saying I was doing so because Goldenson had returned my calls.

It was quite a service, with about a thousand broadcasters filling up Temple Emanuel on Fifth Ave. Speakers included Barbara Walters and Marlo Thomas. The man who had invited me also spoke and mentioned that Goldenson had returned phone calls, adding "not like some executives we know." Everybody in the audience knew who he was talking about.

Now, why have I made such a big point about this? The reason I'm telling you to answer your phone is that you will *make more money*, and develop many more worthwhile contacts, if you do. A lot of people say they would like to return all their calls, but just don't have the time to do so. That's just an excuse. If a call turns out to be unproductive, it's easy enough to terminate it. I suppose you could say the same about e-mail and texting.

When I published the newsletter, my staff had orders to put through every caller who asked for me. That policy made me thousands of dollars. That's how I met Michael Levy whom I discussed in the chapter on women. He told me he had called several financial advisors before finding one, me, who would speak to him. I sold a lot of subscriptions to his class. Alas, there are many newsletter editors who won't take calls from subscribers. What a mistake! Subscribers find it very reassuring to be able to talk to the "head man" if they want to.

Not only that, I took subscriber calls when my staff was busy. This was easy to do given that I had the company's general number on my extension. In those cases I identified myself as "Don Ashe," assistant to Sheldon Jacobs. This way I could stay on top of subscriber concerns without subjecting myself to the lengthy conversations that I knew would ensue if the caller knew he was talking to the head man.

Happily, I'm not alone in taking all calls. Vanguard's top executives have long answered shareholder lines during times of high call volume. Regular shifts are scheduled during the busy IRA season (January through April) and other stints when market conditions warrant. Jack Brennan, Gus Sauter, and Bill McNabb (the current CEO) serve, as did Bogle years ago. Vanguard calls this contingency phone force the "Swiss Army," in recognition of Switzerland's army of citizen volunteers.

Not to belabor the point but here's one other experience, this one from my newsletter days. The *Investor* always carried detailed mutual fund performance tables. To compute fund performance you need not only prices but also the dividends declared in the measured period. We needed cooperation from the funds to obtain these dividends. One month my statistician told me the data were not forthcoming from the Charles Schwab funds, and we only had a two-hour window before our publishing deadline.

I hit the panic button calling five people at Schwab. One was to the errant clerk, three were to mid-level executives, and one was to the then President of Schwab, David Pottruck (Chuck is the chairman). Now who do you suppose got back to me first? Guess—it's not hard. Of course it was Pottruck, and when he heard the problem he made sure the clerk provided the data, which arrived in about 10 minutes. And the other three mid-level executives? Only one ever bothered to return the call. Frankly, I was surprised I didn't get more attention from the three mid-level executives. Since we had a lot of managed clients' money at Charles Schwab at the time, this should have ensured great service. But it didn't.

As I indicated previously, Roone Arledge, the storied president of ABC News and Sports, was the exception to the rule. Thus I found it interesting that Barbara Walters, in her memoir, *Auditions,* also complained about Roone's phone manners. It would be one thing to ignore low-ranking Sheldon Jacobs. It is quite another thing to ignore one of his biggest stars, who not only reported to him, but is the Barbara Walters!

Just because Roone Arledge got away with this behavior doesn't mean it's smart for you to do it. Answer your phone calls when you can. Return them when you cannot.

Similarly, a lot of senior corporate executives have assistants who read and sort their mail, directing much of it to other staffers. I can tell you from personal experience that these executives run the risk of missing a lot of opportunities.

Don't Leave Your Business to Your Children

It's human nature to want your children to take over your business after you're gone. It's the major argument for repealing the so-called "death tax." Proponents of repeal of the federal estate tax, say that the tax interferes with carrying on a "way of life." This is considered a particularly cogent argument if you are a farmer, even a poor farmer, but not if your father owns, say, a shoe store, a distinction I don't get.

If a child sincerely wants to take over his or her parent's business, fine. But without ever seeing any kind of a study, let alone a good one, I tend to believe that these children are a minority. Based on my own experience and those of people I know, I believe most children would be far better off working in a field or profession that really interests them, rather than a field that interested their parents.

I could have taken over my father's business, but I never seriously considered it. To his everlasting credit, my father never pressured me to do so. He had taken over the stores from his father because my grandfather had become sick. But my father knew there were other lives. In 1932, when he made this decision, he was a salesman working for the Van Heusen Shirt Company and living in Milwaukee. He once told me that if he had stayed with Van Heusen, he believed that eventually he could have become head of sales. (Today, Phillips-Van Heusen is a huge clothing conglomerate that owns Calvin Klein, Tommy Hilfiger, Arrow, Izod, and others.)

I know many people in my generation who did go into their parents' businesses. A frightfully high percentage of them were never really happy—or successful.

One case I will never forget was a man, a chemical engineer by education, who was inveigled into taking over the clothing store owned by his in-laws. He ran the store for many years. Then, the day after the second in-law died, he sold the store and got a job teaching math in a local school.

How many Rockefellers are in the oil business? How many Kennedys are in the movie production, liquor importing, real estate businesses, or working on Wall Street? Very few, if any. And thank goodness that Alan Jay Lerner never entered his family's business, the 700 store women's apparel chain Lerner Stores. Instead he enriched all our lives by writing the lyrics and libretto, with composer Frederick Loewe, for such beloved classics as *My Fair Lady, Brigadoon, Camelot,* and *Gigi.*

Another inheritor, Steve Forbes does a great job running the magazine. But I strongly suspect his heart is really in politics. Ask yourself this question. Would Steve have chosen a career in publishing if his father had been in some other field? And to all you potential inheritors, what field would you choose if you didn't have a family business to enter?

Please parents . . . forget your dynastic ambitions. Don't pressure your children to enter your business. If your business is worth anything, it can be sold, and your children will be happier with the money than with the business. Trust me. Let them find their own calling. And if your business is unsalable, why would you want your children to enter it in the first place?

Here are some other problems you will avoid: In the case of families with several children, you won't have to decide which one gets the business, who runs it, and how the ones who don't want to work in the business will be fairly compensated. Finally, chances are your children won't run the business as well as you do. But someone you choose to sell it to very well might.

The same holds true for professions. Just because your father or your mother is a doctor or a lawyer, doesn't mean you should be one too.

Both of my own children had the smarts to succeed in my newsletter business. But neither chose to do so. So, I sold the business, and because of timely estate planning, everybody was happy.

One final thought to your kids: Even if you have no desire to ever take over your parents' business, don't pass up the opportunity to work for it after school and during summers. It could be the best and most useful education you could ever get.

Really Going Your Own Way

I have always respected people who grabbed life and did what was right for them, no matter what other people, or even (dreaded) "society" thought of them. I want to profile two such people who live fulfilling lives by doing what is right for them.

The Corporate Life Was Not for Him

A number of years ago I did a major renovation on my house. The custom cabinet maker I hired to do several installations did incredibly good work. He was a real artisan. He also charged top prices for everything he did, even insisting on charging for minor things that many workmen would have thrown in free. If what I paid him was any indication, the man made a very good living.

I didn't think much about it until three years later, when I saw an obituary in *The New York Times* for a person with the same name. My cabinet maker had an unusual name, let's call him Spitzy Forritzy, Jr. The obit was for a person named Spitzy Forritzy. With a name so close, I figured there had to be a connection. In reading the obit, I found out that the deceased had been the CEO and chairman of the board of a Fortune 500 company. And sure enough, my cabinetmaker was his son.

I often wondered how much courage it took for the son to carve out such a radically different life for himself, and how the father took it. The son may have been able to succeed in a large corporation; he did look the part. But I'm sure that his decision to work with his hands was the right one for him.

Many years later I saw the cabinetmaker and asked him how his father had taken it. He told me that the father had strongly believed in letting his children make their own career choices, and had been very supportive.

The Gardner Who Loved Economics

When I lived in Irvington-on-Hudson, New York, I employed a handyman from time to time. I would guess he was in his forties.

In the winter he plowed my driveway. In the summer he maintained the sprinkler system, trimmed hedges, and cleaned out gutters.

Whenever I saw him working I always stopped to chat with him for a few minutes. I soon found that he liked discussing current economic issues, and was really very knowledgeable on the subject. We had many intelligent conversations. Eventually my curiosity got the best of me, so I asked him how he had come by this interest. He told me that in his youth he had attended New York's City College for a couple of years. While at City, he had taken an introductory course in economics and enjoyed it. He told me that his course instructor had been Alan Greenspan.

It's important to love your work. If you're not happy with your current job ask yourself the following questions: If I had more than enough money to live on for the rest of my life, what would I do with the rest of my life?

Would I stay in my current job? Would I change jobs within my field? Would I change fields?

Advice from Jonathan Clements

For 14 years Jonathan Clements wrote a personal finance column for *The Wall Street Journal*. His final column on April 9, 2008, was one of his best. Here's a short summary of it.

> Having wealth is not just so you can spend more money at the mall. More importantly, it can deliver three key benefits:
> 1. If you have money, you don't have to worry about it [financial security].
> 2. Money can give you the freedom to pursue your passions.
> 3. Money can buy you time with friends and family. Money allows you to go out to dinner with friends, travel to see old friends, vacation, and go to the theater with your spouse.
>
> Do these things and your life will be far richer.

Success is a journey, not a destination. The doing is often more important than the outcome.

—Attributed to Arthur Ashe

Die Broke

There are people who for whatever reason want to spend every cent they have while they are still living. They are not concerned with leaving bequests to children, relatives, charities, or anybody else after they are gone. These people want to die broke. But, for understandable reasons, they don't want to outlive their money either.

Surprisingly, there's a simple way to do it. It's called an immediate annuity without refund. You give a financial institution a designated lump sum of money, and they pay you a monthly stipend for life. When you die they keep what's left. These annuities are a form of insurance.

To give you an idea how it works, here is Vanguard's product. Let's say you are a male, age 65, and your worldly wealth totals $100,000. You give the $100,000 to Vanguard. In return Vanguard sends you a check for $593 each month for life. Simple! Even better, the monthly return is only partly taxable. The part of the $593 that is return of capital is tax-free. Only the income is taxable.

The return varies with age, interest rates, and insurance carrier. It's also possible to inflation-adjust these payouts, and to get a joint and survivors policy that covers your spouse's life as well.

Checking out an annuity can also help you with that most important decision, how much do you need to retire. Let's say you've saved a half-million dollars. Ask an insurance agent how big a monthly payment a half-million will buy. Then determine if that's enough to cover your estimated living expenses. Warning: Buying an annuity at the bottom of the interest-rate cycle may not be a good idea.

Important Lessons in This Chapter

- As much as I would like to show you how to get super rich investing in other peoples' businesses, I can't. The best way I know to make really big money is to start your own business. Your age is immaterial. It's the idea and the drive that count.
- The other lesson: Be careful about interfering too much in your children's lives.

Whether you think that you can or you can't, you're usually right.
—Henry Ford

Epilogue

Journey's End

Dear Reader: Thank you for accompanying me on my journey. This book has been a labor of love for me, and I hope you enjoyed reading it as much as I enjoyed writing it.

Looking back, by 1972, my parents' clothing business had grown to six stores in various towns in the Black Hills and they were ready to retire. I, and my brother who had followed me to New York, showed no interest in taking over the stores. So the clothing chain was offered for sale. Although my parents tried for many months, they couldn't find a buyer. The problem was that the business was too big for local buyers to afford.

My wife said, "What we need is publicity." We noodled around with it, and decided that my parents' plight might be of general interest. I found a contact at *The Wall Street Journal* and pitched the story of how two sons had gone to the big city and rejected the family business back in the small town. (For those of you not familiar with the term, I guess I am showing my age: Noodling is slang. A good synonym would be "brainstorming.")

The Journal liked the idea. They sent one of their ace Chicago-based reporters, Frederick Klein, out to Deadwood to interview my parents. On July 26, 1973, the story appeared on *The Journal's* front page, above the fold, in that great center column *The Journal* had for so many years. It was titled: "The Jacobs Brothers Opt Not to Go Home to Deadwood, S.D." The subtitle was: "So Who Will Take Over Stores the Parents Have Operated? Common Plight for Families."

The article generated about 200 letters and calls and 50 serious buyers. The stores were sold for the asking price, which *The Journal* had generously included in the article.

Well, that's it, I thought. There goes my back-up occupation.

But I needn't have worried. A year later, *Put Money in Your Pocket* was published and I was off and running on my second career as a financial newsletter editor/publisher, one that exceeded any entrepreneurial expectations I had ever had. I learned that writing and advising was in my blood—and small-town retailing wasn't.

But I still have one tie to Deadwood. . . .

Soaring almost vertically above Deadwood is a mountain with two large rock outcroppings. The first set, rising about 600 feet above Main Street's 4,250 foot elevation, is called Brown Rocks. The second, another 450 feet above that, majestically capping the mountain, is called White Rocks.

Between the two, overlooking Deadwood, lies Mount Moriah, the prettiest boot hill in the entire West.

There, in a section of the cemetery known as Hebrew Hill, about a hundred yards from where Wild Bill Hickok and Calamity Jane are buried side-by-side, is the Jacobs family plot. There lie my great grandparents, Simon and Dora Jacobs, who came to Deadwood in 1886, four years prior to the nearby battle of Wounded Knee and three years before South Dakota became a state.

Next to them are my grandparents, Sidney and Jennie Jacobs Jacobs (this is not a typo). Sidney gave up a promising career in vaudeville (he worked for Weber and Fields and actually knew Sam Harris and David Belasco) to move to Deadwood to marry his true love.

Just below them on the hill are my parents, Bert and Ruth Jacobs, who could have made it anywhere but chose to live out their lives in the small town where he had been born and that they dearly loved.

There are still two empty plots. That's where my journey will end, some day. The West is still in my blood.

Sheldon Jacobs
Paradise Valley, Arizona
Hartsdale, New York

If you would like to contact me, my e-mail address is shelnl@aol.com. I also invite you to visit on my website: www.sheldonjacobs.com.

The Two Meanings of Life

The first is *relationships,* the relationships with your familial loved ones, your friends, your colleagues, and your acquaintances.

The second is *shopping.* By that I mean consumption and the production necessary to sustain it.

Shelton Jacobs

Appendix

Directory of Newsletters with Model Portfolios

Newsletter	Editor	Investment focus	Phone/Email
All Star Fund Trader	Ronald E. Rowland	Mutual funds, ETFs	800-299-4223
Almanac Investor Newsletter	Jeffrey A. Hirsch	Stocks, ETFs	800-762-2974
AlphaProfit Sector Investors' Newsletter	Sam Subramanian	Fidelity Sector funds	281-565-6963
Bernie Schaeffer's Option Advisor	Bernie Schaeffer	Options	800-448-2080
Blue Chip Investor	Steven Check	Stocks	860-710-5777
Bob Brinker's Marketimer	Robert J. Brinker	Mutual funds	303-660-8686
Bob Carlson's Retirement Watch	Robert C. Carlson	Mutual funds, insurance, annuities	800-552-1152
Brinker Fixed Income Advisor	Robert M. Brinker	Fixed Income funds, ETFs, bonds, CDs	303-688-2555
Buyback Letter	David R. Fried	Stocks	888-289-2225
Cabot Market Letter	Michael A. Cintolo	Growth stocks	800-729-7967
(The) Chartist	Dan Sullivan	Stocks	800-942-4278
(The) Chartist Mutual Fund/ETF Letter	Dan Sullivan	Mutual funds, ETFs	800-942-4278
(The) Complete Investor	Stephen Leeb	Stocks, funds, gold	888-833-2070
Coolcat ETF Report	Kevin Kennedy	ETFs	559-875-0613
(The) Dines Letter	James Dines	Stocks, gold	800-845-8259
Doug Fabian's ETF Trader	Doug Fabian	ETFs	800-950-9262

(Continued)

Newsletter	Editor	Investment focus	Phone/Email
Doug Fabian's Successful Investing	Doug Fabian	Mutual funds, ETFs	800-950-8765
Dow Theory Forecasts	Richard J. Moroney, CFA	Stocks, funds	800-233-5922
ETF Trader	James H. Lowell III	ETFs	orders@ marketwatch .com
Fidelity Independent Adviser	Donald R. Dion, Jr	Mutual funds	800-548-3797
Fidelity Insight	John Boyd	Fidelity mutual funds	800-444-6342
Fidelity Investor	James H. Lowell III	Fidelity funds	800-290-6577
Fidelity Monitor	Jack Bowers	Mutual funds	800-397-3094
Fidelity Navigator	Mark A. Grimaldi	Fidelity Mutual funds	877-585-2785
Fidelity Sector Investor	James H. Lowell III	Fidelity sector funds	800-290-6577
Forbes/Lehmann Income Securities Investor	Richard Lehmann	Bonds, preferred stocks, convertibles, closed-end funds	800-472-2680
Fosback's Fund Forecaster	Norman G. Fosback	Mutual funds	561-417-5000
Fund Advice	Paul A. Merriman	Mutual funds	fundadvice.com
Good Fortune	William Ragsdale	Mutual funds	530-867-6241
Independent Adviser for Vanguard Investors	Daniel P. Wiener	Vanguard mutual funds	800-211-7641
Index Rx	Dr. Lawrence Czelusta	Mutual funds, ETFs	877-374-6339
Invest by Model	Alan J. Brochstein	Stocks	713-344-0826
InvesTech Research Portfolio Strategy	James B. Stack	Stocks, mutual funds, & ETFs	800-955-8500
Investor's ETF Report	Mark Salzinger	ETFs	800-706-6364
(The) Investor's Guide to Closed-End Funds	Thomas J. Herzfeld	Closed-end Funds	800-854-3863
Investor's Intelligence	Michael L. Burke	Stocks, currencies, commodities, futures	914-632-0422
Investor's Intelligence ETF Review	Michael L. Burke	ETFs	914-632-0422
Mark Skousen's Forecasts & Strategies	Mark Skousen	Stocks, funds, precious metals, real estate	800-211-7661
Moneyletter	Walter S. Frank	Mutual funds, ETFs	800-890-9670
Morningstar Fund Investor	Russel Kinnel	Mutual funds	866-910-1145
Mutual Fund Prospector	Eric W. Dany	Mutual funds	866-541-5299

Newsletter	Editor	Investment focus	Phone/Email
Mutual Fund Strategist	Holly Hooper-Fournier	Mutual funds, ETFs	800-355-3863
National Trendlines	Douglas Jimerson	Stocks, bonds, funds, gold	800-521-1585 x
NoLoad FundX	Janet Brown	Mutual funds, ETFs	800-763-8639
No-Load Fund Analyst	Steve Savage	Mutual funds	800-776-9555
No-Load Fund Investor	Mark Salzinger	Mutual funds, ETFs	800-706-6364
No-Load Mutual Fund Selections & Timing	Stephen L. McKee	Mutual funds	800-800-6563
NoLoad Navigator	Mark A. Grimaldi	Vanguard Mutual funds	877-585-2785
Oberweis Report	James W. Oberweis	Stocks	800-323-6166
On The Money	Dennis Slothower	Mutual funds, ETFs	800-772-5789
Peter Dag Portfolio Strategy & Mgmt	George Dagnino	Stocks, funds, ETFs	800-833-2782
Peter Eliades' Stockmarket Cycles	Peter G. Eliades	Mutual funds	800-888-4351
Professional Timing Service	Curtis Hesler	Stocks, bonds, gold, futures	888-891-4326
Prudent Speculator	John Buckingham	Stocks	877-817-4394
Real Wealth Report	Larry Edelson	Gold stocks, gold bullion, natural resources	800-604-3649
(The) Relevant Investor	Bill Wysor	Mutual funds	336-793-6004
Reminiscences	Laszlo Birinyi, Jr.	Stocks	800-357-4468
Richard E. Band's Profitable Investing	Richard E. Band	Stocks, bonds, funds & ETFs	800-211-8566
Safe Money Report	Mike Larson	Stocks, funds, ETFs, options	800-236-0407
Sector Navigator	Mark A. Grimaldi	Mutual funds	877-585-2785
Sound Mind Investing	Austin C. Pryor, Jr.	Mutual funds	877-736-3764
Stealth Stocks Daily Alert	Dennis Slothower	Stocks	800-524-4832
Sy Harding's Street Smart Report	Sy Harding	Stocks, funds, bonds, gold	888-427-3464
Systems and Forecasts	Dr. Marvin Appel	Mutual funds, stocks, ETFs	800-829-6229
Timer Digest	Jim Schmidt	Mutual funds, stocks, gold	800-356-2527

Source: Hulbert Financial Digest.

Glossary

active investing: An investing approach that seeks to exceed the returns of the financial markets. Active managers rely on research, market forecasts, judgment, and experience in making investment decisions.

advisor: The organization employed by a mutual fund to manage assets and provide research and related services. Advisors must register with the Securities and Exchange Commission and state securities commissions as Registered Investment Advisors.

all-weather fund: A fund that long-term investors can hold with relative safety throughout a complete market cycle. Market timing, low volatility, and asset allocation funds may be all-weather.

alpha: A portfolio's performance minus the performance of a hypothetical benchmark portfolio of equivalent risk. A positive alpha is considered a measure of management's ability. In Wall Street vernacular, "searching for alpha" means an advisor is seeking above average returns relative to a benchmark.

asset allocation: The process of dividing up one's securities among broad asset classes such as stocks and bonds.

asset class: A group of securities that share common characteristics and tend to trade in similar patterns. Stocks, bonds, cash, and real estate are common asset classes.

average maturity: A measure of the risk in a bond or bond fund. In the case of a fund, it's the dollar-weighted average of all the current maturities of individual bonds in the fund. Generally, the longer the maturity, the greater the volatility, and thus the risk in holding the bond. *Also see* **duration**.

averages: Stock price measures that are calculated and distributed by a number of organizations including Dow Jones and

Standard & Poor's. Also called market averages, market index, stock averages, stock indexes.

back-testing: The process of testing a trading strategy using historical data.

balanced fund: A mutual fund that has an investment policy of always balancing its portfolio, by holding relatively fixed portions of common stocks, bonds, and preferred stocks.

basis point: A value equaling one one-hundredth of a percent (0.01 percent). It's commonly used to measure changes in interest rates, bond yields, expense ratios, and equity returns.

bear: An investor who believes a security or some other asset or the security markets in general will follow a broad downward path.

bear market: A sustained period when stock prices, as shown in major equity indexes, are generally falling. One common (although not universally accepted) definition is a decline in major benchmarks such as the S&P 500 Index or Dow Jones Industrial Average of 20 percent or more from a previous peak.

benchmark: An appropriate standard against which actively managed funds can be judged.

beta: A leading statistical measure of risk in securities. It divides an asset's total risk into its market risk and its specific risk. For most U.S. stocks, beta is a measure of its risk vis-à-vis a common benchmark such as the S&P 500 Index. A stock with a beta of .80 can be expected to increase or decrease by 80 percent of the change in the index. A stock with a beta of 1.00 can be expected to increase or decrease at the same rate as an index. A beta of minus 1.00 moves in perfect opposition to the market. High-beta stocks or mutual funds (those with betas above 1.00) can be expected to have greater fluctuations in price than the broad market.

black swan: A term that alludes to the once widespread belief that all swans are white. This was proven false when European explorers discovered black swans in Australia. A black swan event is something that is remote but highly risky. The term was popularized in a book by Nassim Nicholas Taleb. It is sometimes defined as an "outlier."

blend: A style designation indicating a fund holds both growth and value stocks.

bubble: A mass speculation in which prices rise out of all proportion to intrinsic worth, only to burst (or crash) as investors finally come to their senses. They occur when investors believe that investments bought at the current price can subsequently be sold at even higher prices. Syn: **mania**.

bull: An investor who believes a specific security or security markets in general will follow a broad upward trend.

bull market: A sustained period when stock prices, as shown in major equity indexes, are generally rising.

capital gain distributions: Cash amounts paid to mutual fund shareholders that represent gains realized on the sale of the fund's portfolio securities. Most mutual funds pay a capital gain dividend once per year, toward the end of each year.

cap-size: *See* **market capitalization.**

cap-weighted: A portfolio that weights its component securities in proportion to their market capitalization.

closed-end fund: Closed-end funds may be actively managed (like mutual funds) but they issue a fixed number of shares, which are traded on exchanges (or in the OTC market) like stocks. Supply and demand factors determine the prices of closed-end funds. If the market price of shares is below the fund's net asset value (NAV), as is commonly the case, the fund is said to trade at a "discount." The amount of the discount is the difference between market price and NAV. If the fund's market price is higher than its NAV, the fund is said to be selling at a "premium."

closet index fund: An investment company that claims to actively manage its portfolio, but in reality emulates a market index such as the S&P 500. These funds generally charge sales fees and expenses that are typical for an actively managed fund, which are significantly higher than a true index fund. Investors pay large fees for minimal differentiation.

collectible: An asset of limited supply that is sought for a variety of reasons including a possible increase in value. Stamps, coins, and art are usually considered collectibles.

commodities: Assets that can be grown, raised, drilled, or mined. They include agricultural products such as corn, metals such as gold, and energy, that is, oil. Commodities do not provide an income stream; their value depends on what a buyer will pay for them. While they are generally considered an inflation hedge, ultimately their prices depend on supply and demand.

compounding: The process that occurs through the reinvestment of interest, dividends, or profits. Growth thus occurs at the same rate that the investment itself earns, allowing the reinvested money to multiply, rather than simply adding to the investment.

consol: A perpetual bond that never pays back principal so it has no maturity. Interest payments continue in perpetuity. They fluctuate widely in price with changes in long-term interest rates.

contrarian: An investor who does the opposite of what most investors are doing at a particular time.

correction: A short downturn in prices during a longer bull market trend. Corrections are of a lesser magnitude and lesser duration than bear markets.

correlation: A statistical measure with a range between −1 and +1 demonstrating similarity between the movements of two variables. The extremes represent perfect inverse and direct relationships and 0 indicates no relationship at all.

day trading: Trading with the intention of profiting from short-term moves, sometimes buying and selling the same security within hours.

derivatives: An asset which derives its value from another asset. A derivative may be exchange-traded (such as a listed option contract) or it may involve a private negotiation between two parties (such as a forward delivery contract).

diversification: An investment principle in which a portfolio is divided among different securities or investments with different characteristics, so that the whole portfolio is not exposed to similar risks. A stock portfolio may be divided among different companies, industries, or economic sectors.

dividend: Distinct from a capital gain distribution, it represents distributions from investment income. *Also see* **yield.**

dollar-cost averaging (DCA): The discipline of investing fixed dollar amounts at regular intervals in markets with fluctuating prices. The discipline can reduce the investor's average share cost over time as more shares are acquired when prices are low (for the same fixed dollar amount) than when prices are high. To work effectively, DCA must be pursued systematically over time, and it does not guarantee against losses in falling markets.

Dow Jones Industrial Average: *See* **price weighting.**

duration: A measure of fixed-income risk similar to average maturity, except that unlike average maturity, duration takes into account cash flows from current interest payments. Thus a bond with sizeable interest payments will have a lower duration than another bond with the same maturity that doesn't pay as much current income. The higher the duration, the riskier the bond.

EAFE Index: An abbreviation for the Morgan Stanley Capital International Europe, Australasia, Far East Index. It's a market-capitalization-weighted index representing approximately 70 percent of market capitalizations of 21 developed countries. The United States and Canada are excluded. Most international funds allocate their investments by referencing this index. When an international fund manager says he is underweighting or overweighting a country, he means compared to the EAFE Index.

economics: The study of how people use limited resources— personal, commercial, national, or international—to achieve maximum well-being.

efficient market: The theory that the stock market quickly and efficiently prices in all known information, so future price changes are random.

efficient market theory: The theory that market prices reflect the knowledge and expectations of all investors. Believers of the theory hold that any new development is quickly reflected in a company's stock price, making it impossible for an investor to beat the market over the long run. *Also see* **random walk.**

equities: Common stocks; an ownership interest in a corporation.

exchange-traded fund (ETF): Funds that own baskets of stocks or bonds that can be traded on a stock exchange at any time throughout the day. A brokerage account is needed to buy and sell shares. ETFs can be shorted in margin accounts. Because they are index funds, their portfolios are transparent. You know exactly what you are getting. In 2008, the SEC approved the first actively managed ETF, provided it disseminates its portfolio composition daily. The ETF structure allows for a diversified, low-cost, low-turnover investing with some tax advantages over conventional mutual funds.

expense ratio: The percentage of a fund's average net assets used to pay fund expenses. It takes into account management, administrative, and 12b-1 fees if any. It does not take into account brokerage commissions.

fiduciary: A person, such as an investment manager or the executor of an estate, or an organization, such as a bank, entrusted with the property of another party and in whose best interests the fiduciary is expected to act when holding, investing, or using that party's property.

Financial Industry Regulatory Authority (FINRA): The largest non-governmental regulator for all securities firms doing business in the United States. It was formerly known as the National Association of Securities Dealers (NASD).

fixed income security: A debt security such as a bond and a preferred stock with a stated return in percentage or dollars.

FTSE 100 Index: The Financial Times-Stock Exchange Index. It's a market-weighted index of the 100 leading companies traded in Great Britain on the London Stock Exchange. It's known phonetically as the "footsie."

fundamental analysis: Analysis of corporate balance sheets, income statements, management, sales, products, and markets in order to forecast future stock price movements.

fundamental indexing: A method of constructing an index or index fund in which components are chosen and weighted based on criteria that indicate a company's fundamental operational data, not market value.

fund-of-funds: A fund that invests in other funds. Also called multi-funds.

fund supermarket: A financial institution that offers a large number of mutual funds from many different sponsors. Usually refers to brokerage firms offering no-load funds.

global asset allocation fund: A broadly diversified fund that typically invests across a number of markets to provide a hedge against declines in the U.S. stock market. Their holdings may include U.S. stocks; international stocks; U.S. bonds, often governments; international bonds; gold or gold mining shares; cash equivalents, and sometimes real estate securities.

global fund: A fund that invests in the securities of the United States as well as those of foreign countries.

greater fool theory: A theory that postulates that no matter how much you overpay for an asset, there will be a buyer (the greater fool) who will pay even more.

gross domestic product (GDP): A basic measure of an economy's economic performance, it is the market value of all final goods and services produced within the borders of a nation in a year.

growth fund: A mutual fund whose primary investment objective is long-term growth of capital. It invests principally in common stocks with growth potential.

hedge: To offset. To safeguard oneself from loss on a risk by making compensatory arrangements on the other side. For example, to hedge one's long positions with short sales, so that if the market declines the loss on long positions will be offset by profit on the short positions.

hedge fund: A type of investment fund designed for wealthy individuals and institutions. Most hedge funds are not required to register as securities because they may not be sold or advertised to the public. They are characterized by specialized investment strategies that are not generally accessible in mutual funds, including high uses of leverage and short positions. Hedge funds typically charge shareholders substantially higher fees than mutual funds.

hindsight bias: A cognitive error causing investors to exaggerate the quality of their foresight, while conveniently forgetting initial errors.

immediate annuity: An annuity that is purchased with a lump sum and that begins making payments one period after the purchase.

income distribution: A payment made by a mutual fund that represents a pass-through of interest and dividends collected by the fund to shareholders on a pro rata basis.

incubator fund: A fund supposedly run on a small scale in-house for a period of time, and then publicly offered to investors if its in-house record has been good. (*Note:* I have never seen any statistics documenting how prevalent this practice is, nor do I know any rating service that includes performance before a fund is publicly offered.)

index: A figure in a system or scale that represents the average value of specified prices, shares, or other items as compared to some reference figure such as a previous date. Computation of indexes can involve many types of averages and weightings.

index fund: A mutual fund containing either all or a statistically valid sample of the stocks or bonds in a stated market index. Because index funds do not employ in-depth research to select securities that might outperform benchmarks, they are called "passively managed." Index funds may have "tracking errors," slight differences between the fund and the underlying index, caused by technical factors.

institutional investor: A bank, insurance company, mutual, pension fund, foundation, or endowment that invests large amounts of money on behalf of others. Institutions typically trade securities in larger volume than do individuals.

investment advisor: *See* **advisor.**

investment company: A corporation, trust, or partnership in which investors pool their money to obtain professional management and diversification of their investments. Mutual funds, closed-end funds, and most ETFs are popular types of investment companies.

Investment Company Act of 1940: The federal law setting forth the registration and regulation of investment funds. Mutual funds, ETFs, closed-end funds, and REITs fall under this act.

investment objective: The goal—long-term capital growth, current income, and so forth—that an investor or a mutual fund pursues.

investment return: The business return from equities (dividends plus the growth in corporate earnings). Investment return is a component of total return. *Also see* **speculative return**.

large-cap fund: A fund holding common stocks with market capitalizations of $10 billion or more.

leverage: The use of borrowed money, primarily to increase volatility.

limit order: To avoid buying or selling a stock at a price higher or lower than you wanted, you can place a limit order rather than a market order. A limit order is an order to buy or sell a security at a specific price. A buy limit order can only be executed at the limit price or lower, and a sell limit order can only be executed at the limit price or higher.

liquidity: The ability to turn your investments into cash, easily and quickly, without having to accept a fire-sale price.

load fund: A fund whose shares are sold by a broker or salesmen with a sales charge.

long: Ownership of a security. Securities purchased for price appreciation in a rising market. *See* **short sale** for opposite.

long-term: 1. A holding period of 12 months or longer for purposes of calculating capital gains tax. 2. An investment strategy of holding an investment for a year or longer. 3. A bond with a maturity of 10 years or longer.

long-term funds: All funds except money market funds and bond funds with maturities of approximately less than two years.

management fee: The amount paid by a mutual fund to the investment advisor for its services. Industrywide, management fees for actively managed funds generally range from 0.5 to 1.5 percent a year of a fund's assets.

mania: *See* **bubble**.

margin: Investing with borrowed money.

market capitalization: The value of a company, as determined by its current stock market price. The "market cap" calculation multiplies the total number of shares outstanding by the current market price. Funds are generally categorized as large, mid, small, and micro caps. Also called *market value.*

market-neutral investing: A strategy of attempting to assemble an investment portfolio with a return that is unaffected by the returns of the overall market. This is accomplished by both buying long and selling short securities.

market timer: An investor who attempts to time the market so that shares are sold before they decrease in value and bought when they are about to increase in value.

market timing: A strategy that attempts to predict the market's ups and downs by using technical and fundamental indicators. The strategy may call for frequent buy and sell decisions.

mark-to-market: Also known as fair value accounting, refers to accounting for the fair value of an asset or liability based on the current market price of the asset or liability, or for similar assets and liabilities, or based on another objectively assessed "fair" value.

micro-cap fund: A fund holding stocks with market capitalizations in the $50 million to $250 million range.

mid-cap fund: A fund holding stocks with market capitalizations in the $2 billion to $10 billion range, although the cutoff points are fuzzy at both ends.

model portfolio: A portfolio suggested by an investment advisor or newsletter publisher to guide the decisions of investors. In most cases, it is possible to duplicate the model by buying all of its holdings in the same proportions.

Modern Portfolio Theory (MPT): Developed by Harry Markowitz in 1952, it states that the risk in a portfolio of diversified stocks is less than the risk inherent in any one of the stocks, provided the right combination of non-correlated stocks is chosen. According to the theory, it's possible to construct an "efficient frontier" optimal portfolio that offers the maximum possible expected return for a given level of risk.

money market fund: Also called a liquid asset or cash fund, it is a mutual fund whose primary objective is to make short-term, interest-bearing securities available to investors who want safety of principal, liquidity, and current income.

M squared (M2): A measure of risk-adjusted performance that is essentially a better way of expressing the Sharpe ratio. M2 provides a risk-adjusted return figure by putting all equity funds on a level playing field. Using a complicated formula, M2 determines how each fund would have performed if it had exactly the same risk as the S&P 500. This makes it possible to compare the performance of funds with different objectives on an apples-to-apples basis. Looking at regular performance data, it might appear that an aggressive fund is outperforming a conservative one. However, when M2 takes risk into account, the reverse may be true. The conservative fund may have been the risk-adjusted winner. Just as with raw performance data, the higher the M2 gain, the better. M2 can be computed for bond funds by relating performance to a fixed-income index. The measure was originally developed by Leah Modigliani (who was working on Wall Street) and her grandfather, Franco Modigliani, a Nobel Prize–winning economist, hence the measure's name: Modigliani/Modigliani or M2. (The family is also related to Amedeo Modigliani, the painter and sculptor.)

multi-fund: A fund that invests in other mutual funds. They are now usually called fund-of-funds, or fund-of-hedge-funds.

municipal bond fund: A mutual fund that invests in a mix of tax-exempt bonds issued by states, cities, and other local governments. The interest obtained from these bonds is passed through to share-owners free of federal tax and sometimes state/local income tax. The fund's primary objective is current tax-free income.

municipal debt: A catchall term for all government borrowing below the federal level—by states, cities, localities, and their agencies.

mutual fund: An investment company that pools investors' money and is managed by a professional advisor. The fund stands ready to buy back (redeem) its shares at their current net asset value. The value of the shares depends on the Net Asset Value (NAV) of the fund's portfolio securities, as updated after the close of each trading day. Most mutual funds continuously offer new shares to investors. Mutual funds can invest in almost any liquid security: stocks, bonds, and cash. The term is *not* synonymous with equity investing.

NASDAQ: An automated information network that provides brokers and dealers with price quotations on securities traded over-the-counter. NASDAQ is an acronym for National Association of Securities Dealers Automated Quotations.

National Association of Securities Dealers, Inc. (NASD): *See* **Financial Industry Regulatory Authority (FINRA)**.

nest egg: Assets put aside to provide for a secure standard of living after one's retirement.

net asset value per share (n.a.v.): A fund's total assets—securities, cash and any accrued earnings—after deduction of liabilities, divided by the number of shares outstanding. It is synonymous with the bid price, and, for no-load funds, it also is the offering or market price.

no-load fund: A mutual fund selling its shares at net asset value, without the addition of front-end or back-end sales charges. The fund may have a redemption fee and/or a 12b-1 fee of no more than .25 percent.

passive investing: A buy-and-hold approach characterized by lower portfolio turnover, lower operating expenses and transaction costs, greater tax efficiency, a long-term perspective, and being full invested at all times.

performance: *See* **return**.

perma bull (bear): An investor or outlook that consistently predicts either a strong market (bull) or a weak market (bear). Many media analysts and authors develop "perma" characteristics so that the audience clearly understand their role or niche in market debates and commentaries.

price/earnings (P/E) ratio: An important measure of a stock's value, obtained by dividing the current market price by a measure of earnings, typically trailing 12-month earnings. Projected forward earnings over the next year are also used by analysts. The lower a stock's P/E ratio, the less investors must pay for each dollar of earnings and the more attractively valued the stock may be.

price weighting: The Dow Jones Industrial Average is price weighted. It is calculated by summing the prices of all 30 stocks, then dividing by a divisor that is no longer 30 because it has been adjusted for splits and spinoffs in order to ensure that such events do not in themselves alter the numerical value of the DJIA. After many adjustments, the divisor is now less than one (meaning the index is actually larger than the sum of the prices of all 30 component stocks before dividing). The defect of price weighting is that the higher a stock's price, the higher its weight. There is no logic to this. The practice began in an age before calculators were invented. The DJIA will be around for a long time because it is owned by the subsidiary of the News Corp. that publishes *The Wall Street Journal* and *Barron's*, which has a vested interest in keeping the Dow industrials in the limelight.

prospectus: The official disclosure document describing the terms of a registered security or fund and offering its shares for sale. A more detailed document known as "Part B" of the prospectus or the Statement of Additional Information is available upon request. A profile prospectus is a short summary document.

random walk: A theory stating that from any given point in time, movements in the stock market are likely to be random and unpredictable when compared to past movements. The theory explains why it is very difficult to predict stock market movements or returns, especially over short intervals. *Also see* **efficient market theory**.

Real Estate Investment Trust (REIT): A type of investment company that invests in real estate properties or mortgages. A REIT, like other types of investment companies, passes through most of its gains and earnings to investors.

real return: Investment return adjusted for inflation.

rebalancing: Adjusting a portfolio so that consistent disciplines (such as asset allocation guidelines) are maintained. Rebalancing often involves transferring assets among different portfolio components periodically to correct for market price changes.

registered investment advisor: A designation representing that a financial consultant's firm is registered with the appropriate state regulators and the RIA representatives for those firms have passed the required exams.

retail funds: Mutual funds that are sold to the general public, as opposed to institutional investors.

return: Usually short for average annual compound rate of total return. Also called *performance*.

risk premium: The difference between a risk-free return (usually a three-month Treasury bill) and the total return from a risky investment. The risk premium is the extra return to compensate for extra risk.

R-squared (R^2): Shorthand for "coefficient of determination." It computes the percentage of a fund's return that can be explained by the movement of an index. An S&P 500 fund has an R-Squared of 1.00. That's because the S&P index explains 100 percent of its movement. A gold fund may have an R-Squared of 0.10 to 0.20 because a domestic index explains only a tenth to a fifth of the gold fund's movement.

Securities and Exchange Commission (SEC): The agency of the U.S. government that administers federal securities laws.

semi-variance risk measures: They focus on downside risk on the theory that most investors welcome upside volatility, and only want to avoid downside volatility. The well-known Morningstar stars rank risk-adjusted performance with the emphasis on downward variation.

sentiment indicators: Measures of bullish or bearish moods of investors.

Sharpe ratio: A measure of reward per unit of risk. Reward is considered to be the fund's performance minus a constant (U.S. Treasury bills) that reflects a risk-free rate of return. Risk is the fund's standard deviation. The ratio is computed by dividing reward by risk. The higher the resulting ratio, the better the compensation for the risk taken. The measure was named after Stanford professor William F. Sharpe.

short sale: The sale of a security that is not owned in the hope that the price will go down so it can be repurchased at a profit.

small-cap fund: A fund holding stocks with market capitalizations less than $2 billion. This cutoff point has grown over the years with the advancement of bull markets. In the 1970s the cutoff was generally considered $1 billion. *Also see* **micro-cap fund**.

smid (cap): An amalgam of the words small and mid.

speculative return: The changes in the prices of stocks due to changes in investors' willingness to pay more for a dollar of earnings (commonly denoted by changes in the P/E ratios). Speculative return is a component of total return. *Also see* **investment return**.

standard deviation: The variations in performance from a long-term average. Standard deviation differs from beta in that it measures variability within a fund, while beta measures it in relation to an outside index.

style drift: The moving away from the original asset allocation either by purchase of securities outside a particular asset class, or by not rebalancing.

survivorship bias: The bias introduced into long-term mutual fund averages by the elimination of liquidated funds that are usually underperformers. Virtually all fund averages are based on only those funds currently in existence.

tactical asset allocation: The attempt to move into and out of various stocks, bonds, and cash as market conditions change.

target date maturity fund: A type of fund in which the mix of assets and risk/return profile is periodically adjusted as the investor moves closer to a given target date, such as retirement. These funds may be broadly diversified among securities and asset classes (stocks, bonds, and cash). The investor is not required to make decisions or take actions because portfolio adjustments are made by formula.

tax-managed strategies: Investing strategies designed to minimize taxes.

technical analysis: Research into the supply and demand for securities based on trading volume and price studies. Technical analysis uses charts or computer programs to identify price trends and predict future price movements. Unlike fundamental analysts, technical analysts do not concern themselves with the financial position or operations of a company, such as assets and revenues, earnings.

time value of money: The concept that holds that a specific sum of money is more valuable the sooner it is received. The time value of money is dependent not only on the time interval being considered but also the discount rate used in calculating current or future values.

total return: A comprehensive measure of investment performance that includes price changes, realized capital gains, and dividend distributions.

tracking error: The extent to which an index fund fails to track its selected index.

Treasury bill (T-bill): A short-term debt security of the U.S. Government sold with 13-, 26-, and 52-week maturities. They are considered risk-free since they are guaranteed by the government. However, if held over time, they are subject to the inflation risk.

Treasury Inflation-Protected Securities (TIPS): Treasury bonds that provide protection against inflation. The principal of a TIPS increases with inflation and decreases with deflation, as measured by the Consumer Price Index.

turnover: The rate at which a fund buys and sells securities over the course of a year. The turnover ratio is calculated by dividing the lesser of purchases or sales of portfolio securities over a full year by the monthly average of the value of the portfolio securities owned by the fund during the year.

12b-1 fee: A continuing asset-based fee charged by some mutual funds to their shareholders to reimburse the fund for distribution and marketing expenses. The fee must be disclosed by prospectus and may not exceed limits set by regulations. It is commonly used to provide continuing compensation to sales representatives who service the account. 12b-1 fees paid to sales reps are also called "trails" or "trailing commissions."

unrealized gain: The appreciation in value of an asset that has not been sold.

unrealized loss: The depreciation in value of an asset that has not been sold.

value fund: A fund that invests in stocks that are judged to have attractive values relative to their prices. Value funds and value styles often focus on low price/earnings ratios, low book values, and high dividend yields.

volatility: The relative rate at which an investment's price tends to move up or down. For example, a highly volatile fund is one that usually rises or declines far more than the average of similar investments or a benchmark index.

yield: Income received from investments expressed as a percentage return. It is computed by dividing per share income by the market price. Also referred to as current yield. Bond and money market mutual funds are required to quote yields using standard calculation methods.

yield-to-maturity: The yield earned on a bond over its full life. Includes capital gains if the bond was bought at a discount from its face value.

zero-sum gain: A situation in which one person's gain must be matched by another person's loss. Ignoring transaction costs, options, futures, and gambling are examples of zero-sum gains.

Acknowledgments

I began to write this book from memory. Then I discovered my memory for facts, statistics, and stories, some decades old, was less than perfect. This meant I had to talk to a number of people in order to get my facts right. Some people took or returned my calls (see Chapter 19), and some responded to my e-mails. Most made minor contributions; but a few did more. I thank you all from the bottom of my heart. I couldn't have done it by myself.

Frederick Pierce

I do want to thank one person who had no direct involvement whatsoever with this book.

My first real exposure to writing came when I was hired by ABC-TV to research television. The results of my research had to be written up, so I was very fortunate to have had a boss who took the time to work with me on my memos. Fred Pierce, then the manager of research, taught me to write with the patience of Job. Sometimes he would edit, correct, and improve two, three, and even four drafts of my memos before he deemed them ready to be sent to management. His criticisms were always positive; he never raised his voice. And the memos always went out under my name. I would never have developed into a writer without him.

About the Author

Sheldon Jacobs wrote, in 1974, the first self-help book ever on no-load mutual funds, *Put Money in Your Pocket*, introducing thousands of investors to no-load funds. It launched a notable career that enabled Jacobs to found a popular investment newsletter in 1979. *The No-Load Fund Investor* went on to become the number-one financial newsletter in America for risk-adjusted performance for the 15 years ending in 2006. In 1987, Jacobs co-founded—along with Bob Brinker, an ABC radio host and newsletter publisher—the BJ Group, a Registered Investment Advisor. Over 1,000 clients entrusted $600 million of assets to the BJ Group, which the firm managed on a discretionary basis. The *Investor* newsletter was later sold, but Jacobs continues as a contributing editor.

In July 1993, Jacobs was one of five nationally recognized mutual fund advisors chosen by the *New York Times* for a mutual fund portfolio competition. The portfolio he selected produced the highest returns for almost seven years.

Jacobs is a member of *Bottom Line*'s investment advisory panel. He was a founding advisor to Charles Schwab's Financial Advisory Service Board, and has been listed in *Who's Who in America*.

The *Investor* is also the only investment newsletter in America to earn recognition on the annual *Forbes/MarketWatch/Hulbert* Honor Roll in 10 of the past 11 years that Sheldon edited the newsletter.

Civic activities: Jacobs is on the Board of Directors of Westchester Community College Foundation in New York, and a member of the Finance Committee managing the college's multimillion-dollar endowment portfolio.

Index